Learning .NET High-performance Programming

Learn everything you need to know about
performance-oriented programming for
the .NET Framework

Antonio Esposito

BIRMINGHAM - MUMBAI

Learning .NET High-performance Programming

First published: June 2015

Production reference: 1260615

Published by Packt Publishing Ltd.
Livery Place
35 Livery Street
Birmingham B3 2PB, UK.

ISBN 978-1-78528-846-3

www.packtpub.com

Credits

Author
Antonio Esposito

Reviewers
Altaf Hussain

Thomas Krause

Chad D. Morgan

Newton Sheikh

Commissioning Editor
Dipika Gaonkar

Acquisition Editor
Larissa Pinto

Content Development Editor
Amey Varangaonkar

Technical Editor
Rohith Rajan

Copy Editors
Charlotte Carneiro

Ameesha Green

Pulu Lalvani

Vikrant Phadke

Project Coordinator
Suzanne Coutinho

Proofreaders
Stephen Copestake

Safis Editing

Indexer
Rekha Nair

Graphics
Jason Monteiro

Production Coordinator
Melwyn D'sa

Cover Work
Melwyn D'sa

About the Author

Antonio Esposito has been an experienced software developer, architect, and trainer since 2002. He started programming in BASIC on MS-DOS 3 at the age of 8 and still loves programming on Microsoft products. An expert in .NET, he has a lot of knowledge of SOA techniques and architectures as well as WCF and Microsoft Azure. He also has extensive knowledge of application production frameworks, such as WPF, MVC, and so on.

Antonio has worked with prominent companies as a freelance consultant, speaker, and trainer. These companies include UniCredit Banca, Microsoft Italia, IBM Italia, Ferrari, Tenova Pomini, Cornér Banca, and many others.

As a speaker, he has had the opportunity to contribute to events such as the MCT Summit Europe, WPC Italia, Community Days Milano, Codemotion, and many more from his own user group, DotNet Lombardia.

I thank my lovely baby and wife for always being in my heart.

About the Reviewers

Altaf Hussain is a student pursuing a master's course from Saint Francis Xavier University in Nova Scotia, Canada. Prior to this, he received his undergraduate degree in computer science and engineering from Shahjalal University of Science and Technology in Sylhet, Bangladesh. He is researching in the field of semantic web and cloud services. He is also into developing a framework for context-aware service discovery and selection, providing decision-making support for healthcare scenarios, using parallel computing and semantic technologies.

Altaf is also working as a senior software engineer for Logistics Software Corp., Canada, where he develops distributed web and desktop applications in C#, ASP. NET, and contemporary technologies. Prior to beginning his master's course, he also worked as a full-stack distributed application developer, implementing e-forms, citizen services, and public sector workflow integration. Altaf has also published several research papers in the fields of grid computing, cloud computing, and the Semantic Web.

Thomas Krause is an independent software developer, author, and consultant. He specializes in high-performance solutions, algorithms, and artificial intelligence. Most of the projects he has worked on have leveraged the productivity of the Microsoft .NET framework while still aiming to be highly performant and efficient. One example of this is his work on a message-based backend processing system based on BizTalk for a Fortune 500 company. This system manages the administration of over 200,000 employees in that company worldwide.

Thomas has also served as a consultant and developer on an automated infringement system that handles tens of millions of offenses in traffic every year worldwide and processes terabytes of data. As an author, he wrote a book about large-scale duplicate detection algorithms using indexing technologies, similar to those used by Google and other major search engines.

Thomas lives and works in Cologne, Germany, where he enjoys Metthappen and Kölsch (ground pork on bread and the typical Cologne beer). Cologne is also home to a company called Akzente.IT, which he founded for his consulting work. He is always looking for new and interesting projects, so don't hesitate to contact him. You can find more information about him at `http://akzente.it/`.

First and foremost, I want to thank my parents, my girlfriend, and the rest of my family, who have always supported me.

Special thanks also go to Sophie for being my funny neighbor; my colleague Oliver for bringing everything in apple-pie order as well as delivering an awesome product to our friends overseas; and my colleague Manuel for playing with me for FC Klostein (local soccer team). Seriously, you guys are great and it's always fun working with you!

Chad D. Morgan is currently the director of technology at MapGraphiX, a software company that focuses on mapping solutions for the transportation industry. Additionally, he owns a consulting company, Pelican Creek Consulting, and has 14 years of professional experience, developing software across various industries. He has had a strong focus on web technologies. His credentials include Microsoft Certified Professional Developer, Microsoft Certified Application Developer, and Microsoft Certified Technology Specialist, among others.

Newton Sheikh is a consultant on cloud computing and distributed computing with focus on Microsoft Azure. He is also a .NET developer and game programmer. He has a lot of interest in the field of mathematics and complex algorithms.

Newton enjoys most of his day coding, working on business solutions, and designing architecture for the cloud. He also loves working on compiler design.

When he is not in front of a computer, he loves to spend time with his friends and family and hang out at different places with a camera in his hands.

He has reviewed *XNA 4 3D Game Development by Example Beginner's Guide*, *Packt Publishing*.

You can get in touch with him at `https://in.linkedin.com/pub/newton-sheikh/33/391/910`.

I would like to thank my colleagues with whom I work for helping me with the review process.

www.PacktPub.com

Support files, eBooks, discount offers, and more

For support files and downloads related to your book, please visit www.PacktPub.com.

Did you know that Packt offers eBook versions of every book published, with PDF and ePub files available? You can upgrade to the eBook version at www.PacktPub.com and as a print book customer, you are entitled to a discount on the eBook copy. Get in touch with us at service@packtpub.com for more details.

At www.PacktPub.com, you can also read a collection of free technical articles, sign up for a range of free newsletters and receive exclusive discounts and offers on Packt books and eBooks.

https://www2.packtpub.com/books/subscription/packtlib

Do you need instant solutions to your IT questions? PacktLib is Packt's online digital book library. Here, you can search, access, and read Packt's entire library of books.

Why subscribe?

- Fully searchable across every book published by Packt
- Copy and paste, print, and bookmark content
- On demand and accessible via a web browser

Free access for Packt account holders

If you have an account with Packt at www.PacktPub.com, you can use this to access PacktLib today and view 9 entirely free books. Simply use your login credentials for immediate access.

Instant updates on new Packt books

Get notified! Find out when new books are published by following @PacktEnterprise on Twitter or the *Packt Enterprise* Facebook page.

Table of Contents

Preface

For most of us, "performance" is a word with a single meaning. When it comes to software production, this meaning usually corresponds to something fast. A fast program is a good program. Although this is not is a wrong assertion, the meaning of the word "performance" is wider and deeper.

Writing a responsive UI actually means writing a performing UI. Deploying a worker role across Microsoft Azure, which is able to scale up to 100 cores, and handling millions of messages per hour actually means writing a performing workflow. The two examples show two different kinds of performance, and more exist.

Other than multiple meanings, the word "performance" also refers to multiple implementation levels. For example, a developer has to keep the security aspect of his application in mind right from the outset, because using a simple X509 certificate does not make an insecure web application secure. The same is true when it comes to performance.

If we want to create a high-performance application, we have to design a high-performance architecture right from the start, implement performance-oriented strategies, and bring up a good performance-engineered project that is able to assist the wider development project to create valid performance requisites and tests.

As developers, we cannot avoid mastering all the techniques required to help us face day-to-day challenges. Asynchronous programming and parallel programming are two examples. Mastering such techniques helps us create good software in terms of responsiveness and scalability. A clear understanding of the .NET Framework has to become part of the knowledge arsenal for any .NET developer; understanding memory management, process isolation, and thread life cycle are examples.

Lots of real-world examples will be available in this book. They will be about the most widely used programming techniques and scenarios, together with special-case programming recipes for big data, engineering, and database integration.

All of these topics are covered here with enthusiasm and expertise.

What this book covers

Chapter 1, Performance Thoughts, gives you an overview of the term "performance" and related concepts.

Chapter 2, Architecting High-performance .NET Code, describes the various architectural concerns of software related to performance, with practical real-world examples.

Chapter 3, CLR Internals, gives you in-depth knowledge of the internals of CLR, from memory management to thread life cycle management.

Chapter 4, Asynchronous Programming, equips you with the ability to program methods that will never keep the user waiting.

Chapter 5, Programming for Parallelism, gives you many details of parallelism, and covers scenarios such as this one: a lot of data items are available for our business logic. Mastering parallelism techniques brings any application throughput to extremely high levels, with little effort by the developer.

Chapter 6, Programming for Math and Engineering, shows you real-world examples for specific cases related to scientific elaboration.

Chapter 7, Database Querying, demonstrates working with databases. Any business-related application or enterprise application deals with a lot of data. This chapter also provides good knowledge of all persistence-layer access frameworks and techniques that make such accesses fast and reliable for all kinds of applications.

Chapter 8, Programming for Big Data, covers working with huge and fast-growing datasets that have specific issues and difficulties, with a simplified presentation and a lot of examples.

Chapter 9, Analyzing Code Performance, proves that good programming and design are not enough if we don't always monitor our software performance results in design time and runtime.

What you need for this book

The only requirement to use all that this book offers is Microsoft Visual Studio 2013, with related updates and some experience in the C# programming language.

Who this book is for

Any developer will benefit from reading this book because of the many practical examples and the related advanced explanations. Software architects and project managers will also benefit from reading this book in the fields of performance engineering, architecture, and designs.

Conventions

In this book, you will find a number of text styles that distinguish between different kinds of information. Here are some examples of these styles and an explanation of their meaning.

Code words in text, database table names, folder names, filenames, file extensions, pathnames, dummy URLs, user input, and Twitter handles are shown as follows: "We can include other contexts through the use of the `include` directive."

A block of code is set as follows:

```
var previousTiming = GCSettings.LatencyMode;
try
{
    //switch to LowLatency mode
    GCSettings.LatencyMode = GCLatencyMode.LowLatency;

    //your code
    //never use large short-living objects here
}
finally
{
    GCSettings.LatencyMode = previousTiming;
}
```

New terms and **important words** are shown in bold. Words that you see on the screen, for example, in menus or dialog boxes, appear in the text like this: "Clicking on the **Next** button moves you to the next screen."

 Warnings or important notes appear in a box like this.

 Tips and tricks appear like this.

Reader feedback

Feedback from our readers is always welcome. Let us know what you think about this book — what you liked or disliked. Reader feedback is important for us as it helps us develop titles that you will really get the most out of.

To send us general feedback, simply e-mail feedback@packtpub.com, and mention the book's title in the subject of your message.

If there is a topic that you have expertise in and you are interested in either writing or contributing to a book, see our author guide at www.packtpub.com/authors.

Customer support

Now that you are the proud owner of a Packt book, we have a number of things to help you to get the most from your purchase.

Downloading the example code

You can download the example code files from your account at http://www.packtpub.com for all the Packt Publishing books you have purchased. If you purchased this book elsewhere, you can visit http://www.packtpub.com/support and register to have the files e-mailed directly to you.

Downloading the color images of this book

We also provide you with a PDF file that has color images of the screenshots/diagrams used in this book. The color images will help you better understand the changes in the output. You can download this file from https://www.packtpub.com/sites/default/files/downloads/8463EN_ColorImages.pdf.

Errata

Although we have taken every care to ensure the accuracy of our content, mistakes do happen. If you find a mistake in one of our books — maybe a mistake in the text or the code — we would be grateful if you could report this to us. By doing so, you can save other readers from frustration and help us improve subsequent versions of this book. If you find any errata, please report them by visiting http://www.packtpub.com/submit-errata, selecting your book, clicking on the **Errata Submission Form** link, and entering the details of your errata. Once your errata are verified, your submission will be accepted and the errata will be uploaded to our website or added to any list of existing errata under the Errata section of that title.

To view the previously submitted errata, go to `https://www.packtpub.com/books/content/support` and enter the name of the book in the search field. The required information will appear under the **Errata** section.

Piracy

Piracy of copyrighted material on the Internet is an ongoing problem across all media. At Packt, we take the protection of our copyright and licenses very seriously. If you come across any illegal copies of our works in any form on the Internet, please provide us with the location address or website name immediately so that we can pursue a remedy.

Please contact us at `copyright@packtpub.com` with a link to the suspected pirated material.

We appreciate your help in protecting our authors and our ability to bring you valuable content.

Questions

If you have a problem with any aspect of this book, you can contact us at `questions@packtpub.com`, and we will do our best to address the problem.

1
Performance Thoughts

In software engineering, the most misused word is *performance*. Although anyone may like a performing application or website, the word itself hides a lot of meanings, each with specific pros and cons.

A professional programmer must have a deep understanding of the various facets of the term *performance*, as the term assumes different meanings in different scenarios.

A well-performing application should comply with different kinds of performance requirements, which usually change according to the application's architecture and design. It should also focus on the market expectations and (sometimes) what the current development trend is.

As C# programmers, we must add to the generic knowledge about performance-oriented programming. All these skills let us achieve the best results from coding. Choosing the best architecture solution or design pattern will give a boost to long- or short-term performance results (explained later in this chapter). However, implementing these architectures with the wrong design, will nullify expectations of speed or quality we planned. This chapter will guide you on the meanings and facets of the term *performance*, as implied when programming for **Microsoft .NET Framework**:

- Understanding performance
- Performance as a requirement
- Performance engineering
- Performance aspects
- Class of applications
- Technical overview

Understanding performance

When you talk about performance with respect to the results of an application being developed, it is a word that means *good results* for the *given expectations*.

Without diving into the details of the meaning, it is clear that the keyword here is not the search for *good results* but the comparison between those results with a specific reference value. No static, relative, or ranged value can have any significance without some kind of a legend associated with it.

Diving into the meaning of the phrase *good results for the given expectations*, there is another hidden important key concept: the availability to measure, in *technical terms*, any given aspect of our application. Such terms must be numerically defined, such as a time, a size expressed in Bytes (or multiples), and so on.

In other words, performance is associated with all the measurable aspects of an application.

As software developers, we have to understand client needs. We cannot be simply code writers or technical enthusiasts.

Although we have to mine technical requisites between use cases and user expectations, we have to guide the client to give us useful information regarding their expectations. I know they do not know anything about software engineering, but it is up to us to let them learn at least the basics here. Sometimes, we have to mine requisites by ourselves, while other times we can try to get the client to use the right requisite formula with suggestions, questions, and indications.

Any requisite with no relative or absolute reference value exposed is invalid.

Subtle to define as *not valid* is any performance requisite with some generic numeric needs, without specifying any context or value legend. An example will be a request like a web page response time, without specifying the server load or page computational complexity.

Taking some time to reflect on what we just read, we found another aspect of the term *performance*, which is a technical value and may become a performance indicator only if it's compared to a valid *expected range*.

Let's evaluate another client need. A client asks for a web page to be able to respond in less than 1 second in a low load time window (less than 1,000 active users) or not more than 10 seconds with heavy load equal to or more than 10,000 active users.

Here, we do have a valid request against a value range and environment, but there is still something missing, such as a *shared and documented test case*, which acts as a reference to everyone working on the project.

An example on a valid client's need for performance requirement would be that a client asks for a web application to execute `Test001` in less than one second with less than 1.000 active users online, or be able to execute the same test case in less than 10 seconds with no more than 10.000 active online users.

Performance as a requirement

Talking about performance as a need for a client (or buyer), it is easy to infer how this is definitely a requirement and not a simple need that a client may have.

In software engineering, the requirement collection (and analysis) is called *Requirements engineering*. We found a couple of specific requirements that we should properly understand as software developers: the **functional** and **non-functional** requirements.

Under the functional requirement, we can find *what* a software must do, and this (and other specifications) codes what we call **software design**. While with a non-functional requirement, we focus on *how* the system (and hence, the software) has to work. This (and other specifications) codes what we call **system architecture**.

In other words, when a client asks for an application to compute something (and if the computation hides a proprietary logic, the formula is part of the requirement as a technical detail), they are asking for a function, so this is a functional requirement.

When a client asks for an application to work only if authenticated (a non-functional requirement), they are definitely asking that an application works in a specific manner, without asking the application to produce a target or goal in the results.

Usually, anything about security, reliability, testability, maintainability, interoperability, and performance guidelines, are all non-functional requirements. When the client asks the software what needs can be satisfied with respect to their business, it is actually a functional requirement.

Although a client may ask for a *fast* or *responsive* application, they are not actually asking for something related to their business or what to do with the software, they are simply asking for some generic feature; in other words, a wish. All such technical wishes are non-functional requirements. But what about a scenario in which the client asks for something that is a business requirement?

Let's say that a client asks for an application to integrate with a specific industrial bus that must respond in less than 100 milliseconds to any request made throughout the bus. This now becomes a functional requirement. Although this is not related to their business, logically, this is a technical detail related to their domain, and has become a proper functional (domain-related) requisite.

Performance engineering

Performance engineering is the structure behind the goal to succeed in respecting all the nonfunctional requirements that a software development team should respect.

In a structured software house (or enterprise), the performance engineering is within system engineering, with specific roles, skills, tools, and protocols.

The goal here is not only to ensure the availability of the expected performance requirements during the development stage, but also how these requirements evolve when the application evolves, and its lifecycle up to the production environment, when continuous monitoring of the current performance against the initial requirements gives us a direct and long-range analysis of the system running.

We live in a time when an IT team is definitely an asset for most companies. Although there are still some companies that don't completely understand the definition of IT and think of it as an unnecessary cost, they will at least see the importance of performance and security as the most easily recognizable indicators of a well-made application.

Performance engineering has objectives that cover the easy goal of how to write a *fast* application. Let's take a look at some of these objectives, as follows:

1. Reducing software maintenance costs.
2. Increasing business revenue.
3. Reducing hardware acquisition costs.
4. Reducing system rework for performance issues.

Here, the focus is on all aspects of software development that good performance engineering may optimize. It is obvious that a more powerful application leads to lesser hardware requirements, although it is still obvious that a well-made application needs less reworks for performance issues. The focus is not on the time or money saved, but the importance of thinking about performance from the beginning of the development project up to the production stage. Writing a performing piece of code is an easy task compared to a complete software development project, with *performance* in mind. I know that coding is loved by any developer, but as a professional, we have to do something more.

Reducing the work to fix issues and the cost of having developers working on performance optimization or system tuning after an application is deployed in the production stage enforces the contract with the client/buyer who commissioned the software development. This respects the performance requisites and builds trust with the customer as well as leading to a sensible reduction in maintenance costs.

In performance engineering, a formal performance requisite is coded at the beginning of the development stage, together with software and system architects. Multiple tests are then executed during the development lifecycle in order to satisfy requisites (first) and maintain the level of success at the time. At the end of the production stage, the performance test analysis will act as proof of the work done in programming, testing, releasing, and maintaining of the software, as well as an indicator for various kind of issues not related directly to performance (a disk failure, a DoS instance, a network issue, and so on).

Performance aspects

When working on performance requirements, in the development stage or for the complete application lifecycle, we have to choose the performance aspects that influence our software and development project. Before writing the code, many decisions will be taken, such as what architecture the software must have, what design to implement, what hardware target will run our software, and so on.

As said previously, anything technically measurable and comparable with a valid value range may become a performance indicator and therefore a performance requirement. The more this indicator becomes specific to the application that is being developed, the more its requirements becomes domain related, while for all the others, they are generic non-functional requirements.

We have to always keep in mind that a lot of things may become performance indicators from the technical standpoint, such as the ability to support multithreading or parallel programming, also system-specific indicators, such as the ability to support multicore or a specific GPU's programming languages, but these are only details of a well-formed performance requisite.

A complete performance requisite usually covers multiple aspects of performance. Many aspects do exist. Think of this requirement as a map, as follows:

Latency	Magnitude					
	0%	20%	40%	60%	80%	100%
Latency						X
Throughput			X			
Resource usage					X	
Availability		X				
Scalability	X					
Efficiency				X		

A performance aspect map is a simple grid, exposing the importance of performance aspects

The first thing to keep in mind is that we cannot have every aspect that is shown in the preceding figure as our primary performance goal. It is simply impossible for hardware and software reasons. Therefore, the tricky task here is to find the primary goal and every secondary or less important objective that our application needs to satisfy. Without any regret, some aspect may become completely unnecessary for our application. Later in this chapter, we will cover a few test cases.

 Putting extreme focus on a single kind of performance may lead to a bad performing application.

A desktop or mobile application will never scale out, so why focus on it? A workflow never interacts directly with a client; it will always work in an asynchronous way, so why focus on latency? Do not hesitate to leave some of this aspect in favor of other, more critical aspects.

Let's look at the most important and widely recognized performance aspects.

Latency

The latency is the time between a request and response, or more specifically, the time between any action and its result. In other words, *latency is the time between a cause and its effect*, such that a user can feel it.

A simple example of latency issues is someone using an RDP session. What lets us feel that we are using an RDP session is the latency that the network communication adds to the usual keyboard and mouse iteration.

Latency is critical in web applications where any round-trip between the client's browser and server and then back to the browser is one of the main indicators about the website's responsiveness.

Throughput

One of the most misused words, a synonym for power, or for the most part, the synonym for good programming, is throughput. Throughput simply means that the speed rate of anything is the main task of the given product or function being valued.

For instance, when we talk about an HDD, we should focus on a performance indicator to reassume all the aspects of HDD speed. We cannot use the sequential read/write speed, and we cannot use the seek time as the only indicator to produce a throughput valuation. These are specific performance indicators of the domain of HDD producers. The following guidelines are also mentioned at the beginning of the chapter. We should find a good indicator (direct, indirect, or interpolated) to reassume the *speed* of the HDD in the real world. Is this what a performance test suite does for a system and HDD? We can use a generic random 64K read/write (50/50 percent) test to produce a single throughput indicator.

Talking about software, the ability of a workflow to process transactions in a timely manner (such as per second or per hour) is another valid throughput performance indicator.

Resource usage

This is another key performance indicator that includes everything about resource usage such as memory, CPU, or GPU (when applicable).

When we talk about resource usage, the primary concern is memory usage. Not because the CPU or GPU usage is less important, but simply because the GPU is a very specific indicator, and the CPU usually links to other indicators such as throughput.

The GPU indicator may become important only if the graphical computation power is of primary importance, such as when programming for a computer game. In this case, the GPU power consumption becomes a domain-specific (of game programming) technical indicator.

[A memory leak may occur when the memory is partially or totally unreleased within a process, when unused]

That being said, it is easy to infer that for the resource usage indicator, the most important feature is memory consumption. If we need to load a lot of data together (in the following chapters, we will see alternatives to this solution), we will have to set up hardware resources as needed.

If our application never releases unused memory, we will face a memory leak. Such a leak is a tremendous danger for any application. `OutOfMemoryException` is an exception, which in the .NET programming world means that no more memory is available to instantiate new objects.

The only chance to find a memory leak is by profiling the entire application with a proper tool (we will see the integrated profiling tool of Visual Studio in *Chapter 9*) to show us how an application consumes memory on a subroutine basis.

Availability/reliability

This is a key performance indicator for any software serving multiple users, such as a web service, web application, workflow, and so on.

Availability is also the proof of how a performance indicator may also be something not directly related to speed or power, but simply the ability of the software being in up-time, actually running, without issues in any condition. Availability is directly related to reliability. The more a system is available, the more it is reliable. However, a system may become available using a good maintenance plan or a lot of rework. A reliable system is always a strong one that does not need special maintenance or rework because it was well developed at the beginning, and meets most of the challenges that the production stage can produce.

Scalability

When talking about scalability, things come back to some kind of power — the ability of a single function or entire application to boost its performance — as the number of processors rise or the number of servers increases. We will focus a lot on this indicator by searching for good programming techniques such as multithreading and parallel programming in this and the following chapters, because at the time of writing this book, CPU producers have abandoned the path of single processor power, in favor of multicore CPU architectures. Today, we see smartphones with a CPU of four cores and servers with a single socket of twenty cores each. As software developers, we have to follow market changes, and change our software accordingly to take the most advantages possible.

Scalability is not too difficult to achieve because of the great availability of technologies and frameworks. However, it is not something we can always achieve and at any level. We can neither rely only on hardware evolution, nor on infinite scalability, because not all our code maybe scalable. If they are, it is always limited by the technology, the system architecture, or the hardware itself.

Efficiency

Efficiency is a relatively new kind of performance indicator. The existence of mobile devices and computer-like laptops since 1975, with the release of **IBM 5100**, opened the way to a new performance indicator of efficiency. Absolute power consumption is a part of the meaning of efficiency, with a new technical indicator named **performance per watt**, an indicator that shows the computation level that consumes a single watt of power.

As software developers, we will never focus on hardware electrical consumption, but we have to reduce, at the most, any overhead. Our goal is to avoid wasting any computational power and consequently, electrical power. This aspect is critical in mobile computing, where battery life is never enough.

Speaking of cloud computing, efficiency is a critical indicator for the cloud provider that sells the virtual machines in a time-based billing method, trying to push as many billable VMs in the same hardware. Instead, for a cloud consumer, although efficiency is something outside of their domain, wasting CPU power will force the need to use more VMs. The disadvantage of this is to pay more to have the same results.

In my opinion, always take into consideration this aspect, at least a bit, if you want to reduce global electrical consumption.

Class of applications

The performance requirement analysis is not easy to obtain.

A lot of aspects actually exist. As explained at the beginning of the last paragraph, we have to strike the right balance between all performance aspects, and try to find the best for our target application.

Trying to get the best from all the aspects of performance is like asking for no one at all, with the added costs of wasting time in doing something that is not useful. It is simply impossible reaching the best for all aspects all together. Trying to obtain the best from a single aspect will also give a bad overall performance. We always must make a priority table like the aspect map already seen in preceding paragraphs.

Different types of applications have different performance objectives, usually the same per type. Here are some case studies for the three main environments, namely desktop, mobile, and server-side applications.

Case study: performance aspects of a desktop application

The first question we should ask ourselves, when designing the performance requirements of a desktop class application, is *to whom is this application going to serve?*

A desktop class application serves a single user per system.

Although this is a single-user application, and we will never need scalability at the desktop level, we should consider that the architecture being analyzed has a perfect scalability by itself.

For each new user using our application, a new desktop will exist, so new computational power will be made available to users of this application. Therefore, we can assume that scalability is not a need in the performance requisite list of this application kind. Instead, any server being contacted by this kind of application will become a bottleneck if it is unable to keep up with the increasing demands.

As written by Mr. Jakob Nielsen in 1993, a usability engineer, human users react as explained in the following bullet list:

- 100 milliseconds is the time limit to make sure an application is actually reacting well
- 1 second is the time limit to bring users to the application workflow, otherwise users will experience delay
- 10 seconds is the time limit to keep the users' attention on the given application

It is easy to understand that the main performance aspect composing a requisite for a desktop application is latency.

Low resource usage is another key aspect for a desktop application performance requisite because of the increasingly smaller form factor of mobile computing, such as the Intel Ultrabook®, device with less memory availability. The same goes for efficiency.

It is strange to admit that we do not need power, but this is the truth because a single desktop application is used by a single user, and it is usually unable to fulfil the power resources of a single desktop class system.

Another secondary goal for this kind of performance requirement is availability. If a single application crashes, this halts the users productivity and in turn might lead to newer issues such that, the development team will need to fix it. This crash affects only a single user, leaving other user application instances free by any kind of related issues.

Something that does not impact a desktop class application, as explained previously, is scalability, because multiple users will never be able to use the same personal computer all together.

This is the target aspect map for a desktop class application:

Latency	Magnitude					
	0%	20%	40%	60%	80%	100%
Latency						X
Throughput			X			
Resource usage					X	
Availability		X				
Scalability	X					
Efficiency				X		

The aspect map of a desktop application relying primary on a responding UI

Case study: performance aspects of a mobile application

When developing a mobile device application, such as for a smartphone device or tablet device, the key performance aspect is resource usage, just after Latency.

Although a mobile device application is similar to a desktop class one, the main performance aspect here is not latency because on a small device with (specifically for a Modern UI application) an asynchronous programming model, latency is something overshadowed by the system architecture.

This is the target aspect map for a mobile device application:

Latency	Magnitude					
	0%	20%	40%	60%	80%	100%
Latency		X				
Throughput				X		
Resource usage						X
Availability			X			
Scalability	X					
Efficiency				X		

The aspect map of a mobile application relying primary on low resource usage

Case study: performance aspects of a server application

When talking about a server-side application, such as a workflow running in a completely asynchronous scenario or some kind of task scheduler, things become so different from the desktop and mobile device classes of software and requirements.

Here, the focus is on throughput. The ability to process as many transactions the workflow or scheduler can process.

Things like Latency are not very useful because of the missing user interaction. Maybe a good state machine programming may give some feedback on the workflow status (if multiple processing steps occurs), but this is beyond the scope of the Latency requirement.

Resource usage is also sensible here because of the damage a server crash may produce. Consider that the resource usage has to multiply for the number of instances of the workflow actually running in order to make a valid estimation of the total resource usage occurring on the server. Availability is part of the system architecture if we use multiple servers working together on the same pending job queue, and we should always make this choice if applicable, but programming for multiple asynchronous workflow instances may be tricky and we have to know how to avoid making design issues that can break the system when a high load of work comes. In the next chapter, we will look at architectures and technologies we can use to write a good asynchronous and multithreaded code.

Let's see my aspect map for the server-side application class, shown as follows:

Latency	Magnitude					
	0%	20%	40%	60%	80%	100%
Latency	X					
Throughput						X
Resource usage					X	
Availability			X			
Scalability				X		
Efficiency		X				

The aspect map of a server-side application relying primary on high processing speed

When dealing with server-side applications that are directly connected to user actions, such as a web service responding to a desktop application, we need high computation power and scalability in order to respond to requests from all users in a timely manner. Therefore, we primarily need low latency response, as the client is connected (also consuming resources on the server), waiting for the result. We need availability because one or more application depends on this service, and we need scalability because users can grow up in a short time and fall back in the same short time. Because of the intrinsic distributed architecture of any web service-based system, a low resource usage is a primary concern; otherwise, the scalability will never be enough:

Latency	Magnitude					
	0%	20%	40%	60%	80%	100%
Latency						X
Throughput				X		
Resource usage						X
Availability			X			
Scalability				X		
Efficiency		X				

A user invoked server-side application aspect-map relying primary on latency speed

The aspect map of a server-side web service-based application carefully uses cloud-computing auto-scale features. Scaling out can help us in servicing thousands of clients with the right number of VMs. However, in cloud computing, VMs are billable, so never rely only on scalability.

It is not necessary to split the aspects trying to cover each level of magnitude, but it is a good practice to show the precedence order.

Performance concerns as time changes

During the lifecycle of an application living in the production stage, it may so happen that the provisioned performance requisite changes.

 The more focus we put at the beginning of the development stage in trying to fulfil any future performance needs, the less work we will need to do to fix or maintain our application, once in the production stage.

The most dangerous mistake a developer can make is underestimate the usage of a new application. As explained at the beginning of the chapter, performance engineering is something that a developer must take care of for the entire duration of the project. What if the requirement used for the duration of the development stage is wrong when applied to the production stage? Well, there is not much time to recriminate. Luckily, software changes are less dangerous than hardware changes. First, create a new performance requirement, and then make all brand new test cases that can be applied to the new requirements and try to execute this on the application as in the staging environment. The result will give us the distance from the goal! Now, we should try to change our code with respect to the new requirements and test it again. Repeating these two steps until the result becomes valid against the given value ranges.

Talking, for instance, about a desktop application, we just found that the ideal aspect map focuses a lot on the responsiveness given by low Latency in user interaction. If we were in 2003, the ideal desktop application in the .NET world would have been made on Windows Forms. Here, working a lot with technologies such as **Thread Pool** threads would help us achieve the goal of a complete asynchronous programming to read/write any data from any kind of system, such as a DB or filesystem, thus achieving the primary goal of a responsive user experience. In 2005, a `BackgroundWorker` class/component could have done the same job for us using an easier approach. As long as we used Windows Forms, we could use a recursive execution of the `Invoke` method to use any user interface control for any read/write of its value.

In 2007, with the advent of **Windows Presentation Foundation (WPF)**, the access to user controls from asynchronous threads needed a `Dispatcher` class. From 2010, the `Task` class changed everyday programming again, as this class handled the cross-thread execution lifecycle for background tasks as efficiently as a delegate handles a call to a far method.

You understand three things:

- If a software development team chose not to use an asynchronous programming technique from the beginning, maybe relying on the DBMS speed or on an external control power, increasing data over time will do the same for latency

- On the contrary, using a time-agnostic solution will lead the team to an application that requires low maintenance over time

- If a team needs to continuously update an old application with the latest technologies available, the same winning design might lead the team to success if the technical solution changes with time

Technical overview

Until now, we have read about what performance requirement analysis means, how to work with performance concerns, and how to manage performance requirements against the full life cycle of a software development project. We will now learn more about the computing environment or architecture that we can leverage while programming for performance. Before getting into the details of the architecture, design, and C# specific implementations, which will be discussed in the following chapters, we will have an overview of what we could take as an advantage from each technique.

Multithreaded programming

Any code statement we write is executed by a processor. We can define a processor as a stupid executor of binary logic. The same processor executes a single logic every time. This is why modern operating systems work in time-sharing mode. This means the processor availability is frequently switched from virtual processors.

A thread is a virtual processor that lives within a process (the .exe or any .NET application) that is able to elaborate any code from any logical module of the given application.

Multicore processors are physical processors, which are all printed in the same metallic or plastic package. This helps reducing some cost and optimizing some external (but still internal to the package) devices such as memory controller, system bus, and often a high-speed cache.

Multithreading programming is the ability to program multiple threads together. This gives our applications the ability to use multiple processors, often reducing the overall execution time of our methods. Any kind of software may benefit from using multithreaded programming, such as games, server-side workflows, desktop applications, and so on. Multithreading programming is available from .NET 1.0 onward.

Although multithreading programming creates an evident performance boost by multiplying the code being executed at the same time, a disadvantage is the predictable number of threads used by the software on a system with an unpredictable number of processor cores available. For instance, by writing an application that uses two threads, we optimize the usage of a dual-core system, but we will waste the added power of a quad-core processor.

An optimization tries to split the application into the highest number of threads possible. However, although this boosts processor usage, it will also increase the overhead of designing a big hardly-coded multithreaded application.

Gaming software houses update lot of existing game engines to address multicore systems. First implementations simply used two or three main threads instead of a single one. This helped the games to use the increased available power of first multicore systems.

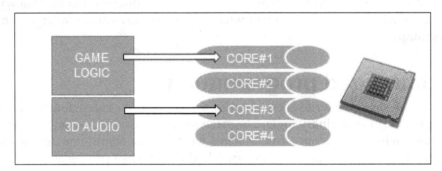

A simple multithreaded application, like most games made use of in 2006/2007

Parallel programming

Parallel programming adds a dynamic thread number to multithreading programming.

The thread number is then managed by the parallel framework engine itself according to internal heuristics based on dataset size, whether or not data-parallelism is used, or number of concurrent tasks, if task parallelism is used.

Parallel programming is the solution to all problems of multithreaded programming while facing a large dataset. For any other use, simply do not use parallelism, but use multithreading with a sliding elaboration design.

Parallelism is the ability to split the computation of a large dataset of items into multiple sub datasets that are to be executed in a parallel way (together) on multiple threads, with a built-in synchronization framework, the ability to unite all the divided datasets into one of the initial sizes again.

Another important advantage of parallel programming is that a parallel development framework automatically creates the right number of sub datasets based on the number CPU cores and other factors. If used on a single-core processor, nothing happens without costing any overheads to the operating system.

When a parallel computing engine splits the initial dataset into multiple smaller datasets, it creates a number, that is, a multiple of the processor core count. When the computation begins, the first group of datasets fulfils the available processor cores, while the other group waits for its time. At the end, a new dataset containing the union of all the smaller ones is created and populated with the results of all the processed dataset results.

When using parallel programming, threads flow to the cores trying to use all available resources:

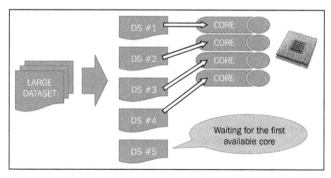

Differently from hardcoded thread usage with the parallelism of Task Parallel Library items flow to all available cores

In parallel programming, the main disadvantage is the percentage of the use of parallelizable code (and data) in the overall application.

Let's assume that we create a workflow application to read some data from an external system, process it, and then write the data back to the external system again. We can assume that if the cost of input and output is about 50 percent of the overall cost of the workflow, we can, at best, have an application that is twice as fast, if it uses all the available cores. Its the same for a 64-core CPU.

The first person to formulate this sentence was Gene Amdahl in his *Amdahl's law* (1967). Thinking about a whole code block, we can have a speed-up that is equal to the core count only when such code presents a perfect parallelizability; otherwise, the overhead will always become a rising bottleneck as the number of cores increases. This law shows a crucial limitation of parallel programming. Not everything is parallelizable for system limitations, such as hardware resources, or because of external dependencies, such as a database that uses internal locks to grant unlimited accesses limiting parallelizability.

The following image is a preview of a 50 percent parallelizable code across a virtually infinite core count CPU:

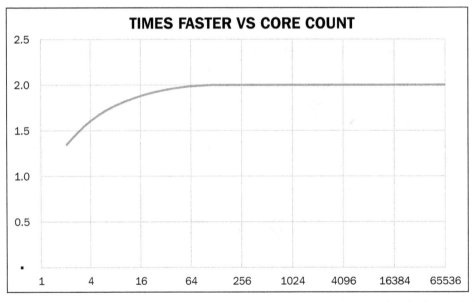

The execution speed increase of a 50 percent un-parallelizable code. The highest speed multiplication (2X) is achieved about at 100 cores.

A software developer uses the Amdahl's law to evaluate the theoretical maximum reachable speed when using parallel computing to process a large dataset.

Against this law, another one exists, by the name of *Gustafson–Barsis' law*, described by John L. Gustafson and Edwin H. Barsis. They said that because of the limits software developers put on themselves, software performances do not grow in a linear way. In addition, they said that if multiple processors work on a large dataset, we can succeed processing all data in any amount of time we like; the only thing we need is enough power in the number of processor cores.

Although this is partially true only on cloud computing platform, where with the right payment plan, it is possible to have a huge availability of processor count and virtual machines. The truth is that overhead always will limit the throttling multiplication. However, this also means that we have to focus on parallelizable data and never stop trying to find a better result in our code.

Distributed computing

As mentioned earlier, sometimes the number of processor cores we have is never enough. Sometimes, different system categories are involved in the same software architecture. A mobile device has a fashionable body and may be very nice to use for any kind of user, while a server is powerful and can serve thousands of users, it is not mobile or nice.

Distributed computing occurs every time we split software architecture into multiple system designs. For instance, when we create a mobile application with the richest control set, multiple web services responding on multiple servers with one or more databases behind them, we create an application using distributed computing.

Here, the focus is not on speeding up a single elaboration of data, but serving multiple users. A distributed application is able to scale up and down on any virtual cloud farm or public cloud **IaaS** (infrastructure as a service, such as **Microsoft® Azure**). Although this architecture adds some possible issues, such as the security between endpoints, it also scales up at multiple nodes with the best technology its node can exploit.

The most popular distributed architecture is the **n-tier**; more specifically, the **3-tier** architecture made by a user-interface layer (any application, including web applications), a remotely accessible business logic layer (SOAP/REST web services), and a persistence layer (one or multiple databases). As time changes, multiple nodes of any layer may be added to fulfil new demands of power. In the future, technology will add updates to a single layer to fulfill all the requirements, without forcing the other layers to do the same.

Further reading:
http://en.wikipedia.org/wiki/Distributed_computing

Grid computing

In grid computing, a huge dataset is divided in tiny datasets. Then, a huge number of heterogeneous systems process those small datasets and split or route them again to other small processing nodes in a huge **Wide Area Network (WAN)**, usually the Internet itself. This is a cheaper method to achieve huge computational power with widely distributed network of commodity class systems, such as personal computers around the world.

Grid computing is definitely a customization of distributed computing, available for huge datasets of highly parallelized computational data.

In 1999, the University of California in Berkeley released the most famous project written using grid computing named *SETI @ home*, a huge scientific data analysis application for extra-terrestrial intelligence search. For more details, you can refer to the following link:

http://setiathome.ssl.berkeley.edu/

Summary

In this chapter, you read about the meaning and aspects of the term *performance*, the importance of performance engineering, and about the most widely used techniques available to fulfil any performance requirement.

In the next chapter, you will focus on the software architecture and designs that can produce well-performing applications, good-looking solutions, and avoid common mistakes.

2

Architecting
High-performance
.NET Code

Software architecture is something that is hard to define in a single statement. However, to summarize, the architecture of an application is its whole design, together with how its blocks/modules/layers interact with each other and with the related documentation.

As explained in the previous chapter, different designs produce different pros and cons in terms of the various aspects of performance. Here, we will dive into the most used/misused architectural techniques and solutions, in search of the best for our performance goals.

In this chapter, we will focus on the following topics:

- Software architecture
- Performance concerns about the architecture
- Object-oriented design principles
- Common designs and architectures
- Common platform architectures
- Performance considerations

Software architecture

A software architecture is something a development team must share, together with the person in charge of the architecture itself (even better if someone who constructs software architectures as their main job), to achieve the goal of producing an application with standard methods, techniques, and tools driving the team as standardized industry-level workers.

A software architect is someone who designs software in a real sense. He understands and addresses business (functional) and technical (non-functional) requisites that drive the development team in the right direction during the entire software development lifecycle. A software architect is also someone who makes the software writable by multiple developers simultaneously, by writing a global design at the beginning of the development of a new software, and hence, enables it to work homogeneously. This is why, often, a software architect is in charge of internal framework development, and so, useful in simplifying and standardizing team working.

This happens by writing documentation about overall architecture and design, defining all boundaries that any module must comply with, all technologies to be used by those modules, all standards to apply to, any authentication and authorization logic, and any choice about the interaction between those modules or layers depending on the kind of application.

Software architecture: A widely accepted definition of software architecture is that it deals with anything that software developers perceive as hard to change. As foundations are unchangeable once we build the building, the same applies to those guidelines and rules that build software architecture. Software architecture is not about technical whole-application level choices; it is the art of making a choice.

Although creating multiple modules in an agnostic way and never trying to fulfill single specific business needs, such modules may help the company to reuse the software by creating a corporate code base. However, dividing software into multiple modules does not imply architecting it. Different designs and patterns also exist regarding architectures. Any of those designs can alter some project management rate, such as future code reuse (productivity), maintainability, or performance.

At the design stage, anything can produce pros and cons regarding all three different sides of the same cube, which represents the whole work of software development. Architectural decisions affect performance in a way that is sometimes hard to fix with simple future optimization code; so always be particularly careful in the design stage.

In this context, performance thoughts are usually a primary concern. Sometimes the choice of having less manageability instead of a higher throughput can be taken, or vice versa, if that is the need. However, choices such as writing ugly code in the name of extreme performance are usually something to avoid.

Software architecture is some kind of multipurpose design of the whole system, where different decisions are made to fulfill the right balance between all needs and specifications, including performance that a software actually needs. The software should also eventually support future additions/modifications.

A big deal when designing the architecture is the use of design patterns.

The most diffused definition of pattern (applicable also to software patterns) is the following one made by Christopher Alexander in his book *A Pattern Language: Towns, Buildings, Construction*, published in year 1977:

> *Each pattern describes a problem which occurs over and over again in our environment, and then describes the core of the solution to that problem, in such a way that you can use this solution a million times over, without ever doing it the same way twice.*

Always remember that a software architecture is not a design pattern, although a design pattern (usually multiple) may become a part of a software architecture. A design pattern is a *commonly used solution to a commonly faced problem*. Though the definition is simple, the most important aspect of design patterns is their ability to standardize the market regarding how professionals talk to each other. Talking in terms of patterns between professionals helps one understand it technically. For instance, saying, I *made a layered architecture*, helps—it avoids always explaining what a layered architecture is. The same can happen when, instead of saying, I *prepared an instance of a class to be used in any case and from anywhere*, a professional simply says, I *made a singleton of such class*.

Thus, outside this, the only reason is to choose a design pattern, simply create your own, or use no design pattern, is the need to develop the software. Sometimes, the market enforces its fashions, such as the use of **Model-View-Controller (MVC)** or **Model-View-ViewModel (MVVM)** patterns. An example is Microsoft's development web environment: since ASP.NET in 2010, MVC has become the standard for web applications. As a pragmatic developer, I can only state that this does not mean that **Web Forms** is dead and that we cannot use it anymore in the future! Both MVC and Web Forms have different pros and cons, and the choice of which fits our software best should be the only (or principal) motivation to adopt one web presentation pattern over another.

Performance concerns about architecture

The goal of architecture is to provide the best structure to fulfill all functional and non-functional requirements, and to achieve the best results in terms of customer satisfaction with a bit of overhead to, we have to manage any future need the application may have during the release.

Decisions about selecting software architecture are about performance. An important distinction is between decisions that affect the whole software and decisions that can be made as optimization or tuning.

There is a *performance architecture* that focuses on the performance concerns that always persist as time changes, and an optimization time, when performance concerns fit the underlying system and its configuration (OS version, middleware version, .NET version, the database version, and so on). After a system change, the architectural vision should not change, whereas the optimization against the new system must be made to fit the requirements. When dealing with software architecture, performance concerns may change from time to time. Let's take a look at a couple of instances.

Suppose that we have a web application that serves hundreds of users, and we need to decide how to store data in single or multiple relational repositories. A simple solution is to use a single relational DB for all the data, because using an association to retrieve data from referenced tables is easy with an object-relational mapping (OR/M) and because a **DBMS** is fast at executing joins. We might say that this solution brings very good latency and throughput in data extraction from 100 to 10,000 users online. This is what usually happens in 2-tier architectures.

However, as time changes, things may become different because as powerful as a system may be, scaling up (with all the trouble of changing the hardware of a critical system) is not always possible. Think about when we already have the fastest system available. Splitting the data persistence on different DBMS breaks constraint-based associations between entities, but gives us great scalability over time. This is what usually happens in 3-tier architectures. Adding new modules to the whole application will also mean adding more module-oriented DBs, so the application scalability need is linear to the available persistence storage scalability.

In *Chapter 1, Performance Thoughts*, we talked about performance requisites and aspect maps. The two solutions have different maps. The first is winning latency while the second is winning scalability. Different performance requisites might move us away from choosing one solution or another. It depends on how far away the analyst that made the requisite has been able to see the needs of the customer.

Bear in mind that if we used the second option, the one with multiple persistence systems, the system would have performed slightly worse on latency (compared the first option) at the beginning. Further, if the web application would have scaled to 10,000 or 100,000 online users, we could have chosen the winning architecture, after all. Scaling to fulfill thousands of requests is obviously different from responding in as few milliseconds as possible. This is a choice. The architect deals with such choices all days of their life. That is the simplest truth and definition available of a software architect. This shows how difficult it is to find the right design for a system, even if we're talking about a single module, such as the relational persistence module.

Another important aspect is choosing whether to optimize the software to work in the given environment or not, and if yes, how to do it.

If we have to make a software module or tier that can operate indistinctly on a premise (on our systems) or on a cloud **Infrastructure as a Service (IaaS)** or a **Platform as a Service (PaaS)** subsystem, we must create something more system agnostic — a software module that is able to scale up and down from the premise to the cloud. Otherwise, by using idioms of specific systems such as a specific DBMS function (for instance, SQL Server File Table), we cannot ensure that such a feature is always available in all environments. A module that should execute in the same way in our virtual machine or a public cloud virtual machine without configuring nothing more than what is available in a `.config` file is definitely an agnostic software module. On the contrary, when the highest performance is required, by sacrificing some code reusability, we can use all dialects or idioms of any language to get the best from each one.

 An idiom in computer science is something specific to a given language or system, such as C# Interface or Delegate, which is not available in other languages, or SQL Server file streams, which is not available in other DBMS.

In this chapter, we will focus on performance architecture, while in the following chapters, we will focus on code optimization and performance instrumentation.

Object-oriented design principles

C# is a general-purpose language that can work in a managed environment. It is the .NET **Common Language Runtime (CLR)** that handles the most tricky logic for us, such as the lifecycle of variables and their removal from memory, process isolation, thread abstraction, variably safe typing, and so on.

Although we will assume that we will use C# only in **object-oriented programming (OOP)**, the language itself supports other paradigms as well.

In terms of class design, the following tenets are at the basis of OOP:

- **Encapsulation**: Any class can hide its core logic in external items.
- **Inheritance**: Any class can expand the capability of a mother class, by adding more specific properties or adding/changing logics.
- **Polymorphism**: Any object, if extended by inheritance, when compared to other objects of the same parent family, may produce different business results by applying the eventually changed logic as allowed by inheritance, creating what names a polymorphic behavior.

Object orientation is all about abstracting the real world in multiple business-like items that represent any business-related entity, such as a house in the real-estate business domain or a customer in the invoicing business domain. Entities may not only be people or companies. Anything that can be represented in detail with finite properties (data) and the ability to use some logic on inner data or that can interact with other entities is definitely a living entity in terms of OOP. This living entity is called an *object*. An entity is a part of a family of objects that has the same logic but has different related inner data, called a *class*. Therefore, an object is an instance of a class.

Understanding OOP will greatly simplify the understanding of how to subdivide the whole application in multiple modules/layers/tiers. Do the dictates from OOP give all the answers? Actually, no. Another group of OOP design principles made by *Michael Feathers* and *Robert C. Martin* in 2000, named *SOLID*, explains in detail on how to actually program for OOP. Understanding those other principles will give us knowledge about all architecture decisions.

The word SOLID is an acronym of five principles. Let's briefly look at them.

The single responsibility principle

A single class must have a single responsibility, something like abstracting a single business entity or a single communication protocol. It does not matter how easy creating such an entity is or how much coding such an entity needs. This is because if a single class tries to abstract multiple entities, it would be unable to actually abstract any of those entities proposed. This does not mean that multiple classes abstract entities that are more specific. For example, applying an inheritance principle does not inherit a single and a more abstract class (the mother class).

The open-closed principle

This principle states that a class must be open for extension and closed for modification. This is an important principle regarding teamwork and code lifetime management. If a class never changes its contract (public shape) but still grows up in functionality, it then maintains compatibility with the older versions. Later in this chapter, in the *Common designs and architectures* section, we will see how this principle is also applicable in specific high-distributed architectures such as the n-tier or Service Oriented Architectures.

The Liskov substitution principle

This principle states that wherever an object is used, a subtype must be used in the same place, without ever changing any code and without having any different behavior in the application. This tenet extends the OOP inheritance principle by giving us a direct test case to validate how inheritance is applied to our class hierarchy.

The interface segregation principle

This principle states that a *role interface* must be created, based on what a client (the caller of the methods of any object) needs with no more logic (methods) or properties than effectively required. These interfaces help software decoupling between modules, module management, and development because it splits the contract (the shared need of a client in the form of a C# interface) from the concrete implementation. Like creating a facade, this principle helps to simplify the shape of the object to its clients and helps move concrete logic from different classes, if needed, without (actually decoupling) any change in the client usage.

The dependency inversion principle

This principle extends the preceding interface segregation principle by stating that better decoupling and management of software modules happens by inverting references between objects. Without this principle, multiple modules calling each other at the same or from different levels will make up the software. Although abstraction is practically nothing at some level, such as when developing a module with, for instance, classes for low-level network communication, for most other modules, abstraction is significantly useful for reducing coupling. For instance, with a strait dependency, a desktop application using this module will contain a UX module that calls business logic in one module and that in turn calls another system by using another module ($A \to B \to C$).

By inverting the dependency, we will find that module *A* asks for another module (without knowing the concrete name/implementation) that extends any interface that *A* needs. The same occurs between module *B* and the unknown module *C*, when *B* asks for a module to implement its needs (module *C*). A practical implementation of this scenario is the plugin pattern or the **Inversion of Control (IoC)** with the **Dependency Injection (DI)** pattern.

By respecting this principle, the improved decoupling is visible. Less visible is the little drawback this solution has. If used extensively, this solution could create some performance issues, such as added latency and higher resource usage that came from data-mapping usage. Later in this chapter, we will see a case study on Dependency Injection.

Further information about SOLID can be found at:
`http://en.wikipedia.org/wiki/SOLID_%28object-oriented_design%29`.

Common designs and architectures

As mentioned earlier, sharing knowledge and simplifying communication between team members is one of the most common reasons some scientists give names to architectures and designs.

A **layer** is a logical module of software with its own core logic and boundaries.

A **tier** is a physical container of one or more layers, such as a server across a network or multiple instances of the same Virtual Machine, working in a load-balanced way.

Different kinds of architectures and designs exist, such as a single or multiple layered architectures and creational or behavioral design patterns. This book is not about architectures, so we will only provide an overview of the most used software and system architectures while trying to provide more details on performance concerns.

When dealing with a software architecture that relies on multiply systems, such as any n-tier architecture, the whole design takes the name of **system architecture**.

When talking about performance, many system designs are taken into account.

Layered architecture

Most architectures created are layered architectures. A generic layered architecture splits different application modules at different levels (layers) that represent the distance from the application user. The following figure shows a layered architecture:

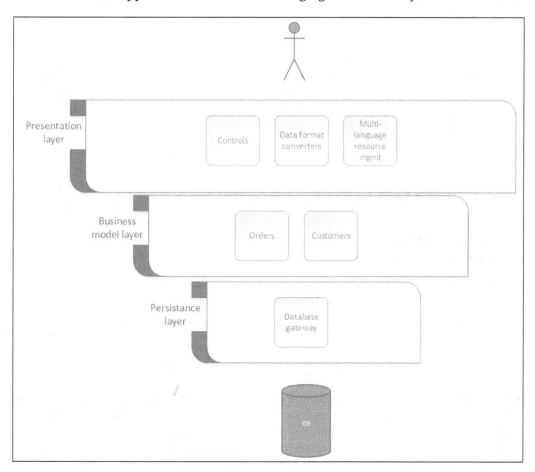

The preceding diagram shows what a generic web application or desktop application design might look like, according to a layered architecture. Layering is one of the older software architectures for OOP. It comes from a time when the critical requirement was to persist data and keep it safe somewhere. This is why the end user is at the opposite of the layer diagram. This approach adds decoupling because coupling only takes place from the top layer to the bottom layer.

Multiple modules can exist in the same layer, sharing the same stage of distance from the application user, because its parts are of the same behavioral module set (presentation, business, and so on). Otherwise, any cross-layer invocation can actually become a message exchange for decoupling needs. In-layer communication does not need to be decoupled, so any living object may talk to any associated object simply by invoking/using each one the brother instance's methods and properties that it needs.

Instead, when the communication breaks the boundary of the layer, we need to use the **data transfer object** (**DTO**) pattern, usually with plain old CLR object (POCO) objects. This kind of plumbing class serves as a container for data transfer, and a messaging scenario may actually use the **request-reply** pattern, which always expects a couple of DTOs, a request, and a response.

DTO, a design pattern as explained by *Martin Fowler* in his book *Patterns of Enterprise Application Architecture*, published by Addison-Wesley, has the objective of grouping data and reducing method calls. However, its main task is to reduce a round trip by frequently calling a remote system. It is also frequently used in **design-by-contract** programming (also known as **contract** programming) when dealing with interfaces as suggested by the *interface-segregation principle* in order to break the dependency and decouple the whole system.

 From more information on design-by-contract, refer to: `http://en.wikipedia.org/wiki/Design_by_contract`.

Performance concerns

As far as performance is concerned, the drawback of such a super-decoupled system is the need of other objects to convert or map (maybe with a **data mapper** pattern) different kinds of DTOs for all message purposes. Although the computational power in terms of CPU power needed to copy value-type data from one object to another is negligible, creating millions of object in memory may create an issue regarding memory usage and release. More critical is the huge cost standardization of such solutions may bring by reducing the availability of some specific language idioms, for instance, the ability to use `IQueryable<T>` idiom manipulations that will produce a single server-side executed query. Other instances are later discussed in this chapter. You will learn database querying later in *Chapter 7, Database Querying*.

As explained earlier, many decoupling techniques are available with layered architecture. The first is creating several contracts to break the knowledge of concrete implementation between associated layers. These contracts are obviously made with .NET interfaces and later implemented in concrete classes, where needed. As mentioned, never underestimate the cost of object creations/destructions and data copying that is generated by intensive data mapping. Though this will not cause a lot of CPU wastage, it will bring up a number of other issues. Later, in *Chapter 3*, *CLR Internals*, in the *Garbage collection* section, a deeper knowledge of this cost will become evident. However, in addition to this cost, think of all the idiom-based increased powerfulness that an architecture based on DTO exchanging with data mapping will simply avoid having at our availability.

A multilayered architecture may be released on a single tier (we usually say that this will flatten the architecture's physical setup) that usually also means a single server because of the restrictions in database balancing. A layered architecture has some pros, such as easy maintainability of layers and easy division of work in a team based on skills— from the upper layer skills of user experience, to the intermediate layer skills of good analysis, to the lower layer's need for expert database developers—it is easily understandable that scalability is still zero until we use a single tier. Latency depends only on DB latency itself. This means we can only optimize the I/O development module to try to take some advantage during this time. Throughput is also limited from one of the DBMS itself.

Flattening a 2-tier architecture will need a single physical tier.

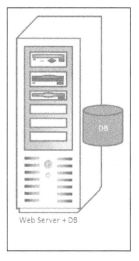

A flattened 2-tier architecture

Although a flattened release of a multilayered architecture is also available for 10-tier architectures, this must be avoided in any production environment. For testing purposes, however, it might be a cheap solution if we are low on space in our virtualization host. However, bear in mind that this choice will alter the similarity between the two environments, for instance powering up any latency time because of the network access time or the avoided network resource authentication time that is not actually required.

 An enterprise application is one that usually involves handling of big databases with several concurrent transactions, frequent data schema changes, customized business rules and logic, and huge integration needs with ubiquitous internal **business-to-consumer (B2C)** or **business-to-business (B2B)** legacy systems.

Most of the enterprise-dedicated applications of order management or customer relationship are made on this layered architecture. Obviously, the worst performance aspect in this scenario is the zero horizontal scalability. This is because this layered architecture is usually released on a 2-tier system, where many improvements in performance arise.

The following figure shows the classic 2-tier physical setup with multiple web servers (or desktop clients) that are using a single RDBMS as a data repository or a state repository:

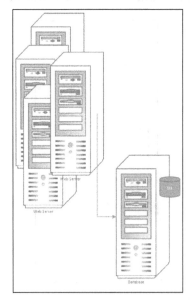

2-tiered architecture

By splitting the physical structure of the layered architecture, multiple groups of systems can be clustered to serve the same web application. This solution drastically changes the performance limitations of the whole architecture, by adding good scalability, although still limited by the unbalanced node (the database). Although this classic physical implementation of 2-tier architecture is the most common in enterprise or **Small office Home office (SoHo)** worlds, this solution usually bases its usage on the easiness of the solution and not on specific performance or reliability needs.

With this physical architecture, latency suffers the added hop, but throughput and scalability balances this (very) small drawback very well.

 A *hop* in computer networking is just another step when a request must be made to achieve the last system in order to be able to participate in a response composition.

Another very big difference that occurs when moving from a single-tier to n-tier (any tier amount) is the creation of a balance between applications/web servers.

Model-View-Controller and ASP.NET MVC

The MVC pattern, which is one of the most widely diffused across various programming languages, is based on a classical layered architecture.

The MVC pattern is at the base of the ASP.NET MVC framework, one of the most used framework in any newborn web application powered by the .NET framework since its first release in 2009, Version 1.0. Previous ASP.NET versions, that was renamed to Web Forms, actually became obsolete without any addition from the developer group (if any still exists) and without any coverage in the official Microsoft learning courseware since the release of Visual Studio 2012. This made ASP.NET MVC the main web-programming framework for Visual Studio.

The MVC pattern is the first layered design pattern for user-interface based applications, made of three layers. Later, **Model-View-Presenter (MVP)** and MVVM joined the group, adding different or specific features from their creators.

The MVC pattern was born in 1988 and was first announced in the pages of *The Journal of Object Technology*. It divides the presentation layer into three main modules or sub-layers: the View is the module concerning the graphical user experience. The Controller is the module concerning the iteration flow from/to the application and the user; and the Model represents the entities needed to fulfill single/multiple Views. The following figure shows an MVC-based web application:

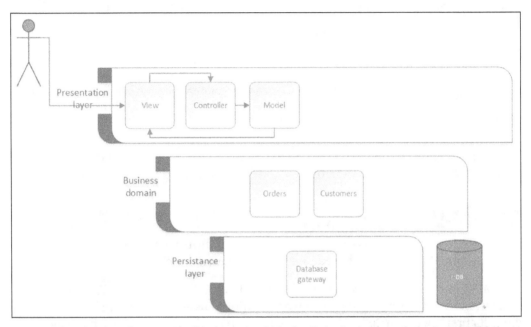

An MVC-based web application with all its layers in which the distinction between the business Model (from domain) and the user-experience oriented model (from MVC) is easily visible

Performance concerns

Using the MVC design pattern in web application development needs more programming work, together with increased testability (because of the more decoupled architecture) in comparison to any **Rapid Application Development (RAD)** approach.

The concrete implementation of the two frameworks ASP.NET MVC and ASP.NET Web Forms behaves very differently in terms of performance.

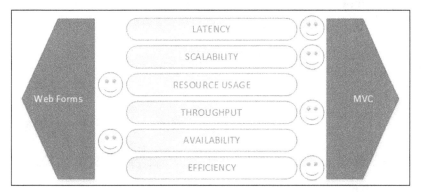

A performance comparative between ASP.NET MVC and Web Forms

Regarding latency, the winner is the MVC-based framework. Web Forms have a verbose page life cycle that increases the page elaboration time with an empty form.

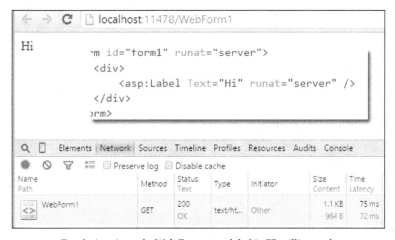

Rendering time of a Web Forms text label in 75 milliseconds

Without diving into the detail of the Web Forms page life cycle, it is enough to say that it must follow more than the simple steps that the MVC framework does. In ASP.NET MVC, any request simply routes from the `MvcHandler` class that creates a `ControllerFactory` class, this creates our controller, which invokes our action method by passing a model that was created by a `ModelBinding` and populated with any input data from the GET or POST request. Then, the controller does its job by executing the logic within the action and producing a new model to bind to the view.

In Web Forms, instead, there are more than 10 events for any page and the same for any child (nested) control. This means that the bigger a page is, the higher the number of wasted objects being created/destroyed and invoked events will be, thus increasing the latency time of rendering the whole page.

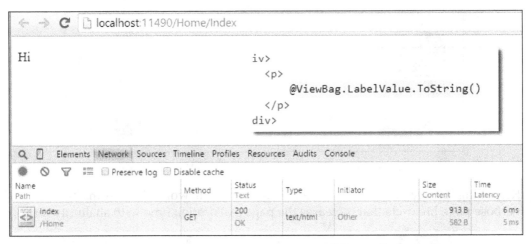

The same preceding page rendered as View in MVC in 6 milliseconds

ASP.NET MVC renders an empty view in not more than 7 milliseconds on my laptop (but in the first application load, the compilation time adds to the rendering time), while Web Forms render the same empty form in not less than 70 milliseconds. Although such absolute values are useless, relative values are the proof of the very different minimum latency times of the two frameworks. Regarding latency, on my laptop ASP.NET MVC is almost 10 times better than Web Forms!

Talking about scalability, MVC bases its architecture on a strong object-oriented design pattern that will guide the programmer to the most modularized application design, instead of the RAD guided approach of Web Forms.

I am not saying Web Forms cannot be used in a good MVP pattern or other layered (non-RAD) architectures, but this is actually not the average scenario. Thus, MVC-based web applications are supposed to become more scalable than Web Forms applications.

Analyzing scalability results in two solutions; this is a big difference that distinguishes MVC from Web Forms. The design of MVC is completely stateless, while a legacy Web Forms application will frequently make use of the session state, the ability to contain some navigational user data that lives in the memory of the web server(s).

Session state is a big bottleneck in scalability because it usually relies on the SQL Server as a persistence provider to contain and share session data between multiple servers that are involved in the same web application.

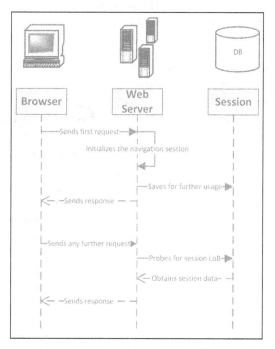

A sequence UML diagram of ASP.NET legacy SQL-based SessionState

Of course, some alternatives to using SQL Server persistence for session state do exist, such as the state server, an in-memory container with the limitation of the RAM available for the server. Another alternative that is greatly scalable from the state server is using a cloud-distributed cache provider, which is also available for local installations, that named **AppFabric Cache**. Using this kind of session provider will boost scalability, but obviously the choice of never using a session grants another level of scalability. It is like what was mentioned in the previous chapter about Amdahl's law. Although a powerful cache provider can give good results in session state persistence, it will also limit this capability, which will, in turn, limit the scalability of the whole architecture. Instead, without using the session state, this limit is virtually nothing when talking about state persistence because other factors limiting scalability could still exist.

A drawback exists in the sessionless approach of MVC. This is the throughput limitation and resource usage amplification due to the need of any request processed by the server to reload (what is usually in the session state) any related data from the persistence storage again. This is a subtle difference between the two designs, but it can make a significant difference in how they perform.

Talking about resource usage, I have to say that although MVC has a smaller footprint in comparison to the page's life cycle of a Web Forms application, the whole architecture needs more decoupling, and as mentioned previously, more decoupling means more abstraction and more mapping/conversion between objects. Another point against all such abstraction is the loss of idiom-based programming, such as the **Entity Framework** materialization or query building, because these are wasted by the DTO pattern being used by layered communication. When using an idiom-based approach, we can take advantage of technologies such as any dynamic expression tree construction that is available with LINQ (explained in the *Querying approaches* section in *Chapter 7, Database querying*). Instead, if we always have to populate a complete DTO, we create multiple DTOs, each for any different request operation, or we always create the DTO with all available data for any given entity. If we create multiple DTOs, we must face issues such as more coding and more requests needed for any case that a single DTO response gives the caller some useful information, but still misses something. If we create the DTO with all available data for the entity, we often waste CPU time and system resources by asking for lot of information, although a caller asks only for one particular piece of information. Obviously, using DTO is not a bad idea. However, simply put, it makes harder to create the right balance between DTO shape and number, which is not an easy task.

Here, a mixed design is desirable but would be hard to implement while respecting all principles of MVC pattern, layered architecture, SOLID, and OOP altogether.

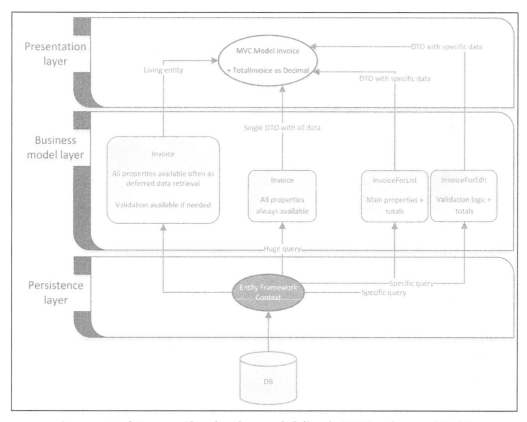

A comparative between an idiom-based approach (left) and a DTO-based approach (right)

As shown in the preceding diagram, a DTO-based approach can waste a lot of computational power, often without any need. Let's take the instance of an invoice materialization with no requirement to summarize the total amount or any other computation logic, such as client aggregations or product statistics and so on. To reduce this kind of limitation to DTOs, a solution could be to create different levels of DTOs of each entity with different details, or use the same type of DTO but with multiple de-persistence methods with the objective of materializing objects with probable empty properties. Another solution may be to use methods to work in an always-lazy calculation mode, sacrificing any massive reading of data.

The most balanced solution between data materialization cost and round-trip reduction is creating two or three business entities (or a single one with multiple DTOs). This solution avoids the extreme cost of using always the single fat DTO. It also avoids using the idiom-based entity, giving an increased ability to customize object materialization outside of the proper layer. This instance is also applicable outside of a persistence/de-persistence scenario.

A common solution to DTO materialization or data mapping is the wide use of caching techniques that can prevent requests from frequently penetrating the layers from the top-most layer to the deep persistence layer. This choice can help latency as well as throughput, but it makes the entire solution harder to maintain because of the difficulty of sharing a common cache object lifetime.

Talking about throughput, the MVC is the best solution because of the very small footprint of its page materialization life cycle, which produces a very low overhead during view rendering. This low overhead, if multiplied by the thousands of views rendered each day compared to the same job done by the classical Web Forms ISAPI, will give us an idea of more such resources that are used in effective throughput in MVC applications.

When analyzing the availability scenario, in a long-range analysis, MVC is the absolute winner. However, in a short-range analysis, Web Forms can produce a good solution, with very little effort from the developer team. This is because of the RAD approach. Once upon a time, old books about Web Forms often said that RAD helps in saving time that will later become available to developers, with the suggestion to use such time for better business analysis.

Another thing to bear in mind about availability regarding ASP.NET MVC applications is that the increased number of layers needs better skilled and experienced developers. Although each layer will become easy to develop by addressing a single (or few) functional needs per instance, integrating all such modules in a well-architected application needs some experience.

Finally, regarding efficiency, MVC is again the winner compared to Web Forms because of the higher throughput it achieves with the same computational power.

Model View Presenter (**MVP**) is not all that different from MVC. In MVP, the Presenter acts as a controller in the middle, between the View and the Model.

In MVC, requests from the View are sent to the Controller, which is in charge of understanding the request, parsing input data, routing such requests to the right action, and producing the right Model object to bind to the View.

On the other hand, the Presenter is more like an object-oriented code behind logic with the goal of updating the View with the Model data and reading back user actions/data.

Model-View-ViewModel and XAML

The MVVM pattern is another descendant of the MVC pattern. Born from an extensive update to the MVP pattern, it is at the base of all **eXtensible Application Markup Language** (**XAML**) language-based frameworks, such as Windows presentation foundation (WPF), Silverlight, Windows Phone applications, and Store Apps (formerly known as Metro-style apps).

MVVM is different from MVC, which is used by Microsoft in its main web development framework in that it is used for desktop or device class applications.

The first and (still) the most powerful application framework using MVVM in Microsoft is WPF, a desktop class framework that can use the full .NET 4.5.3 environment. Future versions within Visual Studio 2015 will support built-in .NET 4.6. On the other hand, all other frameworks by Microsoft that use the XAML language supporting MVVM patterns are based on a smaller edition of .NET. This happens with Silverlight, Windows Store Apps, Universal Apps, or Windows Phone Apps. This is why Microsoft made the Portable Library project within Visual Studio, which allows us to create shared code bases compatible with all frameworks.

While a Controller in MVC pattern is sort of a router for requests to catch any request and parsing input/output Models, the MVVM lies behind any View with a full two-way data binding that is always linked to a View's controls and together at Model's properties. Actually, multiple ViewModels may run the same View and many Views can use the same single/multiple instance of a given ViewModel.

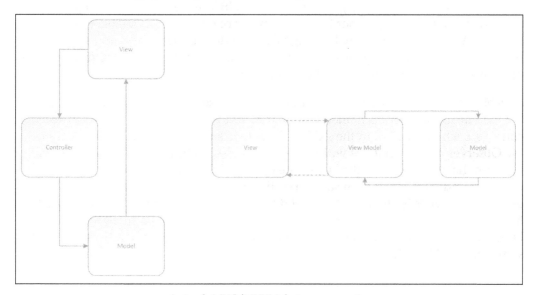

A simple MVC/MVVM design comparative

We could assert that the experience offered by MVVM is like a film, while the experience offered by MVC is like photography, because while a Controller always makes one-shot elaborations regarding the application user requests in MVC, in MVVM, the ViewModel is definitely the view!

Not only does a ViewModel lie behind a View, but we could also say that if a VM is a body, then a View is its dress. While the concrete View is the graphical representation, the ViewModel is the virtual view, the un-concrete view, but still the View.

In MVC, the View contains the user state (the value of all items showed in the UI) until a GET/POST invocation is sent to the web server. Once sent, in the MVC framework, the View simply binds one-way reading data from a Model. In MVVM, behaviors, interaction logic, and user state actually live within the ViewModel. Moreover, it is again in the ViewModel that any access to the underlying Model, domain, and any persistence provider actually flows.

Between a ViewModel and View, a data connection called *data binding* is established. This is a declarative association between a source and target property, such as Person.Name with TextBox.Text. Although it is possible to configure data binding by imperative coding (while declarative means decorating or setting the property association in XAML), in frameworks such as WPF and other XAML-based frameworks, this is usually avoided because of the more decoupled result made by the declarative choice.

The most powerful technology feature provided by any XAML-based language is actually the data binding, other than the simpler one that was available in Windows Forms. XAML allows one-way binding (also reverted to the source) and two-way binding. Such data binding supports any source or target as a property from a Model or ViewModel or any other control's dependency property.

This binding subsystem is so powerful in XAML-based languages that events are handled in specific objects named **Command**, and this can be data-bound to specific controls, such as buttons. In the .NET framework, an event is an implementation of the Observer pattern that lies within a delegate object, allowing a **1-N** association between the only source of the event (the owner of the event) and more observers that can handle the event with some specific code. The only object that can raise the event is the owner itself. In XAML-based languages, a Command is an object that targets a specific event (in the meaning of something that can happen) that can be bound to different controls/classes, and all of those can register handlers or raise the signaling of all handlers.

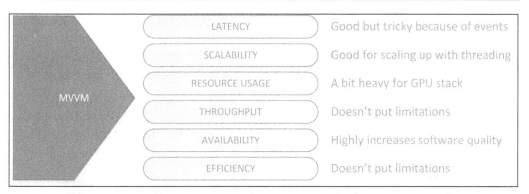

MVVM	LATENCY	Good but tricky because of events
	SCALABILITY	Good for scaling up with threading
	RESOURCE USAGE	A bit heavy for GPU stack
	THROUGHPUT	Doesn't put limitations
	AVAILABILITY	Highly increases software quality
	EFFICIENCY	Doesn't put limitations

An MVVM performance map analysis

Performance concerns

Regarding performance, MVVM behaves very well in several scenarios in terms of data retrieval (latency-driven) and data entry (throughput- and scalability-driven). The ability to have an impressive abstraction of the view in the VM without having to rely on the pipelines of MVC (the actions) makes the programming very pleasurable and give the developer the choice to use different designs and optimization techniques. Data binding itself is done by implementing specific .NET interfaces that can be easily centralized.

Talking about latency, it is slightly different from previous examples based on web request-response time, unavailable in MVVM. Theoretically speaking, in the design pattern of MVVM, there is no latency at all.

In a concrete implementation within XAML-based languages, latency can refer to two different kinds of timings. During data binding, latency is the time between when a VM makes new data available and a View actually renders it. Instead, during a command execution, latency is the time between when a command is invoked and all relative handlers complete their execution. We usually use the first definition until differently specified.

Although the nominal latency is near zero (some milliseconds because of the dictionary-based configuration of data binding), specific implementation concerns about latency actually exist. In any Model or ViewModel, an updated data notification is made by triggering the View with the `INotifyPropertyChanged` interface.

The .NET interface causes the View to read the underlying data again. Because all notifications are made by a single .NET event, this can easily become a bottleneck because of the serialized approach used by any delegate or event handlers in the .NET world.

On the contrary, when dealing with data that flows from the View to the Model, such an inverse binding is usually configured declaratively within the {Binding ...} keyword, which supports specifying binding directions and trigger timing (to choose from the control's lost focus CLR event or anytime the property value changes).

The XAML data binding does not add any measurable time during its execution. Although this, as said, such binding may link multiple properties or the control's dependency properties together. Linking this interaction logic could increase latency time heavily, adding some annoying delay at the View level. One fact upon all, is the added latency by any validation logic. It is even worse if such validation is other than formal, such as validating some ID or CODE against a database value.

Talking about scalability, MVVM patterns does some work here, while we can make some concrete analysis concerning the XAML implementation. It is easy to say that scaling out is impossible because MVVM is a desktop class layered architecture that cannot scale. Instead, we can say that in a multiuser scenario with multiple client systems connected in a 2-tier or 3-tier system architecture, simple MVVM and XAML-based frameworks will never act as bottlenecks. The ability to use the full .NET stack in WPF gives us the chance to use all synchronization techniques available, in order to use a directly connected DBMS or middleware tier (which will be explained later in this chapter).

Instead of scaling up by moving the application to an increased CPU clock system, the XAML-based application would benefit more from an increased CPU core count system. Obviously, to profit from many CPU cores, mastering parallel techniques is mandatory. *Chapter 4, Asynchronous Programming* and *Chapter 5, Programming for Parallelism* will cover such thematic.

About the resource usage, MVVM-powered architectures require only a simple POCO class as a Model and ViewModel. The only additional requirement is the implementation of the INotifyPropertyChanged interface that costs next to nothing. Talking about the pattern, unlike MVC, which has a specific elaboration workflow, MVVM does not offer this functionality. Multiple commands with multiple logic can process their respective logic (together with asynchronous invocation) with the local VM data or by going down to the persistence layer to grab missing information. We have all the choices here.

Although MVVM does not cost anything in terms of graphical rendering, XAML-based frameworks make massive use of hardware-accelerated user controls. Talking about an extreme choice, Windows Forms with **Graphics Device Interface (GDI)**-based rendering require a lot less resources and can give a higher frame rate on highly updatable data. Thus, if a very high FPS is needed, the choice of still rendering a WPF area in GDI is available. For other XAML languages, the choice is not so easy to obtain. Obviously, this does not mean that XAML is slow in rendering with its DirectX based engine. Simply consider that WPF animations need a good **Graphics Processing Unit (GPU)**, while a basic GDI animation will execute on any system, although it is obsolete.

Talking about availability, MVVM-based architectures usually lead programmers to good programming. As MVC allows it, MVVM designs can be tested because of the great modularity. While a Controller uses a pipelined workflow to process any requests, a ViewModel is more flexible and can be tested with multiple initialization conditions. This makes it more powerful but also less predictable than a Controller, and hence is tricky to use. In terms of design, the Controller acts as a *transaction script*, while the ViewModel acts in a more realistic, object-oriented approach.

Finally, yet importantly, throughput and efficiency are simply unaffected by MVVM-based architectures. However, because of the flexibility the solution gives to the developer, any interaction and business logic design may be used inside a ViewModel and their underlying Models. Therefore, any success or failure regarding those performance aspects are usually related to programmer work. In XAML frameworks, throughput is achieved by an intensive use of asynchronous and parallel programming assisted by a built-in thread synchronization subsystem, based on the `Dispatcher` class that deals with UI updates.

The 3-tier architecture

The 3-tier architecture is a layered architecture that is deployed across a physical multi-layered setup. This choice grants extreme layer reusability because each tier (logical representation of a physical layer able to multiple software layers) can participate in multiple applications, if properly developed.

The n-tier architecture is a generic multitier system architecture based on intensive multilayering. 3-tier is the smaller one, which is able to divide the three main tiers (presentation, business, persistence). It is possible to find solutions made of four tiers or six tiers. The architecture itself is the same as 3-tier. The only difference is the number of tiers containing business logic.

In its physical view, it is easily visible that the third tier is that of Web Services. This tier is responsible for containing any business logic by obtaining reusability and higher scalability rates.

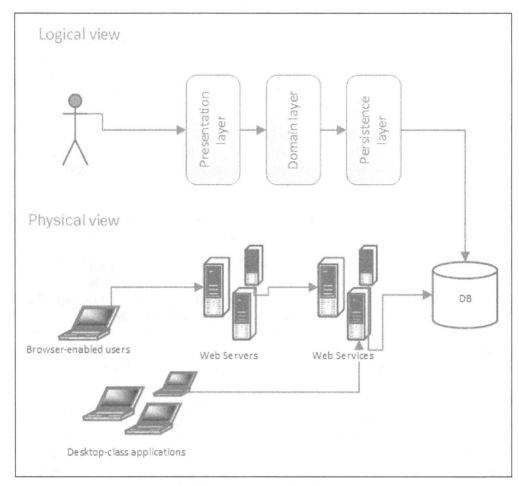

The 3-tier system architecture

Within n-tier architecture, layers are matched on a functional basis. They must share the intent, vision, or objective to be paired in the same tier. An example is the MVC layers paired in the **presentation** tier, all executing in the same web application running on the same web-server tier.

The second tier, as in 2-tier architecture, is the one containing all persistence layers.

The last tier, the one in the middle in the preceding diagram, is the one containing presentation-unaware business logic (logics regarding the presentation are usually interactive logics). Here, software modules such as a web service, a business rule engine, or a state machine workflow, are present to handle whatever the business requirements are. All such logics will run in the application-server tier.

The difference between layered structure and tiered structure is that the latter is a layered architecture with a specific physical layout (system architecture).

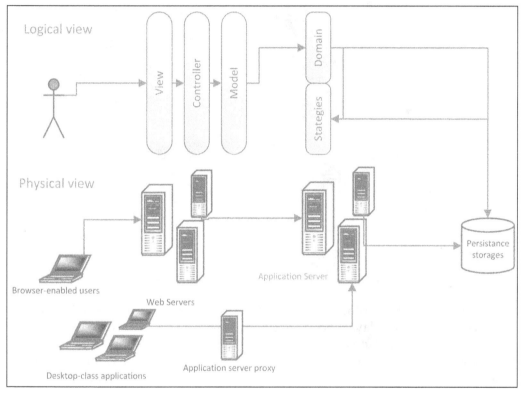

Another 3-tier system architecture containing an external system for business-rule processing (strategies)

Performance concerns

In terms of performance, n-tier architecture gives its best in scalability because each tier, if appropriately designed, could scale individually. Bear always in mind that performance aspects such as network availability, throughput, and latency are a primary concern of 3-tier architecture.

Sometimes, a better result is achieved by isolating the tiers from the main network, apart from the tier that will need this explicit connection, by using a sub-network of grouped systems in a closed network. Because in 3-tier architecture network performances directly affect overall performance, it is a good choice to avoid using the network used to make tiers communicate with each other for other needs of the whole company. This solution reduces the usage of network resources by the addition of corporate network needs, as well as private network ones.

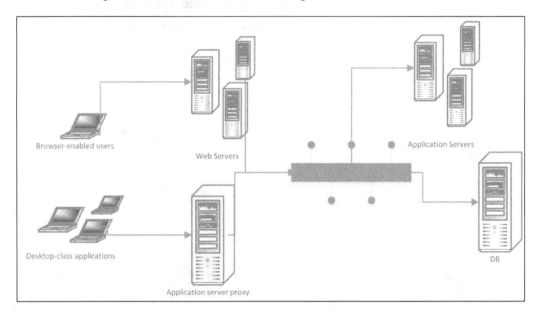

Regarding latency, the multiple round trips happening on the network at each tier cross will add visible delays if no cache systems are used (we will cover caching later in the *Caching, when and where* section of this chapter). Although this issue may be annoying, the great improvements made to other performance indicators usually balance this limitation.

Scalability, as mentioned, will improve greatly using 3-tier architecture, thanks to the ability to balance physical resource usage across multiple systems.

Although a bottleneck that is able to reduce scalability, is the persistence storage provider, usually a DBMS. Balancing the computational power of all systems participating in the architecture is easy to do. Instead, SQL-based persistence providers are usually difficult to balance. Regarding scalability, NoSQL databases are a winning choice compared to classic SQL-based databases.

Resource usage affects the size of the solution. This is why we should not use such architecture to drive simple or small applications. In other words, in small releases, n-tier architecture needs many virtual/physical systems, along with a lot of serialization and creation of DTOs during communication between modules of different tiers. If our target is a small software application, maybe the best architecture would be a 2-tier MVC based web application. Talking again about 3-tier architecture, although it enables us to release the whole solution in a single physical system with multiple virtual machines (or even a single virtual machine), the solution must be designed as a network-based architecture, otherwise eventually scaling out to multiple virtual machines will be impossible. Again, another heavy usage of resources is made by caching providers, which is massively used in 3-tier architecture because of the evident benefit in terms of response time and throughput.

Throughput is another key benefit of such architecture because of the great division made by software modules and layers in all tiers of the whole design. The only limitation is an internal network failure or congestion. It is not just about network bandwidth but also about network backbone availability (within switches), routing/firewall speed (of network appliances), and broadcast/multicast traffic that can saturate all network resources and their availability easily.

The architecture achieves high availability, thanks to the high scalability rate. Multiple nodes of any tier can be released and may work together to balance traffic and obtain a strong failover. The weak tier here is the persistence one that relies on internal persistence-provider solutions in order to achieve availability.

Efficiency is a secondary aspect of n-tier solutions and is a powerful architecture that should address a heavy task such as e-commerce, or a complex human workflow-based solution, such as escalation-based customer care for client services, and so on. High consumption of resources in terms of memory, processor, and network traffic are needed to let n-tier architecture run in the proper way. Therefore, if efficiency is your primary goal when searching for an architecture suited for your new application, simply use another onelike a 2-tier MVC application or any other 2-tiered architecture that has improved efficiency and latency compared to 3-tiererd architecture.

One limitation of n-tier architecture is that the whole system is still a single monolithic application. It is also modularized, layered, divided in tiers to achieve hardware-linked resource configuration per tier, and so on, but the whole system is a single *software*, a single (although big) application. That is why some genius thought of the **Service Oriented Architecture (SOA)**.

Service-Oriented Architecture (SOA)

The service orientation happens when we stop thinking of it as a completely monolithic application, and begin thinking of it as an information system made by the combined usage of multiple small applications.

These small applications that name services are containers of logics with the same functional scope. Although a service does not contain any data by itself, any service has its own persistence storage (or multiple) — a persistence storage is never available to multiple services. The data availability must cross within a service and not behind it.

Services do not have any graphical representation; they are used by other services or end-user applications (with a UI) that need access to service data and logic. In SOA vocabulary, these external applications are used to invoke requests and retrieve response messages from services. Those serialized DTOs that move across the network names are *Messages*.

An important thing to bear in mind is that when talking about SOA, there are no multiple layers released across multiple tiers. In SOA, we definitely have multiple small applications that together compose a huge information system. This does not mean that a single service cannot be developed with a layered architecture by itself. In fact, this is usually what actually happens.

In SOA, there are also special services with the task of grouping data by other smaller services (*service facade*) or special services to maintain, or for service discoverability, such as a corporate **Enterprise Service Bus** (**ESB**).

The following diagram provides a simplified representation of an SOA design with a direct service access, a routed service access by an ESB, and a service aggregator access through a service facade:

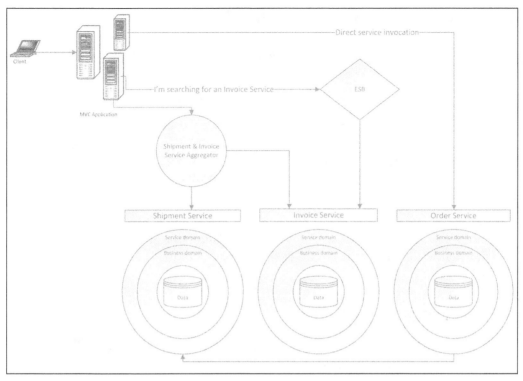

Direct service invocation

Client

MVC Application

I'm searching for an Invoice Service

ESB

Shipment & Invoice
Service Aggregator

Shipment Service

Invoice Service

Order Service

Service domain
Business domain
Data

Service domain
Business domain
Data

Service domain
Business domain
Data

An SOA environment

The most visible unlike SOA and n-tier is that although SOA uses a layered approach, this is confined within the boundaries of any service that acts as a container of the whole logic in terms of the functional behavior of such services.

Another great difference is that different from any other architecture, here, each service has its own data. Any other service needing the same data can only access it by invoking the other service. Thus, this approach increases some latency time, and by utilizing some network resources, it will greatly increase the availability of the whole solution because such integration between logic is done at the service level and not at the raw data level.

Principles of SOA are similar to SOLIDs. A brief description of the most widely accepted standard, as defined by Thomas Erl in his book *SOA Principles of Service Design*, published by Prentice Hall, is provided in the next section.

Standardized service contract

> *Services within the same service inventory are in compliance with the same contract design standard.*

> *– Thomas Erl, SOA Principles of Service Design*

Defining a contract, as is done for the *interface segregation principle* of SOLID, helps in sharing the knowledge of how to use the service, what the service expects on request, and what the service will give as a response, with the difference of adding a network-related standard (as simple object access protocol or SOAP — an XML-based protocol — on HTTP).

This principle is the basis on which all the others principles lie because without a standardized communication and meta-communication (the ability to exchange descriptive information about service design), no autonomous network calls can be placed.

Service loose coupling

> *Service contracts impose low consumer coupling requirements and are themselves decoupled from their surrounding environment.*

> *– Thomas Erl, SOA Principles of Service Design*

Loose coupling is the goal of any OOP-based principle. For SOA, it is exactly the same. This principle states that between the service consumer (a client or another service) and the service, a neutral contract with neutral DTO classes must exist. This choice will break any form of coupling between the client and the service and between the service inner logic and outer DTOs. Never expose a real *Domain* object because it is too powerful and too coupled to internal needs.

This principle helps maintain a neutral layer of objects, that is, the DTOs (already seen in SOLID), which will also help grant a decoupled contract again, in time. When multiple versions of the same service become available in time, new DTOs will be available to fulfill updated service contracts without a direct connection with internal business objects.

Service abstraction

Service contracts only contain essential information and information about services is limited to what is published in service contract.

– Thomas Erl, SOA Principles of Service Design

The decoupling principle states that a service must actually be a kind of a *black box* in the consumer's eyes. The less a consumer knows about the service being used, the more such a service becomes abstract and changeable with other versions or implementations. In SOA, the radical change of the whole service with all that is behind it is actually possible with almost no changes at the consumer level. This is one of the strongest benefits of using SOA.

Service reusability

Services contain and express agnostic logic and can be positioned as reusable enterprise resources.

– Thomas Erl, SOA Principles of Service Design

A service is like a network printer or a network storage server. It is definitely a *resource*. It does not belong to any single application; it is an application itself. It is like any physical resource, always available to any one (human or machine) that needs it within the company network and sometimes, with appropriate security outside the company, in scenarios such as B2B and B2C (usually through a service proxy).

The service reusability principle also slightly states that the ownership of the logic and data behind a service must not be bypassed by anyone.

Service autonomy

Services exercise a high level of control over their underlying runtime execution environment.

– Thomas Erl, SOA Principles of Service Design

This principle definitely enforces the service's single ownership against its core logic and data by dictating that the more a service is isolated by other systems (for instance, it does not call any other service), the more it becomes autonomous. The more a service is autonomous, the more it can be composed of other services to fulfill higher level logic needs or simply to group complex logic behind a single (and easy to invoke) call in what is exposed as a service facade or a service proxy, usually exposed in B2B and B2C solutions.

Service statelessness

Services minimize resource consumption by deferring the management of state information when necessary.

– Thomas Erl, SOA Principles of Service Design

In SOA, the communication state, such as the session state of classic ASP.NET, is useful to reduce network traffic and round trips, providing the ability to reach a more complex interaction level without the need to include anything in a request (for example, as we did in non-SOA compliant services such as RESTfuls).

This principle also states that state information duplication should never happen when a multiple cross-service level access takes place.

For instance, if we are invoking a service that needs accessing three other services that will all need accessing their persistence storage or other helper services, such as an audit service and some other one, with SOA we have the ability to make the request only to the first service while waiting for the whole response. Meanwhile, behind the scenes, the first service will start a session state of the whole operation. All services participating in the same session will be able to access all such data without a direct data exchange between services. Usually, a distributed caching service or session state is the container of all such shared user data.

During a service operation execution, each service should contain only its own state information, relying on the whole session state for any cross-service request.

Service discoverability

Services are supplemented with communicative meta-data by which they can be effectively discovered and interpreted.

– Thomas Erl, SOA Principles of Service Design

A service is a company resource, such as an employee, a printer, or anything else available to the company to reach its goals. So just like an employee has his internal email address or phone number available to every colleague within the company, a service must be found by any application that could ever need it. The principle states that a company service registry, such as an address book of services, must exist. Such a registry (ESB) must contain any available information about the service, such as name, physical address, available contracts, and related versions, and must be available to anyone in the company. Modern ESBs also add functions of DTO conversion in order to achieve version compatibility or to improve compatibility against external standards that are not directly implemented within our services. Other common features include request routing (with priority support), message audit, message business intelligence, and response caching. Within Microsoft's offering, an ESB is available as an optional feature for the **BizTalk Server,** under the name of **BizTalk ESB Toolkit**.

Discoverability is a strong principle to boost service orientation because it helps to see the service as a resource and not as a software module or application piece.

Service composability

> *Services are effective composition participants, regardless of the size and complexity of the composition.*

> *– Thomas Erl, SOA Principles of Service Design*

This principle states that a service must be able to act as an effective composition member of services. This is because an agnostic service can be used to solve different problems, and because a service composition brings the *separation of concerns* to another level, giving the composition the ability to resolve very difficult problems with the participation of the whole system with a little additional work.

This principle may be the soul of the whole principle list. It explains the goal of the entire paradigm. Although services live as autonomous applications, they exist to integrate other services. Indeed, regarding SOA, an information system is definitely a composition of services.

Performance concerns

Regarding performance, it is clear that SOA consumes more resources than the n-tier architecture does. The most widely used standard to drive SOA services is the **Simple Object Access Protocol (SOAP)**. SOAP is based on XML messages that rely on HTTP/POST messaging. This makes all such services definite web services. SOAP supports all the SOA needs, but with a high cost in terms of message size and protocol complexity.

With .NET 3.0, Microsoft introduced **Windows Communication Foundation (WCF)**, which adds support to multiple service communication standards such as SOAP, REST, and the newly `NetTcpBinding` class that extends the old **.NET Remoting** API (a remote-proxy based protocol for distributed programming on TCP — an updated version of **Common Object Request Broker Architecture (CORBA)**) making it able to fulfill all SOA needs. With the ability to support multiple service endpoints (with different protocols), WCF opens the way to a new era of low-footprint SOA services. Switching from SOAP to the `NetTcpBinding` largely reduces network traffic and latency time without any drawbacks, in terms of SOA principles. Unfortunately, this standard is not entirely compatible with no-.NET applications. Obviously, with an ESB converting the messages, such issues disappear.

Developing a performing SOA-driven application needs skilled developers and extensive optimization at multiple levels. Most communication across a network occurs whenever a message flows between services. Moreover, a lot of message validation and business rules are executed at service boundary level, before a service accepts any request and before a client (an application or the service itself) accepts any response from another node. Kindly consider that because of the whole design of the architecture, low latency is never available because of the high number of logical and physical steps any message must pass through to reach the target destination, both as a request and as a response.

High scalability, rather than latency, is definitely a killer feature of SOA. Such an autonomous design for any service produces the maximum scalability level for any service node. The whole architecture itself is made to fulfill thousands of requests from/to any node in the whole design. The eventual bottleneck here is the network itself. Only an extremely well performing network may drive a huge SOA information system. Another key aspect of such a scalability level is persistence decoupling. Although this may create some data duplication, such as the same IDs doubled in each single persistence system, if applicable, it also enables real scaling of such persistence systems. Because of not being bonded to a single (huge and centric) DBMS any more but to multiple different instances made with heterogeneous technologies, addressing the best persistence system depending the kind of data, should be persisted.

Resource usage, as explained, is the Achilles heel of SOA. A saying about SOA is that if you cannot drive SOA because it is missing its hardware resources, SOA is not the right architecture for your company! An SOA system is always a huge system, as the mainframe was a huge system for banking needs 40 years ago (and still is). Maybe SOA is the most complex and powerful architecture for enabling distributed systems to fulfill hundreds or thousands of requests per second of a different kind and complexity level, but such system complexity has some basic requirements, such as high systems resources.

Throughput is another killer feature of SOA because of the quasi-unlimited scalability of the whole system and the extreme modularization that helps in optimizing the code at the core of a service for its only needs. This kind of design also helps maintain the availability of any service because of the great autonomy of each node against other nodes. In addition, testing is easy to drive here because of the great decoupling between nodes that exchanges messages to be substituted with mock (fake data for testing purposes) messages.

Another key feature of SOA is the governance of the whole solution. It is easy to analyze traffic on a per message basis, per functional area basis, per service basis with information regarding consumer metadata, message version, service contract version, and so on.

All such analysis data may be grouped to get an exhaustive overview of the whole system and business without having to fit that logic within a business service, because its agnostic design never should. Information such as the average total amount of an invoice or product price doesn't need to flow from the invoice service to a business analysis workflow; the corporate ESB could simply route this message to the two nodes together. With this, each one could know about the existence of the other.

With Efficiency, the resource consumption of the design is usually a great indicator of the ability of the system to process a huge amount of messages. Keep in mind, as said about resource usage, that SOA has some technical requisites that avoids using easy or small systems. SOA definitely suits complex, huge, or high transaction-rate information systems well.

Architecture comparison

In this section, we provide an analytical view on how different performance indicators relate to different solutions, based on the architectures that we have just discussed.

The two excellent architectures are the 2-tier ASP.NET MVC-based architecture, which is the best performing in terms of latency, and SOA, which definitely wins in terms of scalability.

Another thing that is easily visible is the average low-level result that Web Forms obtains about any performance indicator. Here, the age of the framework (released in 2001) acts as the main bottleneck, together with the RAD approach made to help shorten time release, thus killing long-term maintenance and the life cycle of the whole application.

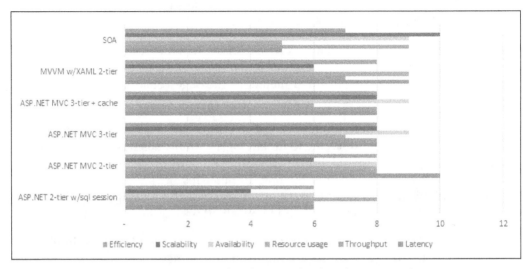

The architectures just analyzed compared with performance results

Common platform architectures

Each type of application has its best fitting software architecture. All modern architectures are somehow derived from layered architecture, although this does not make them all similar in terms of performance. Often, the same logical architecture is performed differently. Accordingly, the applied application kind, and often the same logical architecture, requires some customization to better fit the specific needs of each platform.

Architecting desktop applications

Since the release of Visual Studio 2008, the main desktop platform framework was WPF. Although it is possible to use WPF in an event-driven architecture such as the RAD architecture used in Windows Forms, this is not an efficient solution when fitted across a WPF project. A similar approach will waste long-term programmer productivity, without producing any concrete benefit against performance indicators.

A desktop application requires in low latency, low resource usage, good efficiency, and discrete throughput, while indicators such as scalability and availability are definitely secondary concerns.

For an internal **line-of-business** (**LoB**) data-driven application, the best desktop application relies on a layered MVVM application on the WPF framework, released on a 2-tier system architecture. Because of the great low-latency given by WPF, together with asynchronous programming, maintenance costs of MVVM architecture, together with a direct connection to any corporate DBMS, are low, any other external system nullifies the need for middleware or a middle tier with its own maintenance costs. Obviously, for a corporate application that needs to be accessed by thousands of employees, a 3-tier or SOA architecture will be mandatory in order to fulfill scalability needs, reuse logic, and achieve an improved application decoupling from the underlying database.

The ability to use any multithreading technique in such client applications will also give the right throughput to fulfill any elaboration need.

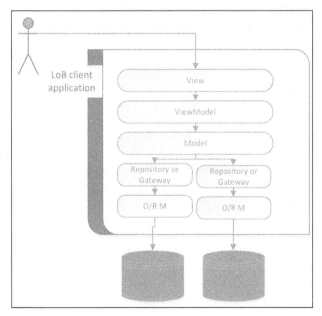

A line-of-business application with multiple DBMS persistence storages

Such architecture will also benefit from the automatic release systems that are offered by Visual Studio with built-in versions and update management, such as **ClickOnce**. Alternatively, a XBAP browser-enabled WPF application may be developed, but this WPF template is slowly being abandoned by Microsoft and by most of the control/component makers on the market.

The alternative is an SOA-powered architecture that totally differs from a data-driven architecture, such as the one explained earlier. SOA does its best when a complex business logic is the primary concern of the whole design.

Find more information about ClickOnce at `http://en.wikipedia.org/wiki/ClickOnce`.

Architecting mobile applications

Mobile applications are similar to desktop applications in terms of performance needs. While the desktop world today is totally confined to enterprise applications, mobile devices, such as smartphones and tablets, need something similar to the desktop application. However, they're different because essentially they're usually consumer-oriented applications.

Mobile applications need very low resource usage, high efficiency, and a good throughput, if applicable. Indicators such as latency and availability are secondary concerns while scalability is unnecessary as any other single-user application relying on external services for data persistence and complex business logics.

Another factor that's important when developing mobile applications, although not regarding performance, is the need for a reactive UX. A mobile user should never find his device frozen; the UI must always do something to acknowledge that the logic is still being executed. Although the same behavior is suggested also for any desktop class applications, mobile applications specifically need such behavior as a primary concern. This need does not deal with latency; it is more like a partial update to the UI, which is made to improve the user experience. Regarding the system architecture, the target solution for a mobile is a 3-tier architecture with the first tier made by a huge number of devices. Usually, because of the high fluctuation of connected devices, a cloud-based release is suggested.

A widely used mobile device web-service based architecture is described in the following diagram. Reusability of services is available for future versions of mobile applications:

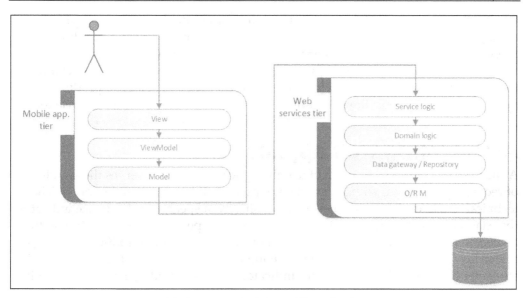

A 3-tier system serving a mobile application

In Visual Studio 2013, new project templates are available and can be used to create multiplatform applications. The **Universal Apps** project helps to create applications that can work on Windows Phone or Windows with a single shared core logic.

Regarding the architecture, creating a mobile application targeted for a single or multiple platforms does not change the architecture needs. Usually, a cloud service provider is used for single mobile applications because Universal Apps may be targeted for a bigger market, made by a more heterogeneous client style.

Regarding performance, the biggest limitation is the one offered by using a portable library logic internally in mobile code where a small .NET framework (with less features) is available. On the other hand, you can execute complex code outside mobile devices in a web service where there is a full .NET framework stack available. It offers better features with more performance optimization techniques, along with virtually infinite computational power.

The usage of a shared logic in a portable library, or using a Universal Apps project that does the same for us, is priceless for the simplicity of creating a single cross-platform application. The drawback is that we have to know the limitations behind such a choice. It is obvious that a shared library can execute only easy tasks with the small .NET framework available. When things become difficult, is time to move the needed computation outside the device.

What is the alternative? Creating a 3-tier architecture catching all the complex logic (see the previous example about the Web) in the middle tier and multiple presentations for devices and other media. Such a presentation may also use Universal Apps as development projects. With this choice, we can process complex logic and huge datasets in a serviced tier without losing the ability to produce a fashioned mobile application for multiple platforms with as few efforts possible.

Architecting web applications

A theoretically perfect definition of a web application is that it serves thousands of requests per second, without letting any users feel the traffic on the server. The technical name for this handling is load sensitivity, a specific performance indicator that stands for how much a system changes its other performance indicators with respect to load change. This indicator is definitely part of our simplified meaning of scalability, because if a system is able to handle millions of requests per second with a huge performance drop in all other indicators, this is definitely not good scalability.

Thus, the target performance requisite for a web application is low latency or asynchronous elaboration of jobs in a state-machine workflow manner. High throughput is necessary, and the same goes for scalability, although this means sacrificing indicators such as resource usage and efficiency. Availability is a critical requisite because although we never desire an easy-to-crash system, when dealing with thousands of requests per second, it is obvious that some of those will fail—such failures should never reduce the robustness of the whole system. Availability means that the web application should maintain its healthy status, although some user requests could fail.

Regarding performance, the most balanced architecture is the 2-tier made on ASP. NET MVC. This layered architecture gives a good response time and good scalability and throughput, along with good long-term maintenance level.

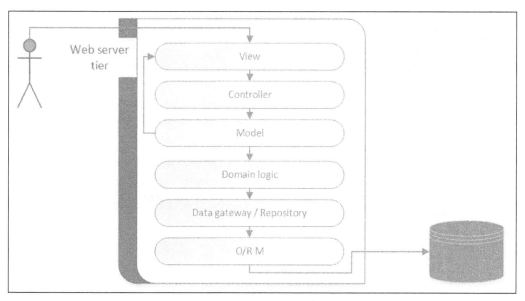

A 2-tier system serving a layered MVC web application

An alternative is to use the SOA to create multiple functional isles with multiple web services and persistence storages. This could support heavy loads, extremely high scalability rate, and very complex logic. Obviously, without any of these specific needs, its drawbacks will waste any benefit with the cost of a high development effort.

Architecting cloud web applications

What differs from a classic, although not legacy, web application and a cloud one is mainly the different technology stacks that sometimes bring different architectural solutions.

Another great difference between these two worlds is the release management. Something actually difficult when working with a 3-tier architecture is handling the service versioning that is needed to fulfill future requirements, along with supporting real time web application subscribed contracts. A typical solution to release the whole software made of all three tiers in a big-bang way, by releasing all tiers together. Although this may seem like a good solution, it is usually difficult to have a new working release of everything, especially when multiple additions are made to the initially designed system architecture.

Here is where a cloud provider such as Microsoft Azure helps us, because all of our application tiers are always in the Cloud Service deployment package. We can say that an Azure Cloud Service always does big-bang releases.

The goal of a 3-tier (and higher) architecture is to externalize core business logic by the presentation layer, which can be updated in time, or reused by serving different frameworks, such as the MVC for web, the MVVM for devices, and so on. With a 3-tier architecture and for SOA too, we have the ability to update only a portion of our application per instance. Obviously, only updates that do not affect other tiers can be made. This gives a great advantage and enables ease of release management and saving time.

Another simplification in release management, scalability, and availability, is the usage of multiple persistence storages, eventually relying on different technologies. A Microsoft Azure 3-tier architecture with multiple persistence storage and asynchronous processing that is made with cloud level queues design is described in the following diagram:

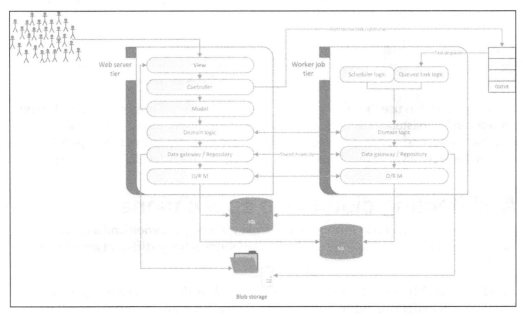

A Microsoft Azure 3-tier architecture

What actually differs from the solution previously seen is the usage of different persistence storages trying to address a winning solution regarding performance, such as relational databases or no-SQL repositories, such as a **BLOB storage** for files.

Another interesting difference here is the usage of asynchronous task registration. An example is the account registration or any high computational or state machine logic-driven task. With this choice, task data is temporarily stored on a **First In First Out (FIFO)** container, a message queue with transactional support and automatic re-attempt logic that guarantees the message processing. This asynchronous design is highly scalable and available because in critical load condition, a message will never be lost or unprocessed; in the worst-case scenario, it might be processed with a bit of delay.

Performance considerations

When dealing with performance, a lot of little design concerns may improve or worsen the overall feel of the application. Let's look at the most used or misused techniques.

Caching, when and where

Caching data means reusing a temporary copy of such data for a short time period, reducing the need to contact a persistence storage or any external system, such as a service.

In respect to performance indicators, caching is something that boosts the throughput and latency of data retrieval by avoiding a round trip to an external server that is running a database. Meanwhile, caching increases client resource usage of CPU and memory. Storing temporary data in a cache is something that is fully handled by a caching framework that has the task of removing old data from the cache when the imposed timeout occurs, or when there is too much data within the cache and older (or less used) data must be removed in order to create space for any new data. This is why when lots of data is deliberately loaded and maintained in memory, to prevent future data loading at application start, we do not use cache. We simply load all data into the memory.

Since .NET 4.0, a new assembly containing caching services has been added to the framework (for old .NET editions, a cache framework was available in the `System.Web` namespace). The `System.Runtime.Caching.MemoryCache` class is used to manage an in-memory configurable data cache. A distributed cache service for on-premise or cloud services is available under the name **AppFabric Cache**.

Caching is a design technique that must work at the boundary of each layer where it is potentially needed. In multi-tier architectures, the cache is always used at the boundary of the tier.

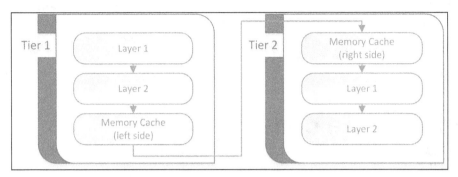

A boundary cache: one at tier 1 and one at tier 2

As visible in the preceding diagram, we find two cache proxies at boundaries of tiers. The one on the left side (at boundary exit) can avoid round trips on the network, along with avoiding data loading from the following tier. Caching at a boundary exit is possibly the biggest performance booster against indicators such as latency and throughput.

The one on the right side (at boundary entrance) can reduce the core logic, and eventually, core data gateways work when the response is already available. An instance of this kind of caching is the *OutputCache* of any ASP.NET application.

In enterprise-level applications, in which many requests are made with a lot of data to handle, it is a good idea to have the two cache levels working together to reduce any kind of already-done logic or data retrieval. This is commonly named multilevel cache.

Be cautious to cached item's lifetime, handled with absolute or relative expiration. Eventually, if a cached item changes it's value before it's cache expiration time then use object poisioning (it is the art of removing a data entry that is not good to be committed), especially in distributed cache systems. Also, take care of item assigned key, expecially when using a multilevel cache, because if such cache has heterogeneous data entries against the same key, a possible data inconsistency may arise.

PLINQ everywhere

The Integrated in-code querying support made by the **LINQ** framework in 2007 with .NET 3.0, changed the mind of developers completely when dealing with data. With these frameworks, any enumerable data available in .NET or externally with specific providers (such as a DB), is available to any object filtering/grouping/reshaping with a single unified querying language.

Task Parallel Library (TPL) and **PLINQ** (LINQ + TPL) did the same thing in 2010, adding parallel elaboration to any enumerable dataset. The TPL, which will be discussed later in *Chapter 4, Asynchronous Programming*, is the basis of all asynchronous programming model on .NET 4.0 or greater. Things such as asynchronous tasks or multicore asynchronous execution of any LINQ query definitely cuts the edge with legacy programming when dealing with computations and iterations.

Dividing thousands of items in to tens of threads may be the best choice when dealing with a very high throughput demanding code; the sooner the code terminates its job, the better it is.

When creating applications such as web or serviced types, where any user request comes across a new thread, creating so many computational threads per user can produce a worse performance than using normal LINQ instead of PLINQ. Such thread usage might let you finish the thread pool provision, further reducing the thread creation time drastically, along with the high resource cost of creating hundreds of threads.

Although definitely needed, such kinds of applications should avoid multiplying thread creation by using standard LINQ queries. A detailed overview about PLINQ and TPL will be available in *Chapter 4, Asynchronous Programming*.

Inversion of Control (IoC)

This design inverts the usage of references between classes. Usually, a class uses its references, thus becoming the orchestrator. Inversely, when using the **IoC** design, a class asks for any implementation of such a desired interface (contract) and waits for the factory to be able to find a suitable external class/component to fulfill this need.

Although this choice can lead to writing winning solutions for design (this depends on the taste of the architect dealing with such architecture), with great modularization and code reusability, and in respect to module reusability, this choice is a bit unpredictable regarding performances.

An application may perform well with a good (or fake for testing purposes) external module and badly with a bad one. It is hard to test something external that was made by someone else. It is also hard to test something that will be made in the future, maybe because in a couple of years, new external components will become available and possibly usable in such applications.

When dealing with such a problem, the performance engineer's job is to isolate the poorly performing modules within the whole application. This helps to identify the reason for such bad performance of the external module and helps maintain a secure application all around, limiting the exploitation made by the assembly injection or cracking.

Lazy loading

Lazy loading is the art of never preloading data or simple class instances. Like caching that prevents duplicated logic from being executed, by saving the result, lazy loading prevents the execution of some logic or data retrieval until it is actually needed. For instance, Entity Framework (EF) definitely uses a lot of lazy loading in query execution and query compilation. *Chapter 7, Database querying*, will focus entirely on data retrieval with EF.

A lot of attention must be given to what logic or data should be delayed in a lazy environment. Never delay data that will be requested just a second later or in massive amounts.

 Never use the lazy loading technique for massive amounts of data; instead, use an asynchronous programming technique.

Regarding performance impact, lazy loading the right data will boost the startup of the application or the response time of a web application. Some general improvement in latency will occur too if unnecessary data is loaded when not needed. Obviously, when an application is completely used by its users, loading all composing modules, any lazy data could be already loaded without altering any performance aspect, compared to a non-lazy approach.

Lazy loading first boosts latency time by trying to delay a secondary logic execution (or data retrieval) to some future time. The drawback happens specifically when a bad design occurs with intensive single data requests (instead of a single complete one) or multiple execution of the same logic for lots of items, without relying on any asynchronous or parallel technique. Lazy loading also alters the execution flow from an imperative instantiation time to a less predictable one. Debugging will suffer because of this.

On the contrary, there is pre-loading data. Although this feels like a legacy option, do not discard it for just this reason. All application level data that can be loaded only once can definitely be loaded at startup. This will increase at such a time, but with the right user acknowledgment, like an old-style initialization bar, the user will feel that the system is loading what is needed, and this is always a good practice, while until the end, such data will grant the best latency time as it wont incur any retrieval cost.

Usually, mixing caching with lazy or pre-emptive loading is always a bad choice because they have opposite goals. Caching is for slow-changing data, increasing initial latency and resource usage for a future improvement in throughput. Lazy loading, on the other hand, reduces (boost) initial latency by delaying tasks to a short timed future by drastically reducing the throughput of data retrieval, which usually lacks any optimization technique.

Reusability of code

It is well known that coding is the love of any developer. It is like a special kind of craziness that takes control of the brain of any developer when a new solution, algorithm, or logic is actually made. Just like how when someone using Microsoft Word presses the Save button when they finish writing something new and important, a developer will try to save the application code when new code is inserted for future usage. Although any code may be reused by cutting and pasting, this is not code reusability.

Writing a good component or control is not easy because most of the code must be reusable. A good component must be autonomous, regarding any eventual implementation. The more autonomous and agnostic the code is, the easier it becomes for any future user of such a control.

For instance, Text Box is a text container. It does not matter if it's usually used for text and not for numbers; it also supports numbers, passwords, and so on. Whoever made the control had to test all possible usage scenarios, without supporting a single use case.

Well-performing code should usually be customized to your specific application or platform needs. Another big deal to face is that eventually, unbelievably complex code structures are made to achieve the best abstraction level without keeping in mind maintainability or any design/architectural guideline. This is where performance optimization cannot be applied. In a certain way, performance and agnosticism are opposites. This is not an always-true rule, but it is the most frequent situation.

This is why most component/control products on the market are usually extremely complex to use and slow at runtime, as some kind of customization in look or behavior is needed.

Agnostic versus idiom-powered implementation

An idiom is a specific technical implementation of a feature provided by a single framework.

For instance, a .NET interface is an idiom because in a lot of other programming languages, it just does not exist. With such interfaces, a lot of designs and paradigms become available. What if we want to write an easily portable (between different languages) application? We would lose all such creational availability.

Entity Framework offers many idioms, such as the ability to have an object-oriented expression tree that represents the query as an object through the `IQueryable` interface. More details can be found in in *Chapter 7, Database Querying*. Any instance of an object query based on such an interface is able to give anywhere, until executed, the ability to alter the query that will be executed, maybe changing requested data or modifying request filters, like in an object-oriented dynamic SQL. Another instance is using EF (an agnostic ORM framework) to add thousands of inserts, instead of using an SQL Client provider's specific feature such as the Bulk Insert. The ability to use any database is a great design goal, but giving a boost of 10 times the insertion time is actually a goal, too.

An agnostic code is some kind of really reusable and application or target unaware code. Agnostic code cannot use any idioms. This is the price to be paid for such reusability.

As seen earlier, in terms of mobile platform architectures, agnostic code is easily movable between platforms or projects. Although a shared assembly is also usable by all platforms, why do we let the more powerful system pay for the limitation of the smaller one? We definitely need to make the right choice regarding our specific priority here.

Short coding

Coding without wasting rows is usually something good for each aspect. It shows the developer's skills, along with the understanding of the business problem. An extremely short code, such as when playing a code-golf challenge, may also produce some drawbacks.

Generally, although short coding may reduce debugging easiness and code understanding to other developers, it may improve better performance results. A single huge LINQ query versus a multiple-step one usually produces better SQL (if applicable) or a better in-memory query.

It's also true that the CLR virtual machine (the details are given in the next chapter) optimizes some code execution to improve code speed at runtime, but such speed can be wasted by a simple academically-styled code that greatly improves the main tenability. Sure, this can happen; but at what price?

Short coding with several comments may be the right balance for real-world programming.

Further reading on short coding:
`http://en.wikipedia.org/wiki/Code_golf`

Remote computation

In the Microsoft programming world, remote computation never had its time. Web services helped a lot, but add a server class system is usually only a bit more powerful than a desktop class system, so we have had to wait for the mobile devices era to need this kind of logic again. Microsoft's Cortana (voice-assistant) or Apple's Siri is a direct example of this design.

The remote computation occurs when we use the device as a console for a more powerful system. In the example of the two vocal assistants, the device uses its microphone and speaker to get the request from the user and then give back the answer in the form of an audio wave.

Local devices cannot process vocal analysis at the same time with the same accuracy and updatability of a remote system that is always available to users through an Internet connection.

Remote computation virtually extends the throughput of any device, because as time changes, new resources are added to the cloud provider that is playing the vocal assistant, along with server-side optimizations eventually.

When we have to face great computational goals, we may use the same solution by using cloud systems or legacy intranet systems. Usually, a secondary, smaller, and weaker edition of the same system is already released at the client's level to maintain the availability of the whole system because of eventual Internet congestion, or simply due to unavailability.

Cloud versus on-premise applications

We have seen cloud architectures and abilities at different points in this chapter.

The choice to use a cloud provider as a system to drive our application is usually based on expected client needs. On premise applications, this might work fine if there is a finite number of clients that usually use a certain kind of logic within corporate level system capabilities. What if we need to load a huge dataset that exceeds internal system capabilities for only two days? Using a cloud provider, we can use an extremely enterprising class of virtual hardware for a few hours.

Talking about performance, a cloud provider has virtually infinite scalability and availability, along with very good efficiency and throughput. Latency and resources usage are based entirely on our design, but features systems as distributed cache and FIFO queues are available immediately via a cloud provider. Asking for these features in a legacy company may need time and lot of IT management effort. In addition, scaling a web server is easy in every company's internal data center by buying some network balancer, while letting scale (in high availability) an SQL Server or an MSMQ cluster virtually without limits is not so easy at all!

Several performance benefits are available through using a cloud provider, along with any new features available in the future through this winning technology.

Summary

This chapter showed the importance of performance within the software architecture design time. An overview of the most widely adopted and responsive platform-oriented design and architectures gave you the vision of how to address emerging software development in the direction of well-performing goals.

In the next chapter, we will dive into the internal architecture of CLR to give the you the ability to understand exactly how to produce well-performing code.

Further reading:

- Fowler, Martin. *Patterns of Enterprise Application Architecture*, Addison Wesley, 2002
- Saltarello. Esposito. *Microsoft .NET: Architecting Applications for the Enterprise*, Microsoft Press, 2014

3
CLR Internals

This chapter will guide you into the knowledge and usage of the virtual machine in which any Microsoft .NET Framework-based language can actually run: the **Common Language Runtime (CLR)**. Good knowledge of such internal functionalities will help any programmer produce better code, avoiding bottlenecks and anti-patterns.

The important aspects that make .NET so easy to use and powerful at the same time have all been explained in depth in this chapter. Go through this exciting chapter and learn how to work with the most beautiful programming language framework there is.

In this chapter, we will cover the following topics:

- Memory management
- Garbage collection
- Working with AppDomains
- Threading
- Multithreading synchronization
- Exception handling

Introduction to CLR

CLR is the environment that actually executes any .NET application. A widely used definition is that the CLR is the virtual machine running any .NET application. Although this simple explanation is somehow correct, we must take a step back and explain in depth what C#, Visual Basic, and CLR are.

.NET is a managed programming language that offers the ability to program any kind of application, target any platform, abstract what is usually said to be low-level programming, such as memory management, object initialization, and finalization, and access any operating system, and so on.

C#, VB.NET, F# and many other high-level languages from Microsoft for the .NET Framework and other non-Microsoft languages such as COBOL.NET are human-oriented languages with proper design pros and cons that are usually linked to historical trade area or scientific needs. For instance, management software was usually made in Visual Basic, while low-level programming in C/C++, scientific programming was done with FORTRAN, and banking programming in COBOL.

When dealing with .NET Framework, all compliant languages (such as C# and VB) are actually only the frontend a programmer uses to interact with real .NET language, such as Microsoft **Common Intermediate Language** (CIL).

When a programmer builds code with Visual Studio, they trigger the compiler to produce the CIL from the source code. The compiler itself is also usable by any command prompt or script because of being a simple console application.

Together with the **Intermediate Language** (IL), any compiler of .NET languages also produces relative metadata that is definitely required for datatype validation in class member invocation, to reflect types, members, and so on.

This module was made by IL and metadata, together with a Windows Portable Executable (PE32 or PE32+ for a 64-bit target platform) header, defines the kind of module (.dll or .exe) and the CLR header. This header defines the version of .NET used and relative options, produce a file package known as Assembly, which also contains the eventually linked resources such as images, icons, and so on.

In the following diagram, we see an assembly with all its layers, showing the .NET physical file structure with the system headers, CLR header, code metadata, and body:

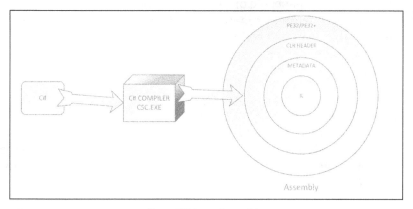

From C# to an Assembly

Once the compilation succeeds, we can launch the application (or link the DLL as a reference to other applications) with the usual double-click. The PE32(+) header will run the executable as an unmanaged application, which will try to load the .NET environment by launching the CLR with relative configuration as available in the assembly file, such as the .NET version, requested target platform, and others. On a system without the proper .NET framework runtime available, the whole application will break execution while on any valid system, the application will run normally.

The following is a simplified block diagram that shows the CLR process execution sequence:

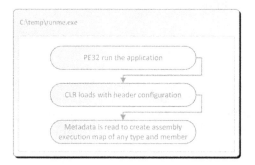

The application startup lifecycle within the CLR

Once the metadata loads successfully, any method is ready to run within the **Just-in-Time** (JIT) compiler of the CLR. JIT compiles the platform-independent CIL language in a platform-specific optimized language that can be executed on the underlying system, method by method, in a lazy fashion. Once a method is actually compiled, this compiled code is injected into the in-memory metadata of the assembly, so as to not have to compile it again until the application remains loaded in the memory.

Although the best performance ever available is provided by using native coding, only experts are able to reach similar results. Otherwise, CLR and its JIT compilation produce great code that often performs fine (and sometimes better) than compared to any unmanaged application, if mid-level programmers are involved in the coding. This is because of the great optimization work done by Microsoft when converting CIL to native code.

This comparison is similar to what happens if we compare an OR/M (such as Entity Framework) querying performance with one of the stored procedures . Although the best-ever results are obtainable only by using specific DBMS features available with specific dialect-SQL coding (such as T-SQL, PL-SQL, and so on), only an expert SQL developer is able to provide such kind of querying.

A moderately experienced C# developer is more able at object querying (and such querying is more platform- and database-producer independent) than in specific SQL coding. This is why, for the most part, object-querying will always produce better performing queries, compared to SQL querying performances. In the future, relational databases will be superseded by NoSQL databases. So, for young developers, learning SQL coding is something actually secondary in their professional growth schedule.

Memory management

When talking about memory management, any code programmer will remember how native languages opened their doors to any kind of issues and bottlenecks. This can also mean that the expert C++ programmer could have access to some customization to produce better memory management than CLR does. However, this relates only to very few people in very few cases.

Theoretically speaking, when a programmer needs to use some memory to store any value in an operation, they need to:

- Define a variable of the chosen type
- Allocate enough free memory to contain the variable:
  - ° Reserve some bytes in the operating system's memory stack to contain the variable
- Use the variable:
  - ° Instantiate the variable with the needed value
  - ° Do whatever is needed with such variable, for example - Define variable, allocate memory, use your variable, deallocate memory
- De-allocate the freed memory:
  - ° Once the variable becomes useless, free the related memory for further usage by this or other applications

Other than the usual generic programming issues with this step sequence, such as using the wrong type, wasting memory, or going against an overflow of the type, the trickiest memory management issues are *memory leak* and *memory corruption*:

- **Memory leak**: This occurs anytime we forget to de-allocate memory, or by letting the application always consume more memory, and offer an easy-to-predict result.
- **Memory corruption**: This occurs when we free memory by de-allocating some variable, but somewhere in our code, we still use this memory (because it is referred by another variable as a pointer), unaware of such de-allocation. This happens because when we de-allocate variables and relative memory, we must always be sure of updating (or de-allocating) all eventually related pointers that otherwise may still point to a freed memory area that could also contain other data.

CLR helps us by managing memory itself. Thus, in the .NET world, the previous list becomes the following:

- Declaring a variable of any type
- Instantiating the variable with a valid value:
  - ° CLR makes the difference between value-types and reference-types regarding initial values of variables before assignation. Reference-types have an initial value of null (Nothing in VB). Value-types (all primitive-types except string and object), instead, are always valued at the default value. Value-types may support a null value through the class Nullable<T> or by adding the character ?at the type ending, like int? (only in C#).
- Using the variable

It is obvious here that memory management is done completely by the CLR, which allocates the needed variable memory plus some overhead (a pointer to a `type` instance and a `sync` block index) as soon as the variable is instantiated. A target-system sized integer pointer that points to an instance of `type` class represents the type of the variable and the another value of the same size used for synchronizing the variable usage. This means that on any 32-bit system, any variable will add 2 x 32-bit values, while for 64-bit systems, a variable will add 2 x 64-bit values. This explains the small additional memory usage that occurs on 64-bit systems. All those objects are arranged in sequence in a memory area called the **managed heap**.

C#/VB variable value assignation is a bit different. C# uses *early binding*, with a built-in type-safe validation for constant and (often) variable values. A down-casting (in terms of numeric type capability) must pass through a *cast* operation such as `int a = (int)longValue;`. When a value outside of the smaller type ranges enters the cast, `-1` becomes the new value. VB, instead, uses late binding that accepts any value assignation (with built-in support for conversions and parsing), by default. Because of the lazy approach, in VB, a numeric conversion must be compliant to the new type's value ranges. Here, a `cast` operation does not occur, so an eventual `OverflowException` is the result of a code like this: `Dim a As Integer = longValue`.

The CLR also manages another internal memory area called the **managed stack**. Each thread handles its own stack (this is why often we refer it as the **thread stack**) by storing all value-types values in a Last-In-First-Out (LIFO) manner. The purpose of CLR is to abstract memory allocation; thus, directly trying to impact that the kind of memory used is actually some kind of inference in CLR itself. To be honest, it's possible to use explicitly stack memory by switching to C# in unmanaged coding (with a proper keyword, such as `unsafe`) using C++ related techniques, or using only value-types such as integers, `double`, `chars`, and so on in managed C#. When using managed C#, the stack memory is available only until we program in a procedural way. This happens because any type within an object (a reference-type) will be stored in the managed heap. Although storing data in the stack will boost the value read/write speed in the memory, it is like programming in the 1960s.

An interesting read is an article by Eric Lippert, the Chief Programmer of C# compiler team at Microsoft. Find it at `http://blogs.msdn.com/b/ericlippert/archive/2010/09/30/the-truth-about-value-types.aspx`.

The heap is a growing list of bytes that contains a First-In-First-Out (FIFO) collection. It is always slightly bigger than needed, as it quickly accepts new values, exactly the same as any .NET `List<T>` collection. The CLR also has a pointer or cursor that is always pointing to the newly available space for any future allocation.

Here is a diagram showing such FIFO-like memory handling with the new-item cursor:

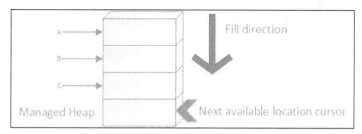

The heap memory allocation model

This heap population job occurs on a portion of memory that is assigned to the application by the CLR, the address space, in which the Windows environment is actually a Virtual Address Space because it can span from physical memory to page files. This whole application's memory space is then divided into regions—small memory portions side by side to assemble table pages for the compiled CIL, plus metadata and other regions that are eventually created as more memory requests occur.

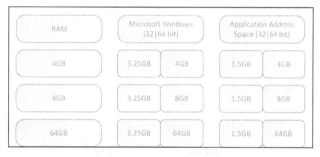

Memory availability in Microsoft Windows systems and CLR

Although for Windows-based systems the theoretic virtual memory available for application address space is 8 TB (64-bit) or 1.5 GB (32-bit), always remember that the address space may be fragmented. This will easily reduce real address space availability for simple variables like huge collections. This is why a CLR running at 32-bit usually raises an OutOfMemoryException error at around 1 GB of memory consumption if we simply populate a huge List<T>.

The difficult part of the job of CLR is freeing such a heap: instead of an unmanaged language in which this job is assigned to the programmer, here, the CLR de-allocates the memory just when the variable exits the scope (if it lives in a managed stack) or when there is no more reference by any other object and it exits the scope (if it lives in a managed heap). This job occurs in a lazy fashion with an internal heuristic that also looks for memory requests. This is why, on a system with high address space available, an application that consumes 100 MB of memory can simply continue consuming the same amount of memory, although it is not used anymore if the application does nothing. However, as soon as possible, when the application needs to create new objects, it could trigger the memory cleanup of the heap by starting an operation named **garbage collection**.

Garbage collection

As mentioned, garbage collection (GC) is the engine that cleans up the memory of managed heap within the CLR with an internal algorithm and its own triggering engine. Although it is impossible to know exactly when the GC will fire, its algorithm is detailed in many articles on MSDN and relative blogs and also has known trigger points, for instance, when CLR needs lots of new memory. The GC memory cleanup operation is named **collect**.

Microsoft gives us the ability to trigger the collector manually, by invoking the GC.Collect method. Although this option is available, manually triggering the GC is something to avoid because every usage will interfere with CLR abstraction of the underlying system.

The GC collection occurs multiple times until the process is alive and running. Its execution has the goal of freeing the memory from objects that are not in use anymore by any code block, or that are not referred by any other living object.

Any surviving object is then marked as a survivor object. This marking phase is crucial in the GC logic. Each survival will increment the survival counter for such an object. The first time an object is analyzed by the GC is in generation zero of its mark counter. Multiple survivals will bring this counter to generation-1 or generation-2. In CLR, the most unchanging objects (survived through all GCs) are marked in generation-2.

Garbage collection always starts by pausing all threads of the application, and then the managed heap is scanned to find unused objects and can service them. Following is a graphical representation of such behavior:

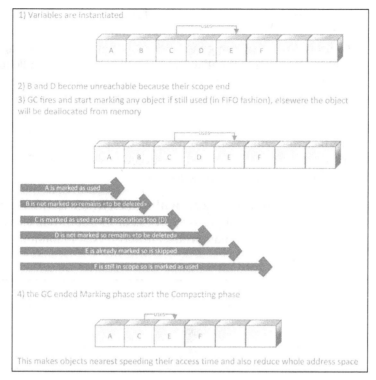

The garbage collection algorithm

Always bear in mind that the variables seen in the preceding diagram are objects that can contain any number of variables, their self-like basic types, and links to other objects, such as the C item that is associated with the E item.

As mentioned, the GC can trigger its job any time that the application needs to instantiate new objects. This occurs because once started, the CLR defines a threshold in bytes, that is, new object breaks to trigger the GC algorithm. Newly-created objects are referred in the GC as gen-0 (generation-0) objects; they are never analyzed for marking. GC has a generational algorithm that focuses on newly-created objects because they are thought to be the most likely to exit the scope; instead, the objects first created when an application starts are thought to be the most enduring ones. Once an object passes the marking phase, it may be promoted to gen-1; thus, it becomes a long-living object. Any generation has its size limit, as defined by the CLR, so it may also happen that the GC analyzes all objects from gen-0 and gen-1. Usually, the GC only collects the generation that exceeds its size limit.

The choice of what generation to collect is ordered from the newer (gen-0) generation up to the older (gen-2) generation. Because of this, it may happen that if a generation always exceeds its limit, the following generations can never be collected, wasting some memory. Obviously, a manual collection trigger will start the collection of all generations. Although this may seem to be an issue, this algorithm is the result of an intensive study that proves this is generally the most efficient way to clean up memory usage.

Once an object survives two collections from gen-0, GC promotes it to gen-1. Once a gen-1 object survives four collections, it is promoted to gen-2. Gen-2 is the less-changing generation; it is also the less-collected one.

Here is a graphical representation of objects within the virtual address space of the managed heap showing different generations. Bear in mind that, as stated previously, physical fragmentation may occur, although virtual memory seems to be a straight collection of objects.

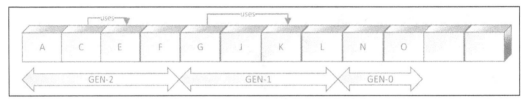

The managed heap with all available generations

When a process starts, the GC logic within the CLR assigns a size limit for each generation. During runtime of a process, the GC increments or decrements the generation size according to the execution of the application. This means that the GC somehow has a self-learning algorithm that tunes itself, based on how many objects it de-allocates or does not de-allocate.

Exceeding of the allocation threshold is not the only trigger for the GC to start collecting dead objects; it may also run when Windows signals low physical memory, when an `AppDomain` class exits (including the main one), or when the code fires `GC.Collect()` method.

 The GC is unable to clean up objects somehow linked to static fields because their scope is the application itself. So use this design carefully, or else a memory leak could happen.

Large object heap

CLR divides objects in two sizes: small (less than 85,000 bytes) and large (equal to or greater than 85,000 bytes). All large objects are allocated in a specific heap, the **large object heap** (**LOH**). The managed heap is valid for each heap, although the LOH has some limitations because of the size of objects contained within.

With the small object heap, the GC can avoid memory corruption, memory fragmentation, and memory leak because any object is only stored once. It's still possible to create thousands of non-useful items, but this is a behavior of the programmer that CLR cannot avoid. Instead of talking about LOH, the GC will avoid the compacting phase, reducing the thread suspend-time and avoiding costly CPU-intensive work, such as moving large objects in memory. This choice boosts the collection latency (time to finish) but obviously does not help memory consumption by never releasing the unused space between adjacent objects. Instead, the unused space at extremes is always released.

Another great limitation to dealing with using LOH is trying to reduce the collection time. All objects within LOH are marked as gen-2. This means that CLR expects that objects always live long. This causes a great impact on application performance if their real usage is short-lived because the great size will easily exceed the gen-2 size limit, starting the collection phase of such an internal, and usually never-changing, heap area.

Collection tuning

By invoking the `GC.Collect` method (or when the CLR responds to the Windows low-memory event), it is possible to force start the collection algorithm of any generation. Although this may happen (I always suggest never invoking it manually), GC usually works in a triggered fashion, trying to balance the lowest application performance impact with the needed memory cleanup.

Garbage collection is divided into two different algorithms that fulfill different application needs. We can choose which *garbage collection type* to use within our application only once in the application configuration file (or Web Configuration File), under the `runtime` node, where we can switch from the *workstation* collection (default) to the *server* collection:

```
<runtime>
  <gcServer enabled="true" /> <!-- enables Server mode -->
</runtime>
```

When the GC works in the workstation mode (default), the CLR tries to balance the overall execution time of the collection with a few resources, by using a single thread at normal priority to analyze and eventually release the unused memory blocks.

When the GC works in server mode (available only for multicore systems), it creates a thread per CPU core and divides the collection work across those threads that will clean up all managed heaps and LOHs related to all application threads executing on the same CPU core.

Using server collection, we can definitely boost memory cleanup throughput by using multiple cores and avoiding a single thread crossing all CPU cores available. The drawback is higher resource usage because of the increased thread count. The server collection should be configured only for applications that are specific to the server side (such as a database or web server), preferring single-application servers.

The LatencyMode property is another configuration available to optimize collection intrusiveness and triggering.

The default collect mode is the **interactive** (or concurrent) mode. With this mode, the collection marking phase works in a background thread (or multiple threads, if using server collection) and only the memory release and compact works by suspending all application threads. This mode is maybe the most balanced one, trying to have good throughput in memory release without consuming too many resources.

The opposite is the **batch** mode (or called as the non-concurrent mode). This mode is configurable within the configuration file, as shown earlier. It can be configured by disabling the concurrent mode, as seen in the following code—the configuration is combinable with the request for using server collection:

```
<runtime>
  <gcConcurrent enabled="false"/> <!-- enables Batch mode -->
</runtime>
```

The batch mode is the most powerful in terms of throughput of memory release because it simply suspends all application thread execution and releases all unused memory. Obviously, this choice can break application latency because an application request must await the completion of the collection.

Other LatencyMode configurations are available only at runtime by setting the GCSettings.LatencyMode property with a value of the GCLatencyMode enum that contains the batch and interactive values, plus the LowLatency, SustainedLowLatency and NoGCRegion values.

By choosing the `LowLatency` mode (available only for workstation collection), gen-2 collection is suspended completely, while gen-0 and gen-1 are still collected. This option should be used only for short periods when we need a very low interference of the GC during a critical job; otherwise, an `OutOfMemoryException` error may occur. When manually triggering the collector with the related `GC.Collect` method, or when a system is low on memory, a gen-2 collection will occur, although in the `LowLatency` mode. One of the best benefit when using the `LowLatency` mode is increase in application responsiveness because of the collection of only small items. The GC itself uses resources minimally, but in the meanwhile, the process can still consume lots of memory because of the inability to collect long-visibility objects from gen-2.

The `LowLatency` mode is configurable, as shown in the following code:

```
var previousTiming = GCSettings.LatencyMode;
try
{
    //switch to LowLatency mode
    GCSettings.LatencyMode = GCLatencyMode.LowLatency;

    //your code
    //never use large short-living objects here
}
finally
{
    GCSettings.LatencyMode = previousTiming;
}
```

The `SustainedLowLatency` mode is similar to an optimized interactive mode that tries to have more memory retention than the interactive mode actually uses. A complete collection usually occurs only when Windows signals a low-on-memory state. Contrary to the `LowLatency` mode, which must be used only for a very short duration, the `SustainedLowLatency` mode can be chosen as an interactive or batch mode without the occurrence of an out-of-memory state. It is obvious that a system with more physical RAM is the best candidate for such a configuration.

 An LOH with short-living large objects (that is never collected) plus the interactive mode and the workstation mode usually equals a high memory-consuming application with great freeze time occurring, because of the slow mono-threading garbage collection.

Within *.NET 4.6* (currently in preview mode), a new mode is available for the extreme purpose of disabling the whole garbage collection process. This mode is named `NoGCRegion`. This choice gives all computational resources to application code, disabling any GC threads. Obviously, such behavior can easily create an `OutOfMemoryException` condition, and its usage should occur only for very short time periods in extreme cases.

This enumeration value (GCSettings.LatencyMode) is in read-only. This means that we cannot write the `GCSettings.LatencyMode` property specifying the `NoGCRegion` value. Instead, we need to signal such a critical section by invoking a couple of methods, one to enter and one to exit this section. Here's a code example:

```
try
{
    var neededMemoryAmount = 1000000000;
    //asks GC to stop collecting
    GC.TryStartNoGCRegion(neededMemoryAmount);

    //do your critical stuffs
}
catch (Exception)
{
    //handle the exception
}
finally
{
    //resume previous collect mode
    GC.EndNoGCRegion();
}
```

Bear in mind that in the .NET history, the GC algorithm has been updated multiple times, and this may occur again in future versions.

To know more about the fundamentals of garbage collection, visit `https://msdn.microsoft.com/en-us/library/ee787088(v=vs.110).aspx`.

Working with AppDomains

An application domain (AppDomain) is a kind of virtual application. It contains and runs code, starts multiple threads, and links to any needed reference, such as external assemblies or COM libraries.

Application domains can be created to isolate portions of an application and prevent them from directly contacting other portions; to configure different kinds of security authorizations, such as with **Code Access Security (CAS)** techniques to limit I/O access, network access, and so on; or to simply increment the whole security level of the application by isolating different application contexts from others.

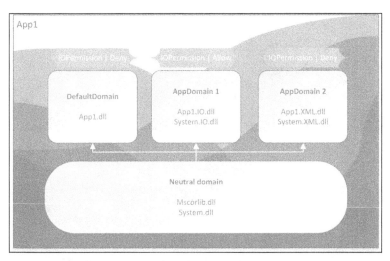

AppDomain usage for reference and/or CAS isolation

The application domains can be unloaded if needed, allowing us to work in a reliable way with multiple external plugins or extensions, like the ones from IoC designs, or simply because we need to load multiple versions of the same assembly all together.

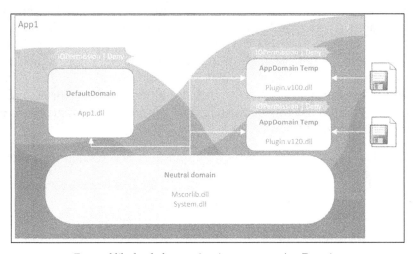

External libs loaded at runtime in temporary AppDomains

Application domains also give us the ability to start multiple applications within a single Windows process that usually consumes several resources in multiple logical applications that are exposed as different application domains, each isolated by others as if they're different processes. The Windows Communication Foundation (WCF) handles its clients in a design similar to the following diagram:

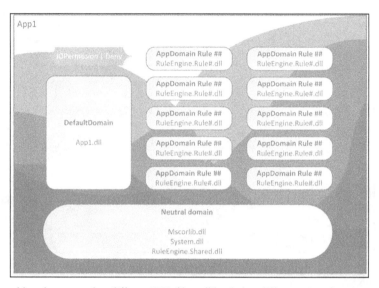

Different assembly rules exposed as different DLL files, all loaded as different virtual processes in the same physical process as AppDomains

Keep in mind that the main goal of using an `AppDomain` class is always isolation. Thus, often some resource usage is incremented. An example is that when loading the same assembly in multiple AppDomains, it will produce multiple instances of the `Type` class for each type that is contained in the referred assembly by each `AppDomain`. Although the JIT is made only once, the compiled IL is copied across the multiple type-and-metadata tables that live within each AppDomain. The only objection is for the neutral `AppDomain`, which is a kind of shared AppDomain across all the processes; it does not waste resources and cannot be unloaded by invoking the `AppDomain.Unload` method.

The creation of an `AppDomain` class is straightforward, as shown in the following code snippet:

```
var d = AppDomain.CreateDomain("AppDomain1");
d.ExecuteAssembly("ConsoleApplication2.exe");
AppDomain.Unload(d);
```

The `Load` method of the `AppDomain` class always loads an assembly in the current application domain. Thus, the best way to load assemblies within a defined `AppDomain` class is within its code using the `Assembly.Load` method or by calling `ExecuteAssembly` method, as shown in the preceding example.

The `CreateDomain` method actually returns a proxy to the real objects, giving the other application domains the ability to invoke some method on the remote one (`AppDomain1`). Those proxies are part of .NET Remoting, a distributed programming framework derived from CORBA. Currently, WCF **TcpBinding** is compatible with Remoting, although it is heavily evolved and optimized to fulfill SOA requirements.

When multiple objects live in multiple AppDomain, some communication may occur between those domains. Other than the option of using an external component, such as a file or service such as any WCF binding, any instance in any AppDomain can produce a `Remoting` proxy to invoke distance methods. Such instances will be marshaled (copied between process boundaries) by value, serializing the object itself, or by reference, with a specific class heritage. Here's an example of this:

```
var domain1 = AppDomain.CreateDomain("domain1");
var domain2 = AppDomain.CreateDomain("domain2");


var byValueType=typeof(MarshalledByValueClass);
var byValue = (MarshalledByValueClass)domain1.CreateInstanceAndUnwrap(
byValueType.Assembly.GetName().FullName, byValueType.FullName);


var byReferenceType=typeof(MarhalledByReferenceClass);
var byReference = (MarhalledByReferenceClass)domain2.CreateInstanceAn
dUnwrap(byReferenceType.Assembly.GetName().FullName, byReferenceType.
FullName);

Console.WriteLine("MarshalledByValueClass -> domain: {0}\
tisProxy: {1}", byValue.DomainName, RemotingServices.
IsTransparentProxy(byValue));
Console.WriteLine("MarhalledByReferenceClass -> domain: {0}\tisProxy:
{1}", byReference.DomainName, RemotingServices.IsTransparentProxy(byR
eference));


AppDomain.Unload(domain1);
AppDomain.Unload(domain2);
Console.ReadLine();
```

These new classes are available, although from another assembly:

```
[Serializable]
public sealed class MarshalledByValueClass
{
    public string DomainName { get; set; }
    public MarshalledByValueClass()
    {
        DomainName = AppDomain.CurrentDomain.FriendlyName;
    }
}

public sealed class MarhalledByReferenceClass : MarshalByRefObject
{
    public string DomainName { get; set; }
    public MarhalledByReferenceClass()
    {
        DomainName = AppDomain.CurrentDomain.FriendlyName;
    }
}
```

In this example, two different objects cross the AppDomain execution. The first object (named byValueType) used the *by-value* marshaling by being decorated with the SerializableAttribute class. This means that when the object crossed boundaries of two AppDomains, it got serialized/de-serialized each time. Bear in mind that the caller is within the default AppDomain class.

The second object (named byReferenceType), instead, used the *by-reference* marshaling by inheriting the MarshalByRefObject class. Actually, such an object never crosses the boundaries of the two AppDomains. A remote proxy is available to remote the AppDomains classes to invoke remote methods and read/write remote properties.

The first difference is that for the marshaled-by-value instance, only the constructor actually works in the other domain. Thus, after it is unloaded, the object copy is still alive in the calling domain, ready to do anything else. For the marshaled-by-reference instance, the object actually lives in the remote domain; hence, any proxy usage after the domain unloads will raise an AppDomainUnloadedException event, proving that a single instance of such an object exists.

This is the execution console output:

```
MarshalledByValueClass -> domain: domain1      isProxy: False
MarhalledByReferenceClass -> domain: domain2   isProxy: True
```

IDisposable interface

The IDisposable interface, when implemented in any class, informs CLR
that such an object will handle some external resource or unmanaged handle.
The best behavior here is to free up or disconnect from such costly resource as
soon as possible, although the object collection will occur later with GC logics.

Once such an interface is implemented, the usage must tell CLR that cleanups
of such resources must occur at a specific time, creating a local scope with usual
parenthesis in C# or a specific End instruction in VB, by using the using keyword:

```
class Program
{
    static void Main(string[] args)
    {
        using (var instance = new ExternalResourceContainer())
        {

        } //here automatically CLR will invoke .Dispose method
    }
}

public class ExternalResourceContainer : IDisposable
{
    private object externalResource;
    public void Dispose()
    {
        //release resource usage
    }
}
```

We may also invoke the Dispose method manually if we cannot use the using block.

Threading

A thread is a virtual processor that can run some c3ode from any AppDomain.
Although at any single time a thread can run code from a single domain, it can cross
domain boundaries when needed. Indeed, in the preceding example, there is only a
single thread that did the entire job for all three AppDomains.

Without diving into the internals of Windows threading, we should know that a CLR thread is actually a Windows thread. This one has a high creation cost (even worse for 64-bit systems) as in any other virtualization technique, although in Windows, creating a process is even worse in terms of resource usage. This is why Microsoft has supported multi-threading programming in its operating systems since the age of Windows NT.

What is important to know is that a thread never has 100 percent of CPU's time because its CPU time is reassigned to any new pending-for-work threads every 30 milliseconds (a time-slice) by acting what we call in Windows a context switch.

This ensures that at the operating system level, no process can harm the system stability by locking every CPU forever and thus stopping critical OS tasks. This is why Windows is definitely a time-sharing operating system.

In the .NET world, a thread can be created by starting the Run method of the Thread class. Thus, the simple instantiation of the object does nothing more than instantiate any other class. A thread must always have an entry point: a starting method that can have an initialization parameter, usually referred to as state— that is actually anything within the .NET class hierarchy.

A Priority configuration is available and mapped to Windows' thread in order to alter the results in the context-switching search for new threads. Usually, priorities higher than normal are dangerous for system stability (in rare cases, letting the OS reach the *starvation* state that occurs when the highest-priority thread prevents context switching), while lower priorities are often used to process no CPU-time critical operations.

An IsBackground property is available to any Thread class instance. Setting this property to True will signal to the CLR that this is a non-blocking thread—a **background thread**—in that its execution does not keep a process in the running state. On the other hand, upon setting it to False (default value), CLR will consider this thread as a **foreground thread**, in that its execution will keep the whole process in the running state.

Operations such as the animation of a clock may surely be made on a background thread, while the non-blocking UI operation of saving a huge file on a network resource is surely a candidate to run in a foreground thread, because although asynchronous against the UI, the foreground thread is also needed, and an eventual process premature exit should not kill such a thread. It is clear that CLR will automatically kill any background thread when a process ends without giving them any time to preserve any eventually needed data consistency.

Here's an example code on creating a background thread with low-priority CPU time:

```
static void Main(string[] args)
{
    //thread creation
    var t1 = new Thread(OtherThreadStartHere);

    //set thread priority at starting
    t1.Priority = ThreadPriority.Lowest;

    //set thread as background
    t1.IsBackground = true;

    //thread start will cause CLR asks a Thread to Windows
    t1.Start();

    //lock current executing thread up to the end of the t1 thread
    t1.Join();
}

private static void OtherThreadStartHere()
{
    //eventually change priority from innerside
    Thread.CurrentThread.Priority = ThreadPriority.Normal;

    //do something
}
```

The Thread class has specific methods to configure (as said) or handle thread lifetime, such as Start, to create a new OS thread and Join to kill a OS thread, and get back the remote thread status on the caller thread, such as any available exception.

Other methods are available, such as Suspend, Resume (both deprecated), and Abort (still not deprecated). It is easy to imagine that by invoking the Suspend or Resume method, the CLR will pause the thread from running or resuming work. Instead, the Abort method will inject a ThreadAbortException event at the current execution point of the thread's inner code, acting as a thread stopper. Although this will actually stop the thread from working, it is easy to infer that it is not an elegant solution because it can easily produce an inconsistent data state.

To solve this issue, CLR gives us the `BeginCriticalRegion` method to signal the beginning of an unable-to-abort code block and an `EndCriticalRegion` method to end such a code portion. Such methods will prevent any `ThreadAbortException` event being raised in such a portion of the atomic code. Here's an example code:

```
static void Main(string[] args)
{
    //thread creation
    var t1 = new Thread(OtherThreadStartHere);

    //thread start will cause CLR asks a Thread to Windows
    t1.Start();

    //do something

    t1.Abort();
}

private static void OtherThreadStartHere()
{
    for (int i = 0; i < 100; i++)
    {
        Thread.Sleep(100);

        //signal this is an atomic code region
        //an Abort will never break execution of this code portion
        Thread.BeginCriticalRegion();

        //atomic code
        //atomic code
        //atomic code
        //atomic code

        Thread.EndCriticalRegion();
    }
}
```

When dealing with iterated functions within a thread, instead of using `Abort` and `Critical` sections to gently signal the thread to exit, simply use a field as a flag (something like `canContinue`) to check within the iterated function, such as `while(canContinue)`. This choice will behave in a similar way to the previous example, without having to raise a useless exception.

Other interesting methods of the Thread class are Sleep (accepts a millisecond parameter) and Yield. The Sleep method suspends the thread for the given time; alternately, when 0 is used as a parameter, it signals a context switch to change the state to suspended, eventually causing higher-priority threads to use the thread time-slice as soon as possible. A better choice—when you want to recycle some of the time-slice time if a thread actually ended its job prematurely—is to use the Yield method that will give the remaining time-slice the next queued thread as soon as possible, waiting for the CPU time of the same processor. Here is an example code:

```
private static void OtherThreadStartHere()
{
    //change state to suspended and wait 1000 ms
    Thread.Sleep(1000);

    //change state to suspended
    Thread.Sleep(0);

    //give remaining time-slice to the next queued thread of current
CPU
    Thread.Yield();
}
```

If we are in search of an alternative to create a thread from scratch with the Thread class, we could use an already created-thread preserved in CLR for any unimportant jobs that we can usually make in a background thread. These threads are contained in a collection named as ThreadPool. Many other CLR classes use threads from the ThreadPool collection, so if a lot of jobs are going to be queued in it, remember to increase the minimum and maximum pool size:

```
static void Main(string[] args)
{
    //set minimum thread pool size
    ThreadPool.SetMinThreads(32, 32);

    //set maximum thread pool size
    ThreadPool.SetMaxThreads(512, 512);

    //start a background operation within a thread from threadpool
    //as soon as when a thread will became available
    ThreadPool.QueueUserWorkItem(ExecuteInBackgroundThread);
}

private static void ExecuteInBackgroundThread(object state)
{
    //do something
}
```

Multithreading synchronization

When dealing with multiple threads, data access in fields and properties must be synchronized, otherwise inconsistent data states may occur. Although CLR guarantees low-level data consistency by always performing a read/write operation, such as an atomic operation against any field or variable, when multiple threads use multiple variables, it may happen that during the write operation of a thread, another thread could also write the same values, creating an inconsistent state of the whole application.

First, let's take care of field initialization when dealing with multithreading. Here is an interesting example:

```
// a static variable without any thread-access optimization
public static int simpleValue = 10;

// a static variable with a value per thread instead per the whole
process
[ThreadStatic]
public static int staticValue = 10;

//a thread-instantiated value
public static ThreadLocal<int> threadLocalizedValue = new
ThreadLocal<int>(() => 10);

static void Main(string[] args)
{
// let's start 10 threads
    for (int i = 0; i < 10; i++)
        new Thread(IncrementVolatileValue).Start();

    Console.ReadLine();
}

private static void IncrementVolatileValue(object state)
{
    // let's increment the value of all variables
    staticValue += 1;
    simpleValue += 1;
    threadLocalizedValue.Value += 1;

    Console.WriteLine("Simple: {0}\tLocalized: {1}\tStatic: {2}",
    simpleValue, threadLocalizedValue.Value, staticValue);
}
```

Here is the console output:

```
Simple: 18      Localized: 11    Static: 1
Simple: 19      Localized: 11    Static: 1
Simple: 18      Localized: 11    Static: 1
Simple: 18      Localized: 11    Static: 1
Simple: 19      Localized: 11    Static: 1
Simple: 18      Localized: 11    Static: 1
Simple: 19      Localized: 11    Static: 1
Simple: 19      Localized: 11    Static: 1
Simple: 19      Localized: 11    Static: 1
Simple: 20      Localized: 11    Static: 1
```

The preceding code example simply incremented three different integer variables by 1. The result shows how different setups of such variable visibility and thread availability will produce different values, although they should all be virtually equal.

The first value (simpleValue) is a simple static integer that when incremented by 1 in all ten threads creates some data inconsistency. The value should be 20 for all threads — in some threads, the read value is 18, in some other 19, and in only one other thread is 20. This shows how setting a static value in multithreading without any thread synchronization technique will easily produce inconsistent data.

The second value (the staticValue) is outputted in the middle of the example output. The usage of the ThreadStaticAttribute legacy breaks the field initialization and duplicates the value for each calling thread, actually creating 10 copies of such an integer. Indeed, all threads write the same value made by 10 *plus* 1.

The most decoupled value is obtained by the third value (threadLocalizedValue), shown at the right of the example output. This generic compliant class (ThreadLocal<int>) behaves as the ThreadStaticAttribute usage by multiplying the field per calling thread with the added benefit of initializing such values with an anonymous function at each thread startup.

C# gives us the volatile keyword that signals to JIT that the field access must not be optimized at all. This means no CPU register caching, causing all threads to read/write the same value available in the main memory. Although this may seem to be a sort of magic synchronization technique, it is not; it does not work at all. Accessing a field in a volatile manner is a complex old-style design that actually does not have reason to be used within CLR-powered languages.

For more information, please read this article by Eric Lippert, the Chief Programmer of the C# compiler team in Microsoft, at `http://blogs.msdn.com/b/ericlippert/archive/2011/06/16/atomicity-volatility-and-immutability-are-different-part-three.aspx`.

More than the standard atomic operation given by CLR to any field, only for primitive types (often limited to `int` and `long`), CLR also offers a memory fence, such as field access utility named **Interlocked**. This can make low-level memory-fenced operations such as increment, decrement, and exchange value. All those operations are thread-safe to avoid data inconsistency without using locks or signals. Here is an example:

```
//increment of 1
Interlocked.Increment(ref value);
//decrement of 1
Interlocked.Decrement(ref value);
//increment of given value
Interlocked.Add(ref value, 4);
//substitute with given value
Interlocked.Exchange(ref value, 14);
```

Locks

Different synchronization techniques and lock objects exist within CLR and outside of Windows itself. A lock is a kind of flag that stops the execution of a thread until another one releases the contended resources. All locks and other synchronization helpers will prevent threads from working on bad data, while adding some overhead.

In .NET, multiple classes are available to handle locks. The easiest is the `Monitor` class, which is also usable with the built-in keyword `lock` (`SyncLock` in VB). The **Monitor lock** allows you to lock access to a portion of code. Here is an example:

```
private static readonly object flag = new object();
private static void MultiThreadWork()
{
    //serialize access to this portion of code
    //using the keyword
```

```
lock (flag)
{
    //do something with any thread un-safe resource
}

//this code actually does the same of the lock block above
try
{
    //take exclusive access
    Monitor.Enter(flag);

    //do something with any thread un-safe resource
}
finally
{
    //release exclusive access
    Monitor.Exit(flag);
}
}
```

Signaling locks

All those locks that inherit the WaitHandle class are signaling locks. Instead of locking the execution code, they send messages to acknowledge that a resource has become available. They are all based on a Window kernel handle, the SafeWaitHandle, this is different from the Monitor class that works in user mode because it is made entirely in managed code from CLR. Such low-level heritage in the WaitHandle class hierarchy adds the ability to cross AppDomains by reference, inheriting from the MashalByRefObject class.

More powerful than the Monitor class, the Mutex class inherits all features from the Monitor class, adding some interesting features, such as the ability to synchronize different processes working at the operating-system level. This is useful when dealing with multi-application synchronization needs.

Following is a code example of the Mutex class usage. We will create a simple console application that will await an operating-system level synchronization lock with the global name of MUTEX_001.

Please start multiple instances of the following application to test it out:

```
static void Main(string[] args)
{
    Mutex mutex;
    try
```

```
        {
            //try using the global mutex if already created
            mutex = Mutex.OpenExisting("MUTEX_001");
        }
        catch (WaitHandleCannotBeOpenedException)
        {
            //creates a new (not owned) mutex
            mutex = new Mutex(false, "MUTEX_001");
        }

        Console.WriteLine("Waiting mutex...");
        //max 10 second timeout to acquire lock
        mutex.WaitOne();

        try
        {
            //you code here
            Console.WriteLine("RETURN TO RELEASE");
            Console.ReadLine();
        }
        finally
        {
            mutex.ReleaseMutex();
            Console.WriteLine("Mutex released!");
        }

        mutex.Dispose();
    }
```

Like the `Monitor` class, the `Semaphore` class enables us to lock a specific code portion access. The unique (and great) difference is that instead of allowing a single thread to execute such a code-block, the `Semaphore` class allows multiple threads all together. This class is a type of a limiter for limiting the resource usage.

In the following code example, we will see the `Semaphore` class is configured to allow up to four threads to execute all together—other threads will be queued until some allowed thread ends its job:

```
class Program
{
    static void Main(string[] args)
    {
        for (int i = 0; i < 100; i++)
            new Thread(AnotherThreadWork).Start();
```

```
        Console.WriteLine("RETURN TO END");
        Console.ReadLine();
    }


    //4 concurrent threads max
    private static readonly Semaphore waiter = new Semaphore(4, 4);

    private static void AnotherThreadWork(object obj)
    {
        waiter.WaitOne();

        Thread.Sleep(1000);
        Console.WriteLine("{0} -> Processed", Thread.CurrentThread.
ManagedThreadId);

        waiter.Release();
    }
}
```

Other widely used signaling lock classes are ManualResetEvent and the AutoResetEvent class. The two implementations simply differ in terms of the manual or automatic switch of the signal state to a new value and back to the initial value.

The usage of those two classes is completely different when compared to all classes seen before, because instead of giving us the ability to serialize thread access of a code-block, these two classes act as flags giving the signal everywhere in our application to indicate whether or not something has happened.

For instance, we can use the AutoResetEvent class to signal that we are doing something and let multiple threads wait for the same event. Later, once signaled, all such threads could proceed in processing without serializing the thread execution, for instance, when we use locks instead, like all others seen earlier, such as the Monitor, Mutex, or Semaphore classes.

Here is a code example showing two threads, each signaling its completion by the manual or the automatic wait handle, during which the main code will await the thread's completion before reaching the end:

```
static void Main(string[] args)
{
    new Thread(ManualSignalCompletion).Start();
    new Thread(AutoSignalCompletion).Start();

    //wait until the threads complete their job
```

```
        Console.WriteLine("Waiting manual one");
        //this method simply asks for the signal state
        //indeed I can repeat this row infinite times
        manualSignal.WaitOne();

        Console.WriteLine("Waiting auto one");
        //this method asks for the signal state and also reset the
value back
        //to un-signaled state, waiting again that some other code
will
        //signal the completion
        //if I repeat this row, the program will simply wait forever
        autoSignal.WaitOne();


        Console.WriteLine("RETURN TO END");
        Console.ReadLine();
    }

    private static readonly ManualResetEvent manualSignal = new
    ManualResetEvent(false);
    private static void ManualSignalCompletion(object obj)
    {
        Thread.Sleep(2000);
        manualSignal.Set();
    }

    private static readonly AutoResetEvent autoSignal = new
    AutoResetEvent(false);
    private static void AutoSignalCompletion(object obj)
    {
        Thread.Sleep(5000);
        autoSignal.Set();
    }
```

In this case, all such functionalities are overshot by the `Task` class and the **Task Parallel Library (TPL)**, which will be discussed throughout *Chapter 4, Asynchronous Programming* and *Chapter 5, Programming for Parallelism*.

Moreover, in .NET 4.0 or later, the `Semaphore` and the `ManualResetEvent` classes have alternatives in new classes that try to keep the behavior of the two previous ones by using a lighter approach. They are called `ManualResetEventSlim` and `SemaphoreSlim`.

Such new slim classes tend to limit access to the kernel mode handle by implementing the same logic in a managed way until possible (usually when a little time passes between signaling). This helps to execute faster than the legacy brothers do. Obviously, those objects lose the ability to cross boundaries of app domains or processes, as the `WaitHandle` hierarchy usually does. The usage of those new classes is identical to previous ones, but with some simple method renaming.

New classes are available in .NET 4 or greater: `CountdownEvent` and `Barrier`. Similar to the two slim classes we just saw, these classes do not derive from the `WaitHandle` hierarchy.

The `Barrier` class, as the name implies, lets you program a software barrier. A barrier is like a safe point that multiple tasks will use as parking until a single external event is signaled. Once this happens, all threads will proceed together.

Although the `Task` class offers better features in terms of continuation, in terms of more flexibility, the `Barrier` class gives us the ability to use such logic everywhere with any handmade thread. On the other hand, the `Task` class is great in continuation and synchronization of other `Task` objects. Here is an example involving the `Barrier` class:

```
private static readonly Barrier completionBarrier = new Barrier(4,
OnBarrierReached);

static void Main(string[] args)
{
    new Thread(DoSomethingAndSignalBarrier).Start(1000);
    new Thread(DoSomethingAndSignalBarrier).Start(2000);
    new Thread(DoSomethingAndSignalBarrier).Start(3000);
    new Thread(DoSomethingAndSignalBarrier).Start(4000);

    Console.ReadLine();
}

private static void DoSomethingAndSignalBarrier(object obj)
{
    //do something
    Thread.Sleep((int)obj); //the timeout flowed as state object
    Console.WriteLine("{0:T} Waiting barrier...", DateTime.Now);

    //wait for other threads to proceed all together
    complationBarrier.SignalAndWait();
    Console.WriteLine("{0:T} Completed", DateTime.Now);
}
```

```
private static void OnBarrierReached(Barrier obj)
{
    Console.WriteLine("Barrier reached successfully!");
}
```

The following is the console output:

```
17:45:41 Waiting barrier...
17:45:42 Waiting barrier...
17:45:43 Waiting barrier...
17:45:44 Waiting barrier...
Barrier reached successfully!
17:45:44 Completed
17:45:44 Completed
17:45:44 Completed
17:45:44 Completed
```

Similar to the `Barrier` class, the `CountdownEvent` class creates a backward timer to collect multiple activities and apply some continuation at the end:

```
private static readonly CountdownEvent counter = new
CountdownEvent(100);
static void Main(string[] args)
{
    new Thread(RepeatSomething100Times).Start();

    //wait for counter being zero
    counter.Wait();

    Console.WriteLine("RETURN TO END");
    Console.ReadLine();
}

private static void RepeatSomething100Times(object obj)
{
    for (int i = 0; i < 100; i++)
    {
        counter.Signal();
        Thread.Sleep(100);
    }
}
```

An interesting overview of all those techniques is available in this article, available on the MSDN website at `http://msdn.microsoft.com/en-us/library/ ms228964(v=vs.110).aspx`.

Drawbacks of locks

Use lock techniques carefully. Always try to avoid any **race condition** that happens when multiple different threads are fighting each other in trying to access the same resource. This produces an inconsistent state and/or causes high resource usage too. When a race condition happens in the worst possible manner, there will be **starvation** for resources.

Starvation happens when a thread never gets access to CPU time because different threads of higher priority take all the time, sometimes also causing an operating system fault if a thread in a loop-state is unable to abort its execution when running at highest priority level (the same of the OS core threads). You can find more details on resource starvation at http://en.wikipedia.org/wiki/Resource_starvation.

With the wrong locking design, an application may fall in the **deadlock** state. Such a state occurs when multiple threads wait forever, each with the other, for the same resource or multiple resources without being able to exit this multiple lock state. Deadlock often happens in wrong relational database designs or due to the wrong usage of relational database inner lock techniques. More details on the deadlock state can be found at http://en.wikipedia.org/wiki/Deadlock.

Instead, with managed synchronization techniques such as spin-wait based algorithms (like the one within SemaphoreSlim class), an infinite loop can occur, wasting CPU time forever and bringing the application into a state called **livelock**, which causes the process to crash for the stack-overflow condition, at a time. For more details on livelock, visit http://en.wikipedia.org/wiki/Deadlock#Livelock.

Exception handling

Exception handling is the black art of doing something to repair an unpredicted error or malfunction. Within CLR, anytime something happens outside our prevision, such as setting an Int16 typed variable with a value outside valid ranges, the CLR will handle such an event by itself, creating an instance of an Exception class and breaking the execution of our code, trying instead to find some other code able to handle (a.k.a catch) such an exception.

Any Exception class is populated with all useful details regarding what just happened, like a simplified error text (within the Message property), the StackTrace that explains exactly the whole method call hierarchy, and other details. Often, instead of a simple Exception class, an inheritance child is instantiated to collect specific additional details or simply to define the kind of exception just raised. Indeed, setting an outranged value within an Int16 typed variable will raise an OverflowException event in place of a simple Exception event.

As just said, an exception is usually handled within a .NET-based application in response to an unpredicted error, although an exception is actually a special GoTo statement that will alter the control-flow of our application. This is the why its called as an *exception* instead of an *error*.

Anytime an error happens, or simply when the flow cannot proceed as normal, an exception is created and raised (raising an exception actually starts the control-flow alteration) to avoid completing a method run, maybe, because its data is inconsistent. We can also create our exceptions regarding our business, components, or helpers/frameworks if special parameters are needed to flow.

Carefully create and handle exceptions because of the cost the CLR incurs when any exception is raised. Although an exception will start a control-flow alteration, at the beginning, CLR will compute the full call stack of the executing thread. This is a CPU-intensive operation that actually stops the thread from running any other code. This is proof that Microsoft considers the entire exception-handling framework as error management. Therefore, it is impossible to create a multiple control-flow application using exception handling without enabling great wastage of resources. This means that, if we still need to be creating multiple control-flow applications, we will still need to use the goto keyword.

Here is a graphical representation that shows the control-alteration made by any exception:

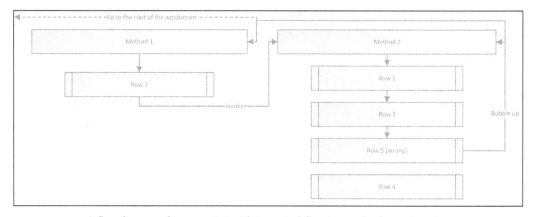

A flow diagram of an exception with its control-flow in search of a continuation

As seen in the preceding diagram, when the control-flow changes, the CLR searches for some catch code-block. This may be locally, or at any calling level, up to the program's Main method. Here is a classical implementation in C#:

```
int a = 0;

try
```

```
{
    //normal control-flow
    a = 10;
    a = a / int.Parse("0"); //this will raise a
DivideByZeroException
}
catch (DivideByZeroException dx)
{
    //altered control-flow if CLR raises DivideByZeroException
    Console.WriteLine(dx.Message);
}
catch (Exception ex)
{
    //altered control-flow if CLR raises any other exception
    Console.WriteLine(ex.Message);
}
finally
{
    //usually used for cleanup resources
    //or restore data state

    a = 0;
}
```

The CLR executes the code within the `try` block; then, when an exception is raised, CLR searches the best-fit altered control-flow by matching handled exceptions (with the `catch` keyword) with the exception raised. The search is from top to bottom and supports class hierarchy. This means that the less specific exception (the one handled with the generic `Exception` class) must be always the last one. Otherwise, other exceptions will never be matched.

In the preceding example, there is a `catch` block for such an exact exception raised, so the flow will continue in that block. After any `try` or `catch` block, the `finally` block is invoked, if present (optional).

A try-catch block can be nested in others if needed, although this may lead to a control flow that is tricky to understand with all those alterations. By nesting exceptions, CLR still goes in search of a `catch` block from the deeper code row where the exception has originated, flowing up to the process' `Main` method. Such exceptions lift, like an air bubble in the water, it lets programmers work with exception-handing search as made by CLR from the deeper code to the most outer one (the `Main` method), the name of *exception bubbling*.

Raising new exceptions is actually simple; it is enough to use the throw keyword and pass the new exception:

```
throw new Exception("HI");
```

Any time an exception is raised somewhere, the related AppPool is notified of the FirstChanceException event that actually runs before the bubbling occurs — in other words, at the start of the bubbling.

During the bubbling, if the CLR cannot find any valid catch block, the related AppDomain (the one where the exception originated) is notified on the UnhandledException event. Although this cannot handle the exception as a super catch block can, it can somehow notify application users or the system administrator gracefully before the critical exit of the process. Here is an such an example:

```
static void CurrentDomain_UnhandledException(object sender,
UnhandledExceptionEventArgs e)
{
    //contains exception details
    var ex = e.ExceptionObject;

    //if true the process will terminate
    var willKillCLR = e.IsTerminating;
}

static void CurrentDomain_FirstChanceException(object sender,
FirstChanceExceptionEventArgs e)
{
    //contains exception details
    var ex = e.Exception;
}
```

After the UnhandledException event occurs, the AppDomain class is unloaded by CLR.

A special case occurs when another compiler raises a non **Common Language Specification** (CLS) compatible exception (such as raising a string exception or int exception — classes that do not inherit from the Exception class). Although this is a rare opportunity, some external vendor language implementation could work with such behavior. In this case, the CLR will raise a RuntimeWrappedException event with the ability to read raw exception data, such as an int value or a string value, as an internal exception.

Another special case to be aware of is that a `finally` block—although it is usually called, anything that can happen within a `catch` block—cannot run if the executing thread is killed by unmanaged code, by invoking the Win32 `KillThread` or `KillProcess` method.

Obviously, in such cases, Windows will also kill the whole process with anything within. The only leak that will still survive will occur when you launch an external process driven by your application that somehow was killed by Windows. In this case, the finally block is avoided and the external process can remain in memory. A widely-used solution is to always check if zombie external processes are still alive from previous executions of the application, when we start a new instance of such an application.

Summary

In this chapter, we looked into CLR internals with regard to compilation and memory management, the two most important abstractions that CLR offers. Thread management, synchronization, and event handling were discussed to give the developer the ability to interact with all specific tools and techniques CLR offers regarding the tricky aspects of programming.

In the next chapter, asynchronous programming techniques such as task creation, maintenance, executing, and tuning will be analyzed in depth.

Further reading:

- Russinovich, Mark. *Windows Internals*, 6th edition, Microsoft Press, 2012
- Richter, Jeffrey. *CLR via C#*, 4th edition, Microsoft Press, 2013

Asynchronous Programming

4

This chapter will dive into the asynchronous elaboration techniques available within the .NET framework.

Here we will explain the following features, techniques, and frameworks:

- Asynchronous programming theory
- Asynchronous Programming Model (APM)
- Event-based Asynchronous Pattern (EAP)
- Task-based Asynchronous Pattern (TAP)
- Async/await operator
- Task optimization and CLR tuning
- Task tweaking
- Task UI synchronization

Understanding asynchronous programming

Multi-threaded programming happens when we use multiple threads to execute our code. The added benefit is the increased CPU power available by using multiple threads.

Asynchronous programming happens anytime we move the execution of any our code from the main thread to another one and then back to the first one to catch any result or acknowledgement. Thus, the difference between multi-threaded and asynchronous programming is that the catching of the result happens within the asynchronous one. Otherwise, it's called multi-threaded programming. For instance, a background thread providing some data in a polling way is simply another multi-threaded one.

Asynchronous programming theory

The first thing to bear in mind when talking about asynchronous programming is what the market actually perceives as asynchronous programming (also because Microsoft tends to drive people in this direction with its frameworks) is the ability to keep the UI unlinked to the code behind the waiting time. A strong proof of such a direction is the obligation to use asynchronous programming for any Windows Phone and Windows Store application. Although this choice is understandable because it drives programmers to create apps as the market expects, it also misguides programmers regarding the concept of asynchronous programming theory.

In multi-threaded programming, we create multiple virtual processors (threads) able to execute our code for *long-time* operations and without the need to participate in the same job. This means that different threads may do different things. In multi-threading, any thread does its job while trying to avoid any resource sharing with other threads, because of the cost of lock synchronization this sharing will imply, as seen in the *Multithreading synchronization* section in *Chapter 3, CLR Internals*. It is like executing multiple applications in the same process or dividing macro features of the same application across available cores.

In asynchronous programming, we create multiple threads to execute a *single short-timed* job (usually involving different external systems) that must end (or continue) all together.

A chat application is an example of a multi-threaded program, an application that consists of two threads. A thread for read data from other participants, and another to write data back to the participants. The two threads have different goals, although they can sometimes exchange or share data. Those threads have a long life and behave as two different applications each integrating with the other only when needed.

An asynchronous programmed example application, instead, creates four threads to save data in four different CSV streams, later compressed into a single ZIP file. What makes such an example perfect for asynchronous programming is the short life of each single thread, the unified software barrier where all threads wait for each other to produce a single ZIP file, and the completely cohesive thread behavior.

Two main asynchronous programming designs are available to developers. A blocking one, which happens when the calling thread waits for all asynchronous threads to proceed all together, or an event signaling based one, where each asynchronous thread acknowledges the main thread by invoking CLR events.

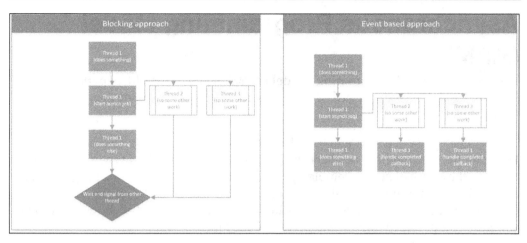

Asynchronous programming approaches – blocking vs. event signaling

As visible in the preceding figure, asynchronous execution may happen in a blocking way with multiple threads that are waited for by the main thread, with signalers such as the `WaitHandle` hierarchy, as seen in the *Multithreading synchronization* section *Chapter 3, CLR Internals*.

Obviously, the .NET framework's observer pattern implementation made with delegates and events is usable and thus, an asynchronous callback handler may be invoked in an operation-starting instance to complete the whole job. If desired, another signaling lock may be used here to continue all together in the blocking way, but again, on another thread.

Before .NET 4, Microsoft allowed asynchronous programming with two main different techniques, one for desktop class applications and another more generic one. Although when programming for .NET 4.5.x, the new frameworks do exist, a lot of SDKs, from Microsoft and other vendors, still support the legacy pattern. Thus, a good knowledge of those techniques is still needed for any programmer who wants to be compliant with all asynchronous designs from Microsoft and also wants to understand the architectural concerns that lie behind the mere technical skill.

Let's look at them in detail.

Asynchronous Programming Model (APM)

The **Asynchronous Programming Model (APM)** is one of the oldest patterns introduced by Microsoft in .NET 1.0 back in 2001 for asynchronous programming handling.

The pattern is easy. To start a deferred job, you simply start such a job by using a **Delegate** (remote method invoker) and then get an object back of type `IAsyncResult` to know the status of such a remote operation. Here an asynchronous programmed application to compute file hashes. The application will add a "`.`" to the `Starting data computation` initial message to acknowledge to the user that the application is still processing. The following examples use the blocking approach:

```
static void Main(string[] args)
{
    //a container for data
    var complexData = new byte[1024];

    //a delegate object that gives us the ability to trigger the
pointed method in async way
    var dataDelegate = new Action<byte[]>(ComputeComplexData);

    Console.Write("Starting data computation...");

    //start retrieving complex data in another thread
    IAsyncResult dataStatus = dataDelegate.BeginInvoke(complexData,
null, null);

    //waiting the completation
    while (!dataStatus.IsCompleted)
    {
        Console.Write(".");
        Thread.Sleep(100);
    }

    Console.WriteLine(" OK");

    //instantiate a delegate for hash elaboration in async way
    var hashDelegate = new Func<byte[], string>(ComputeHash64);

    Console.Write("Starting hash computation...");
```

```
        IAsyncResult hashStatus = hashDelegate.BeginInvoke(complexData,
    null, null);

        //waiting the completion
        while (!hashStatus.IsCompleted)
        {
            Console.Write(".");
            Thread.Sleep(100);
        }

        //this time the async operation returns a value
        //we need to use the delegate again to catch this value from
    the other thread
        var hash = hashDelegate.EndInvoke(hashStatus);

        Console.WriteLine(" OK");

        Console.WriteLine("END");
        Console.ReadLine();
    }

    static void ComputeComplexData(byte[] data)
    {
        var r = new Random();
        Thread.Sleep(3000);
        r.NextBytes(data);
    }

    public static string ComputeHash64(byte[] data)
    {
        using (var engine = new System.Security.Cryptography.
    MD5CryptoServiceProvider())
        {
            Thread.Sleep(3000);
            var hash = engine.ComputeHash(data);
            return Convert.ToBase64String(hash);
        }
    }
}
```

The code is very easy. The class that helps make things asynchronous here is the
`Delegate` class. Here, we use the pre-generated versions, `Action<T>` and `Func<T>`,
compliant with the generic pattern, which helps us use any feature required of such
`Delegate` objects without having to declare a specific one each time.

A `Delegate` object is an object-oriented method pointer with a lot of added features such as asynchronous support and multiple method handlers. Any CLR event is a Delegate too. Such a class gives us the ability to invoke any remote method in a synchronous way (with the usual `.Invoke` method), or in an asynchronous way with `BeginInvoke/EndInvoke`, as visible in the preceding example. As mentioned earlier, the `IsCompleted` property gives us feedback about the remote execution completion of all pointed remote methods.

The usage of such a blocking asynchronous operation, without the need to block the execution of the main thread, helps create respondent UXs as a download popup, or special import/export features.

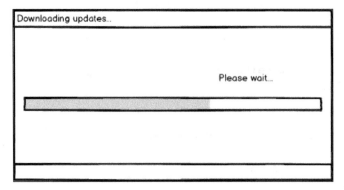

A simple asynchronous download popup

There are a lot of SDKs that give us the ability to use APM patterns like in the preceding example. In .NET 4.0, many core-framework APM implementations have been updated to the new TAP framework (discussed later in this chapter in the *Task-based Asynchronous Pattern (TAP)* section). Here's another APM example showing network communication with the `IDisposable/using` pattern:

```
static void Main(string[] args)
{
    //running in .NET 4.0

    var url = "http://www.google.com";

    Console.Write("Asking for {0}", url);

    //create a new web request for given url
    var request = WebRequest.Create(url);

    //start collecting response in async way
```

```
var responseStatus = request.BeginGetResponse(null, null);

//waiting the completation
while (!responseStatus.IsCompleted)
{
    Console.Write(".");
    Thread.Sleep(100);
}
Console.WriteLine(" OK");

//a size counter
int size = 0;

//catch back on the main thread the response
using (var response = request.EndGetResponse(responseStatus))
//open the stream to access the response data
using (var stream = response.GetResponseStream())
//open a reader for such data
using (var r = new StreamReader(stream, Encoding.UTF8))
    //until data is valid
    while (!r.EndOfStream && r.Read() >= 0)
        size++;

Console.WriteLine("Total size: {0:N1}KB", size / 1024D);

Console.WriteLine("END");
Console.ReadLine();
}
```

In the preceding second code example, we found the ability to use the APM with .NET assemblies. The usage is very straightforward. As visible in the two examples given, the IAsyncResult type gives us the ability to wait for completion in a polling way by repetitively checking the IsCompleted property value. The additional ability to wait for such completion with a WaitHandle class is interesting, as already seen in the *Multithreading synchronization* section in *Chapter 3, CLR Internals*. Here's an example:

```
//alternative 1:
//waiting the completation
while (!status.IsCompleted)
    Thread.Sleep(100);

//alternative 2:
//waiting the completation with the signaling event lock
status.AsyncWaitHandle.WaitOne();
```

Although the WaitHandle class based alternative may seem to be more comfortable than the one that uses the polling property check, the difference is that the polling one also gives us the ability to update the UI while waiting. Instead, the WaitHandle class will simply stop the execution of the thread where such an object is being waited on. Bear in mind that multiple threads can wait together at the same time as the IAsyncResult completion status or wait handle, without any issues (until this brings some other resources to the race condition).

In addition to the blocking wait, as said at the beginning of the paragraph, we have the ability to catch the completion of an asynchronous method execution, to another asynchronous method by passing a Delegate object, which represents a callback method. If multiple callbacks are caught in the same handler, a state parameter can help in its handling. Using a callback method gives us a more event-based approach. Consider that the callback executes in the same thread as the asynchronous processing. Here is an example with a single callback method:

```csharp
static void Main(string[] args)
{
    var invoker = new Func<int>(OnCreateInteger);

    //trigger 3 invocations sending the same invoker as the state
    to the ending handler
    invoker.BeginInvoke(OnHandleInteger, invoker);
    Thread.Sleep(100);
    invoker.BeginInvoke(OnHandleInteger, invoker);
    Thread.Sleep(100);
    invoker.BeginInvoke(OnHandleInteger, invoker);

    Console.WriteLine("MAIN THREAD ENDED");
    Console.ReadLine();
}

private static void OnHandleInteger(IAsyncResult ar)
{
    //the state contains the sent invoker    var invoker =
(Func<int>)ar.AsyncState;

    Console.WriteLine("Async operation returned {0}",
invoker.EndInvoke(ar));
}

private static int OnCreateInteger()
{
    Thread.Sleep(3000);
    //returns a random integer
    return DateTime.Now.Millisecond;
}
```

Event-based Asynchronous Pattern (EAP)

The **Event-based Asynchronous Pattern (EAP)** is a specific design pattern to standardize event-based asynchronous programming features. Such a design is available in multiple classes from .NET itself and is available and suggested in all our implementations if applicable.

Unlike the previously seen APM, in this pattern, any method that supports synchronous execution will add an overloaded method for an asynchronous invocation. The result, instead, will be available only to a specific predefined callback method, one for each available method, within the class itself.

Here is an example showing the `WebClient` class downloading some web page data:

```
static void Main(string[] args)
{
    //a simple web client
    var client = new WebClient();

    //register for result callback
    client.DownloadDataCompleted += client_DownloadDataCompleted;

    //invoke asynchronous request
    client.DownloadDataAsync(new Uri("http://www.google.com"));

    Console.WriteLine("MAIN THREAD ENDED");
    Console.ReadLine();
}

static void client_DownloadDataCompleted(object sender,
DownloadDataCompletedEventArgs e)
{
    //this callback receives the whole response (data and status)

    //data
    byte[] downloadDataResult = e.Result;

    //eventual exception
    Exception ex = e.Error;

    Console.WriteLine("Downloaded {0:N1}KB",
downloadDataResult.Length / 1024d);
}
```

The same features are available in any of our classes by implementing the same pattern. Here is an example:

```
class Program
{
    static void Main(string[] args)
    {
        var instance = new SimpleAsyncClass();

        Console.WriteLine("Sync value: {0}",
instance.ProcessSomething());

        //register an event handler to catch the result
        instance.ProcessSomethingCompleted +=
instance_ProcessSomethingCompleted;
        //invoke async invoke
        instance.ProcessSomethingAsync();

        Console.WriteLine("MAIN THREAD ENDED");
        Console.ReadLine();
    }

    static void instance_ProcessSomethingCompleted(object
sender, int e)
    {
        Console.WriteLine("Async value: {0}", e);
    }
}

public class SimpleAsyncClass
{
    public int ProcessSomething()
    {
        Thread.Sleep(3000);
        //returns a random integer
        return DateTime.Now.Millisecond;
    }

    public void ProcessSomethingAsync()
    {
        //initialize a delegate object to make async call
        var invoker = new Func<int>(ProcessSomething);
        //start async elaboration with callback
        invoker.BeginInvoke(InnerProcessSomethingCompleted,
invoker);
    }

    private void InnerProcessSomethingCompleted(IAsyncResult
ar)
    {
```

```
            //catch the delegate object from async state
            var invoker = (Func<int>)ar.AsyncState;
            //raise the event with computed value
            if (ProcessSomethingCompleted != null)
                 ProcessSomethingCompleted(this,
    invoker.EndInvoke(ar));
        }

        //the event that is usable for intercepting the computed value
        public event EventHandler<int> ProcessSomethingCompleted;
    }
```

This simple implementation gives us the ability to understand how EAP works. The pattern asks us to add some naming conventions such as the syntax Async at the end of the method or the syntax Completed for the acknowledgement event.

The pattern itself, in its pure version, is more verbose than how it was just seen. It also requires a specific Delegate declaration for each method (although all with the same sign), cancellation support, process state notification (the percentage or completion), and a busy indicator. It is at the discretion of the programmer whether to implement a pure pattern or a simplified one, as visible in the example just given.

The BackgroundWorker is a component that supports a full EAP with the ability to run in an asynchronous way and synchronize the UI access by itself (discussed later in this chapter in the *Task UI synchronization* section).

Task-based Asynchronous Pattern (TAP)

The **Task-based Asynchronous Pattern (TAP)** is the newly provided asynchronous programming framework born in .NET 4. TAP provides features of APM and EAP with an added signaling lock like an API that offers a lot of interesting new features.

Task creation

In .NET, this asynchronous job takes the name of a task. A task is also a class of the System.Threading.Tasks namespace. Here is a basic example:

```
var task = Task.Run(() =>
    {
        Thread.Sleep(3000);
        //returns a random integer
        return DateTime.Now.Millisecond;
    });

Console.Write("Starting data computation...");
```

```
//waiting the completation
while (task.Status != TaskStatus.RanToCompletion)
{
    Console.Write(".");
    Thread.Sleep(100);
}
Console.WriteLine(" OK");
Console.WriteLine("END");
Console.ReadLine();
```

The preceding example is similar to the first one shown about the APM. Although a lambda expression is used here to create an anonymous method implementation, it is the same as creating a named method like we did in the previous example with the ProcessSomething instance.

The Task.Run method starts the asynchronous execution of the remote method provided by the Delegate object (the lambda syntax actually creates a Delegate object referring to an un-named method). It immediately returns a Task object that is usable to the query execution status and eventually waits with any wait handle, shown as follows:

```
task.Wait();
```

The preceding lambda-based syntax works on .NET 4.5, while another syntax is available from .NET 4 with more configurations available:

```
var task = Task.Factory.StartNew<int>(OnAnotherThread);
```

Although the two methods are actually the same because the Task.Run method executes the StartNew method of the default TaskFactory class, by invoking the StartNew itself, we can also specify customized options regarding task creation and continuation. In addition, we can create multiple factories, one for each specific group of tasks of a homogenous configuration with less effort and improved manageability.

A special feature of the TaskFactory class is the ability to marshal the result from APM's EndInvoke method in a specific task with the FromAsync method. In such cases, multiple overloads of the same method offer different options such as sending a state parameter or not sending one.

Let's look at a complete example:

```
static void Main(string[] args)
{
    //the usual delegate for APM
    var invoker = new Func<int>(OnAnotherThread);

    //a task catching the EndInvoke in another asynchronous
method
    var fromAsyncTask =
Task.Factory.FromAsync<int>(invoker.BeginInvoke,
invoker.EndInvoke, null);

    //this usage of the result will internally invoke the Wait
method
    //blocking the execution until a result will become available
    Console.WriteLine("From async 1: {0}", fromAsyncTask.Result);

    //this second overload wants the whole IAsyncResult
    var status = invoker.BeginInvoke(null, null);
    //this will catch the EndInvoke in a task
    var fromAsyncTask2 = Task.Factory.FromAsync<int>(status,
invoker.EndInvoke);

    Console.WriteLine("From async 2: {0}", fromAsyncTask2.Result);

    Console.ReadLine();
}

private static int OnAnotherThread()
{
    Thread.Sleep(500);
    return DateTime.Now.Millisecond; //a random int
}
```

Actually, the initial section of the code is the best regarding short coding because the second one also needs an `IAsyncResult` interface with the need for another variable.

Visit the following MSDN link to learn more about the FromAsync method:

`http://msdn.microsoft.com/en-us/library/dd321469(v=vs.110).aspx`

At the end of the page, we can see the following remark:

◢ Remarks

 Tip

The FromAsync overloads that take an *asyncResult* parameter are not as efficient as the overloads that take a *beginMethod* parameter. If performance is an issue, use the overloads that provide the *beginMethod/endMethod* pattern.

This remark warns us about using the overload that wants the whole IAsyncResult. Instead, it suggests using the one that needs the couple Begin/End statements.

Another useful option that is available when using the TaskFactory method is the ability to configure how tasks are created; the following code shows an example:

```
var task1 = Task.Factory.StartNew(() =>
{
    //classic task creation with factory defaults


var task2 = Task.Factory.StartNew(() =>
{
    //task that startup asap
}, TaskCreationOptions.PreferFairness);

var task3 = Task.Factory.StartNew(() =>
{
    //task that will run for a long time
}, TaskCreationOptions.LongRunning);
```

The TaskCreationOptions enum helps us select between different choices (members) for task startups. The most interesting one here is the last one, that is, the LongRunning member. Although this does not change the task startup time, its creation will occur on a special background thread, without consuming a classic thread from the ThreadPool class, where the TaskFactory class usually takes background threads from, for its tasks.

In theory, although TAP can apply for long-running background work, this is actually not asynchronous programming. It is multi-threading. In actual fact, this logic lies in the factory's Scheduler, an instance of the `TaskScheduler` class, the object in charge of handling task execution with the best performance. For the default task scheduler, high throughput is the primary concern. This is why we need to use the `PreferFairness` creation option to specify a low-latency startup scenario.

Generically talking, this is a good option because from .NET 4 onwards, good optimization has been applied on the `ThreadPool` engine that actually handles a single global FIFO queue of pending user jobs available for the whole process without any local or global lock. In addition to this global queue, any nested task will run on another queue instead, a local queue for each application thread that is running in a LIFO way is optimized for fast execution, CPU cache access optimization, and data locality in CLR memory; the following shows an example:

```
var task = Task.Factory.StartNew(() =>
{
    //will enqueue on global AppPool queue
    var inner = Task.Factory.StartNew(()=>
        {
            //will enqueue on local AppPool queue
        });
});
```

An important aspect of the `System.Threading.ThreadPool` class usage is that some default limitation on thread availability does exist. Such limitations can be set both at the default pool size (minimum size) and at the maximum size. These defaults are the logical processor count for the minimum pool size, while the maximum size is dynamically set by the CLR itself (in older .NET frameworks, it was statically set as a multiple of the CPU count).

The `ThreadPool` class exposes static methods to get and set the minimum (`GetMinThreads`) and maximum (`GetMaxThreads`) pool size. Together they expose the `GetAvailableThreads` method, which gives us the actual remaining thread count number that equals the maximum size once it is subtracted from the currently used thread count. Here is a code example:

```
int min, minIO, max, maxIO;
//retrieve min and max ThreadPool size
ThreadPool.GetMinThreads(out min, out minIO);
ThreadPool.GetMaxThreads(out max, out maxIO);

//retrieve actually available thread count
int remaining, remainingIO;
ThreadPool.GetAvailableThreads(out remaining, out remainingIO);
```

```
//set up a new ThreadPool configuration
ThreadPool.SetMinThreads(64, 64);
ThreadPool.SetMaxThreads(2048, 2048);
```

Please bear in mind that all requests against the `ThreadPool` class will remain queued until some threads become available. This is why, if we create infinite tasks, in a little time, we will exceed the minimum thread pool size, and we will receive an `OutOfMemoryException` message. This exception happens because of the unavailability of adding other user tasks to the pool queue. Another important thing to know about the `ThreadPool` thread lifecycle is that CLR preallocates enough threads as the specified minimum size. When we continue adding threads, until we reach the maximum size, the CLR will add threads to the thread pool, as we might expect. The difference is that thread increase happens in a very slow way, adding only one thread per second. Here is a straightforward example:

```
int c = 0;
while (true)
{
    Task.Factory.StartNew(() =>
        {
            Console.WriteLine(++c);
            Thread.Sleep(-1);
        }, TaskCreationOptions.PreferFairness);
}
```

This example will print the number of logical threads on your CPU to a console output in a short amount of time. Later, a new thread per second count will be available (and never released), giving us a raw representation of pool increase timings. Please use this example, because as you learned before, without ever releasing such threads, the pool queue will reach its limit quickly, causing an `OutOfMemoryException` error.

Let's look at a more complete example:

```
static void Main(string[] args)
{
    //creates a listener for TCP inbound connections
    var listener = new TcpListener(IPAddress.Any, 8080);

    //start it
    listener.Start();

    //accept any client
    while (true)
```

```
    {
        //get a task for client connection
        var client = listener.AcceptTcpClientAsync();
        //wait for client connection
        client.Wait();

        //once the connection succeeded, it starts a new task
        //for handling communication with this new client

        Task.Factory.StartNew(HandleClientConnection, client,
TaskCreationOptions.PreferFairness);

        //run again to accept new clients
    }
}

private static void HandleClientConnection(object arg)
{
    var client = (TcpClient)arg;
    //do something
}
```

This example shows you how to use asynchronous programming efficiently to handle thousands of client connections on the same port. This code has virtually no limits on the client connection count (but the limit set by Windows itself is somewhere around 65,000 connections per port). Obviously, as already said before, although the code is able to accept a virtually infinite number of clients, only a small number of them will be available to run on our CPU, because of the ThreadPool timings in its size increase.

The same example made with an old APM instead, will stop accepting clients as soon as it reaches the ThreadPool default limitations:

```
static void Main(string[] args)
{
    //creates a listener for TCP inbound connections
    var listener = new TcpListener(IPAddress.Any, 8080);

    //start it
    listener.Start();

    //accept any client
    while (true)
    {
        //start waiting for a client
```

```
            var status = listener.BeginAcceptTcpClient(null, null);

            //wait for client connection
            status.AsyncWaitHandle.WaitOne();

            //catch the asynchronously created client
            var client = listener.EndAcceptTcpClient(status);

            //once the connection happened, it start a new thread pool
    job
            //for handling communication with such new client

            ThreadPool.QueueUserWorkItem(HandleClientConnection,
    client);

            //run again to accept new clients
        }
    }

    private static void HandleClientConnection(object arg)
    {
        var client = (TcpClient)arg;
        //IMPLEMENTATION OMITTED
    }
```

Task synchronization

Back to the TaskFactory class, going deeper with regards to nested tasks and
their execution in graph synchronization, we have to differ between attached and
detached tasks. Any task may attach itself to its parent task, if any, although this is
not the default behavior. With the default behavior, child tasks are detached from
their parent tasks. This means that the parent does not care about its child tasks,
shown as follows:

```
    var parent = Task.Factory.StartNew(() =>
    {
        var child = Task.Factory.StartNew(() =>
        {
            Thread.Sleep(3000);
            Console.WriteLine("child: ending");
        });
        Thread.Sleep(1000);
    });
```

```
parent.Wait();
Console.WriteLine("parent: ended before waiting for its child");
Console.ReadLine();
```

Here is the result:

```
parent: ended before waiting for its child
child: ending
```

The `TaskFactory` class lets us specify that a child task must attach to the parent one by passing the optional parameter `TaskCreationOptions.AttachedToParent`. In such a case, the parent will care about its child's status and exceptions by waiting for their completion times, shown as follows:

```
var parent = Task.Factory.StartNew(() =>
{
    var child = Task.Factory.StartNew(() =>
    {
        Thread.Sleep(3000);
        Console.WriteLine("child: ending");
    }, TaskCreationOptions.AttachedToParent);
    Thread.Sleep(1000);
});

parent.Wait();
Console.WriteLine("parent: ended after waiting for its child");
Console.ReadLine();
```

As seen in the preceding code, such little differences in code produce a big difference in the result. In two words: *the opposite*:

```
child: ending
parent: ended after waiting for its child.
```

Always use the `Task.Factory.StartNew` method when dealing with child tasks because the `Task.Run` method prevents the child from attaching itself to the parent. The `Task.Run` method is only a shortcut for task creation with the default setup, while the `Task.Factory.StartNew` method gives us the ability to configure our task initialization options.

Such synchronization has its costs. Therefore, although not really useful, please use multiple outer tasks with the required synchronization techniques, such as waiting for the right number of tasks.

Regarding task synchronization, it is imperative that you understand the difference between all available waiting tasks. Waiting for a task is like waiting for a signaling lock, as already seen in the *Multithreading synchronization* section in *Chapter 3*, *CLR Internals*. The `Task` class gives us methods such as `Wait`, `WaitAll`, or `WaitAny` to accomplish jobs as shown in the following example:

```
//Make a Task wait forever
task1.Wait();

//wait for a task to timeout
if (task1.Wait(1000)) //ms
{
    //on time
}
else
{
    //timeout
}

if (task1.Wait(TimeSpan.FromMinutes(1))) { } else { }

//Make tasks wait tasks forever, or timeout
Task.WaitAll(task1, task2, task3);
if (Task.WaitAll(new[] { task1, task2, task3 }, 1000)) { }
if (Task.WaitAll(new[] { task1, task2, task3 },
TimeSpan.FromMinutes(1))) { }

//wait the first one with or without timeout
//others will although complete their job
//wait any always returns the index of the fastest
Task.WaitAny(task1, task2, task3);
Task.WaitAny(new[] { task1, task2, task3 }, 1000);
Task.WaitAny(new[] { task1, task2, task3 },
TimeSpan.FromMinutes(1));
```

Task exception handling

Slightly different from our usual exception handling, as already seen in the *Exception Handling* section in *Chapter 3*, *CLR Internals*, when dealing with tasks, it is impossible to bubble up a raw exception. Any time an exception happens within a task, any tasks waiting, will receive an `AggregateException` error that acts as a container for all the exceptions that happened within the tasks being waited on. This behavior is similar to what happens in exceptions that originate in external threads. If we do not invoke the `Join` method to stop the external thread, such exceptions will never route to the main thread. Here's an example:

```
var task1 = Task.Factory.StartNew(() =>
    {
        throw new ArgumentException("Hi 1");
    });

var task2 = Task.Factory.StartNew(() =>
{
    throw new ArgumentException("Hi 2");
});

try
{
    //the wait will join the two threads exception routing
    //all unhandled exceptions from external threads to the
    //main one
    Task.WaitAll(task1, task2);
}
catch (AggregateException ax)
{
    foreach (var ex in ax.InnerExceptions)
        Console.WriteLine("{0}", ex.Message);
}
```

Task cancellation

Another interesting feature when dealing with tasks is the ability to handle task cancellation. A slight similarity does exist between such a design (task cancellation) and the one from the `Thread.Abort` method. The difference is that for threads, an exception is raised by CLR itself, immediately stopping the thread's execution; while here, although the design may seem the same, all of the implementation is in our hands. The definition of critical section is something to be forgotten here. By the way, because we have cancellation handling in our hands, we can come up with all we need to accomplish a graceful exit from any critical code block. To accomplish state-of-the-art cancellation handling, we must create a `CancellationTokenSource` object to trigger the job cancellation. This source object will create a `CancellationToken` object representing a single-use cancellation token. Once used, a new source must be created and used.

To avoid tasks from being started after a cancellation has already been requested, we must pass this cancellation token to the StartNew method of the TaskFactory class. Together with this optimization, passing the token to the StartNew method that informed the **Task Parallel Library (TPL)** that eventually raised an System. OperationCancelledException from the token within the task code body, must become a TaskCancelledException. Here's a complete example:

```
static CancellationToken cancellationToken;
static void Main(string[] args)
{
    //let us configure a minimal     //threadpool size to slow down
task execution
    ThreadPool.SetMinThreads(2, 2);
    ThreadPool.SetMaxThreads(2, 2);

    //the cancellation token source able to trigger cancellation
    var cancellationTokenSource = new CancellationTokenSource();
    //the cancellation token able to give a feedback on
cancellation status
    cancellationToken = cancellationTokenSource.Token;

    //let's create some task
    //the cancellationToken is here assigned to each task. this
links such two objects
    //avoiding a new task from starting if the token has already been
triggered
    //in addition, passing the token here will convert the
OperationCancelledException thrown by
    the ThrowIfCancellationRequested method in the
    TaskCancelledException class that will inform
    //TPL that such task has been kindly aborted
    var tasks = Enumerable.Range(0, 10).Select(i =>
Task.Factory.StartNew(OnAnotherThread,
cancellationToken)).ToArray();

    Console.WriteLine("All tasks queued for running");
    Console.WriteLine("RETURN TO BEGIN CANCEL TASKS");
    Console.ReadLine();
    cancellationTokenSource.Cancel();

    Console.WriteLine("Cancel requested!");

    try
    {
        //join back all tasks
```

```
            Task.WaitAll(tasks);
    }
    catch (AggregateException ax)
    {
        //all tasks will throw an OperationCanceledException
        foreach (var ex in ax.InnerExceptions)
            if (!(ex is TaskCanceledException))
                Console.WriteLine("Task exception: {0}",
ex.Message);
    }

    foreach (var t in tasks)
        Console.WriteLine("Task status ID {0}: {1}", t.Id,
t.Status);

    Console.WriteLine("END");
    Console.ReadLine();
}


[DebuggerHidden] //avoid visual studio from catching token
exceptions
private static void OnAnotherThread()
{
    Console.WriteLine("Task {0} starting...", Task.CurrentId);

    //do some CPU intensive job
    for (int i = 0; i < 100; i++)
    {
        //prevent a cancelled task continuing doing
        //useless job
        cancellationToken.ThrowIfCancellationRequested();

        //CPU job
        Thread.Sleep(500);
    }

    Console.WriteLine("Task {0} ending...", Task.CurrentId);
}
```

The following is the console output:

```
All tasks queued for running
RETURN TO BEGIN CANCEL TASKS
Task 2 starting...
```

```
Task 1 starting...

Cancel requested!
Task status ID 1: Canceled
Task status ID 2: Canceled
Task status ID 3: Canceled
Task status ID 4: Canceled
Task status ID 5: Canceled
Task status ID 6: Canceled
Task status ID 7: Canceled
Task status ID 8: Canceled
Task status ID 9: Canceled
Task status ID 10: Canceled
END
```

Task continuation

Another useful feature of any task is the ability to attach (with an extension method) any other task.

When dealing with task continuation, the Status property of any task, and eventually the Result property with the internal return value may be valued to apply the right logic for each result.

In such operations, the task continuation helps us by providing a comfortable enumeration used to select the desired Status property when continuation occurs:

```
//a task
var task1 = Task.Factory.StartNew(() =>
    {
        Thread.Sleep(1000);
        //uncomment here for testing the error
        //throw new Exception("Hi");
        return 10;
    });

//a continuation is attached to task1
task1.ContinueWith(task =>
    {
        //this continuation will occur only when previous task
will run without errors
        Console.WriteLine("OK: {0}", task.Result);
    }, TaskContinuationOptions.OnlyOnRanToCompletion);

task1.ContinueWith(task =>
```

```
    {
        //this continuation will occur only if something goes
wrong
        Console.WriteLine("ERR: {0}", task.Exception.InnerException);
//the first inner exception
    }, TaskContinuationOptions.NotOnRanToCompletion);
```

Without waiting for the `task1` completion, although a continuation occurs, it skips the need to handle eventual exceptions in the task-creating code.

With continuation and synchronization techniques used together, complex scenarios of asynchronous programming are available to programmers without having to face difficulties such as manual synchronization with signaling locks or by handling parent-child thread synchronization.

Task factories

As seen previously, the `Task` and `TaskFactory` classes give us the ability to start tasks with special options. Although this is actually an interesting feature, we still use the default factory available, available throughout the `Task.Factory` property.

A `TaskFactory` class can also be instantiated with custom options that will work as the starting configuration for any task made with this factory. This is particularly useful when multiple instances of the same kind of task are going to be created. Here is an example:

```
static void Main(string[] args)
{
    var cancellation = new CancellationTokenSource();

    //a factory for creating int-returning tasks
    //all tasks created by this factory will share this default
configuration
    //all tasks will support cancellation
    //all tasks will start in an attached-to-parent fashion
    //all tasks will accept a continuation occurring only on
success
    //the default TaskScheduler will be used
    var factory = new TaskFactory<int>(cancellation.Token,
        TaskCreationOptions.PreferFairness,
        TaskContinuationOptions.AttachedToParent,
        TaskScheduler.Default);

    //10 tasks
    var tasks = Enumerable.Range(1, 10)
```

```
                .Select(i => factory.StartNew(CreateRandomInt)
                    //all tasks continue as attached (from factory) and
        skipping faulted results
                    .ContinueWith(HandleRandomInt,
        TaskContinuationOptions.NotOnFaulted))
                //always define such query materialization
                //differently, the foreach run could trigger infinite task
        creations
                    .ToArray();

            bool canContinue = false;

            //a single continuation async task
            //will start when all other tasks will end
            //such usage avoid calling WaitAll
            factory.ContinueWhenAll(tasks, allTasks =>
                {
                    canContinue = true;
                    return 0;
                });

            do
            {
                Console.Clear();

                foreach (var task in tasks)
                    Console.WriteLine("Task n. {0}: {1}", task.Id,
        task.Status);

                Thread.Sleep(1000);
            } while (!canContinue);

            Console.WriteLine("END");
            Console.ReadLine();
        }

        //this method executes only if the previous task completed
        successfully
        private static void HandleRandomInt(Task<int> task)
        {
            Console.WriteLine("Handling value: {0}", task.Result);
        }

        static Random random = new Random();
```

```
[DebuggerHidden] //this attribute disables exception debugging
public static int CreateRandomInt()
{
    //wait 1~10 seconds
    Thread.Sleep(random.Next(1000, 10000));

    //throw exception sometime
    if (random.Next(1, 100) % 10 == 0)
        throw new ArgumentException("Unable to produce a valid integer
value!");

    return random.Next(1, 100);
}
```

This example launches multiple tasks to retrieve integers with some complex calculations (the random sleep time). Later, for the only successfully generated integers, a continuation task is assigned to handle these new values. Usually, this application would have used interaction (for/foreach), although in multiple tasks a whole re-join of all such asynchronous executions to catch all results is required. Instead, using continuations, everything is easier because such interaction does not occur.

Another interesting feature visible in the example is the ability to have a continuation task for the whole group of tasks instead of a task-by-task basis. Such usage avoids the WaitAll invocation. Remember that WaitAll works like a Thread.Join method, which opens the door to exception bubbling of all joined tasks in the caller thread.

Task UI synchronization

When dealing with asynchronous programming, the UI experience may achieve great improvement. The first look at any Windows Phone or Windows Store application will easily grant such feedback because of the obligation Microsoft made to SDKs for such platforms.

Dealing with an application that never waits for any external/internal resource or computation, and always remains responsive, is a great feature. The drawback is that Windows Forms and WPF controls are unable to easily update their user data using asynchronous threads (this limitation doesn't exist on ASP.NET).

Both frameworks, Windows Forms and WPF, implement their controls on a **Single Thread Apartment (STA)** with affinity. This means that all objects born on the starting thread will be available only throughout this thread. This affinity works like a firewall that prevents any other thread from accessing the resources behind it. So, although it is possible in asynchronous tasks/threads that do computations or that consume resource usage, when they are exited, any UI update must flow from the initial calling thread that created the UI controls, and maybe the same one that started the tasks.

This is a simple example that produces an exception in WPF:

```
//this is a no-MVVM WPF script
public partial class MainWindow : Window
{
    public MainWindow()
    {
        InitializeComponent();
    }

    private void Window_Loaded(object sender, RoutedEventArgs e)
    {
        Task.Factory.StartNew(() =>
        {
            Thread.Sleep(3000);
            //asynchronously set the Content of a Label on UI
            Label1.Content = "HI";
        });
    }
}
```

When the `Content` property is set, `InvalidOperationException` type is raised with this description: `The calling thread cannot access this object because a different thread owns it`. As said previously, before the preceding example, all UI controls live within a single thread in STA mode. This is why we have such behavior in WPF (and in Windows Forms too).

The solution is easy here because this is a script in WPF code-behind. It is enough to use a `Dispatcher` class, already exposed by any WPF control that works as a bridge to ask the UI thread to do something we want. The preceding task becomes this:

```
Task.Factory.StartNew(() =>
{
    Thread.Sleep(3000);

    var computedText = "HI";

    //asynchronously set the Content of a Label on UI
```

```
Dispatcher.Invoke(() =>
    {
        //this code will execute on UI thread in synchronous
way
        Label1.Content = computedText;
    });

});
```

When working in MVVM, a dispatcher is useless when a notification occurs. When any class that implements the `INotifyPropertyChanged` interface raises its `PropertyChanged` event, any control in binding with any property of this object, will read the underlying data again, refreshing the UI control state. This inverted behavior breaks the need for a direct cross-thread invocation with the dispatcher. The following is an example using the view model:

```
//a simple viewmodel
public sealed class SimpleViewModel : INotifyPropertyChanged
{
    //supporting INotifyPropertyChanged is mandatory for data
changes notification to UI controls with data binding
    public event PropertyChangedEventHandler PropertyChanged;

    //a simple helper method for such notification
    private void Notify([CallerMemberName] string name = null)
    {
        if (PropertyChanged != null && name != null)
            PropertyChanged(this, new PropertyChangedEventArgs(name));
    }

    public SimpleViewModel()
    {
        //the task is fired as view model is instantiated
        Task.Factory.StartNew(OnAnotherThread);
    }

    private string text;
    public string Text { get { return text; } set { text = value;
Notify(); } } //this is how notify fires

    private void OnAnotherThread()
    {
        Thread.Sleep(3000);

        //asynchronously set a text value
```

```
            Text = "HI";
        }
    }
```

To avoid coupling between a ViewModel and a View, we need supporting cross-threaded operations within a ViewModel with the ability to execute some UI update in the proper thread (the UI thread one), although we need using the Dispatcher from within the ViewModel itself, we may use it without having the View passing it to the ViewModel in a direct way. The ViewModel, can simply store the initial creation thread in it's constructor code, and later use such thread to ask for a dispatcher linked to this thread. This choice gives the ability to make cross-threaded operations against object living within the UI thread, without having the ViewModel to directly interact with View. The following is an example:

```csharp
//a simple ViewModel
public sealed class CrossThreadViewModel : INotifyPropertyChanged
{
    //supporting INotifyPropertyChanged is mandatory for data
changes notification to UI controls with data-binding
    public event PropertyChangedEventHandler PropertyChanged;

    //a simple helper method for such notification
    private void Notify([CallerMemberName]string name = null)
    {
        if (PropertyChanged != null && name != null)
            PropertyChanged(this, new
PropertyChangedEventArgs(name));
    }

    Thread creatingThread;
    public CrossThreadViewModel()
    {
        //in the constructor the caller thread is stored as field
        creatingThread = Thread.CurrentThread;

        Texts = new ObservableCollection<string>();
        Task.Factory.StartNew(OnAnotherThread);
    }

    //an observable collection is a self-notifying collection
    //that must be accessed by the creating thread
    private ObservableCollection<string> texts;
    public ObservableCollection<string> Texts { get { return
texts; } set { texts = value; Notify(); } } //this is how notify
fires

    private void OnAnotherThread()
    {
```

```
            Thread.Sleep(3000);

            //asynchronously create a text value
            var text = "HI";

            //add the value to the collection with a dispatcher
            //for the creating thread as stored
            Dispatcher.FromThread(creatingThread).Invoke(() =>
                {
                    Texts.Add(text);
                });
        }
}
```

Another solution is available to access collections from multiple threads within a WPF application in .NET 4.5 or greater. We can request the WPF that is synchronizing an STA object, by using a lock and simply invoking the BindingOperations. EnableCollectionSynchronization method. Here the previous example is modified using the EnableCollectionSynchronization class:

```
tatic object lockFlag = new object(); //the collection accessing
lock
Thread creatingThread;
public CrossThreadViewModel()
{
    //in the constructor the caller thread is stored as a field
    creatingThread = Thread.CurrentThread;

    Texts = new ObservableCollection<string>();
    BindingOperations.EnableCollectionSynchronization(Texts,
lockFlag);
    Task.Factory.StartNew(OnAnotherThread);
}

//an observable collection is a self-notifying collection
//that must be accessed by creating thread
private ObservableCollection<string> texts;
public ObservableCollection<string> Texts { get { return texts; }
set { texts = value; Notify(); } } //this is how notify fires

private void OnAnotherThread()
{
    Thread.Sleep(3000);

    //asynchronously create a text value
    var text = "HI";
    Texts.Add(text);//no more dispatcher needed
}
```

Although this solution will avoid the need of collection synchronization, this will not avoid all of the cross-thread issues, and sometimes we still need to use the dispatcher using the synchronous ViewModel creation thread, as shown in the previous example.

When working in Windows Forms, although the dispatcher is unavailable, a solution always exists for such cross-thread issues. It is enough to ask the control (or Windows Form) to do the cross-thread operation for us, using a delegate identical to the one from the dispatcher.

The following is an example of a wrongly-made cross-thread operation that will generate the same InvalidOperationException exception already seen in the WPF example:

```
public Form1()
{
    InitializeComponent();

    Task.Factory.StartNew(() =>
        {
            //this code will fail
            label1.Text = "Hi";
        });
}
```

The following code example shows the right way to avoid the InvalidOperationException class:

```
public Form1()
{
    InitializeComponent();

    Task.Factory.StartNew(() =>
        {
            //async elaboration
            var text = "Hi";

            //this asks the form to execute such Action on its
creating thread
            this.Invoke(new Action(() =>
                {
                    label1.Text = text;
                }));
        });
}
```

Async/await

Asynchronous programming was first released for Microsoft Visual Studio 2012 as an add-on, and is now natively available in Microsoft Visual Studio 2013. Asynchronous programming is also available with a special pattern called async/await, which is greatly optimized for cross-thread operations.

This pattern helps to achieve asynchronous programming in a simplified way and adds a transparent (to programmers) asynchronous/synchronous jump, row-by-row, with the ability to execute code on the UI, creating threads without having to use any dispatcher or a delegate. The following is an example from the legacy Windows Forms as seen earlier:

```
public Form1()
{
    InitializeComponent();

    OnAsyncWay();
}

private async Task OnAsyncWay()
{
    //running in creating thread

    //async elaboration
    //this starts a new task that returns the required value
    var text = await Task.Factory.StartNew(() =>
    {
        //running on another thread
        Thread.Sleep(1000);
        return "Hi";
    });

    //running again on creating thread
    label1.Text = text;
}
```

As it is visible (although usually the StartNew syntax returns a task), this is executed by the await method that translates it in the asynchronous returned values as the Result property of the task itself.

 Any async method must await something, else it is actually useless.

The `async` keyword specifies that the whole method contains asynchronous calls. The `await` keyword, instead, specifies that the next invocation will execute asynchronously, and when such a task ends, the code must continue again in a synchronous way on the caller thread. Unlike a dispatcher, that requests another thread that is doing something, with `async`/`await` methods we can write code that can work on multiple threads in a very simplified way.

We can also await multiple tasks with the `Task.WhenAll` method, as follows:

```
private async Task OnAsyncWay()
{
    var allValues = await Task.WhenAll(
        Task.Factory.StartNew<int>(TaskRunner1),
        Task.Factory.StartNew<int>(TaskRunner2),
        Task.Factory.StartNew<int>(TaskRunner3)
        );
}

private int TaskRunner3() { return 3; }
private int TaskRunner2() { return 2; }
private int TaskRunner1() { return 1; }
```

When dealing with `async`/`await` methods, if sleep-time is needed, instead of using the `Thread.Sleep` methods that occur on the main thread, use the `Task.Delay` method, which will wait for the same time without having to block the calling thread. The following is an example:

```
await Task.Delay(1000);
```

Keep in mind that `async`/`await` methods add the thread switching feature to the existing task-based asynchronous programming techniques already seen earlier. Everything is still available, from task continuation to factory configuration, task child synchronization, and so on. With such added features, it becomes very easy to deal with UI updates. Asynchronous programming is necessary to achieve a greater user experience and high throughput/scalability for any application.

For further reading, you can refer to the following link `https://msdn.microsoft.com/en-us/library/hh191443.aspx`.

Summary

In this chapter, you saw how asynchronous programming is available to developers with different .NET techniques. Although with the last .NET editions, the TAP (with the `async`/`await` method) will be the main choice when dealing with such programming. A complete knowledge of the available solutions is mandatory anytime we cannot use the newest .NET edition. Moreover, it is actually a plus to know all the available techniques because such a wide knowledge opens the mind of any developer to the asynchronous theory problems and solutions.

In the next chapter, you will learn more about parallelism, another important aspect of high performance programming.

5

Programming for Parallelism

Within the .NET world, **parallel programming** is the art of executing the same job on a collection of data or functions by splitting the desired elaboration over all available computational resources.

This chapter will focus on .NET **Task Parallel Library**'s **(TPL)** implementation of parallel computing, together with the **Parallel Language Integrated Query (PLINQ)** language.

This chapter will cover the following topics:

- Parallel programming
- Task parallelism with TPL
- Data parallelism with TPL
- Integrated querying with LINQ
- Data parallelism with PLINQ

Parallel programming

The goal of any parallel programming is to reduce the whole latency time of the operation by using all the available local resources, in terms of CPU computational power.

Two definitions of parallelism actually exist. **Task parallelism** happens when we execute multiple jobs all together, such as saving data against multiple database servers.

Data parallelism, instead, happens when we split a huge dataset elaboration across all available CPUs, like when we have to execute some CPU demanding method against a huge amount of objects in the memory, like hashing data.

In the .NET framework, we have the ability to use both parallel kinds. Despite that, the most widely used kind of parallelism within the .NET framework's programming is data parallelism, thanks to PLINQ being so easy to use.

The following table shows the comparison between Task parallelism and Data parallelism:

	Task parallelism	Data parallelism
What does it parallelize?	Parallelizable functions	Parallelizable data
Performance boost	Reduces overall execution time by executing multiple functions per time period	Reduces overall execution time by splitting the same algorithm's execution across all the available CPUs
Starting constraint	The same initial data state	The same data set
Ending constraint	Can end up all together in a synchronous or asynchronous way	Must end up all together in a synchronous way
Messaging	If required, any task can message others or can await others with signaling locks, as seen in the *Multithreading Synchronization* section in *Chapter 3, CLR Internals*	Usually nonexistent

There is a tight coupling between **multithreading (MT)** programming and parallel programming. MT is actually a feature of programming languages that helps us by using low-level operating systems threads that give us the ability to run multiple code all at the same time.

Parallel programming, instead, is a high-level feature of programming languages, which will handle multiple operating-system threads autonomously, giving us the ability to split some jobs at a given time and later catch the result in a single point.

Multithreaded programming is a technique in which we work with multiple threads by ourselves. It is a hard-coded technique whereby we split the different logic of our applications across different threads. Opening two TCP ports to make a two-threaded network router is multithreading. Executing a DB read and data fix on a thread and a DB write on another thread is still multithreading. We are actually writing an application that hardly uses multiple threads.

In parallelism, instead, there is a sort of orchestrator, a chief of the whole parallel processing (usually the starting function or routine). The unified starting point, makes all parallel thread handlers share the same additional starting data. This additional data is obviously different from the divided main data that start up the whole parallel process, like a collection of any enumerable.

When dealing with multithreading programming, it is like executing multiple applications that live within the same process all together. They may also talk to each other with locking or signals, but they do not need to.

Task parallelism

Task parallelism happens when we want to split different activities (functions or algorithms) that start from the same point with the same application state (data). Usually, these paralleled tasks end up all together in a task-group continuation. Although this common ending is not mandatory, it is maybe the most canonical definition for task parallelism within the .NET TPL. You should recognize that the choice of continuing with a single task or with multiple tasks, or waiting on another thread of tasks does not change the overall definition. It is always task parallelism.

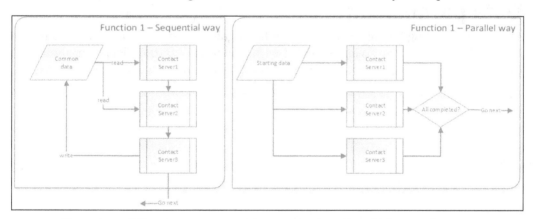

How task parallelism changes a sequential communication with multiple external systems

Any time we need to do different things all together with the same starting data, it is task parallelism. For example, if we need to save data across three different DBs all together, it is task parallelism. If we need to send the same text throughout a mail a file log and a database, those three asynchronous tasks are task parallelism.

Usually, these different things do not need to talk to each other. If this is a requirement, usual locks or (better) signaling locks may give us the ability to drive such multiple asynchronous programming in order to avoid race conditions in resource usage or data inconsistencies with multiple read/writes. A messaging framework is also a good choice when dealing with a multiple asynchronous task execution that needs some data exchanging outside the starting data state.

When using asynchronous programming with multiple tasks (refer to the *Asynchronous Programming Model* section in *Chapter 4, Asynchronous Programming*), it may be that we actually use multiple threads. Although this is task-based multithreading, this is not task parallelism because it misses a shared starting point and overall shared architecture. Parallelism is made by another abstraction level above the abstraction level of Task-based Asynchronous Pattern (TAP).

When we query a **Delegate** object that is executing some remote method asynchronously, we are actually using a thread-pool thread (we may also use those threads by scratch); we are still using simplified multithreading tools. This is not parallelism.

Data parallelism

The art of executing the same function/method against a single (usually huge) dataset is called data parallelism. When working with a huge dataset, parallel programming can bring about an impressive time reduction of the execution of algorithms.

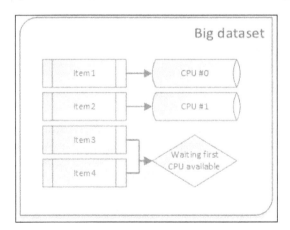

How data parallelism splits data items across CPUs

Within data parallelism, there are more rules; this is different from task parallelism, in which we can actually implement any logic when creating our parallelized functions. Most important of all is that all data must come from a single (usually huge) dataset. This principle is directly coupled to the **set theory**.

A **set** is a uniform group of items of the same type. In the .NET world, a set is any typed array, collection, or the same data type. Like in any relational database, a single table may contain only a homogenous group of items; the same thing happens when we talk about a set. Indeed, a relational table is actually derived from the set theory.

It is not enough to have multiple items all together to create a set. Actually, a set must have any number of items that can be handled as a single unique super-entity. All items that compose a set must be structured as a whole. This means that to practice correctly with data parallelism, a single object type must fill the set once (no duplications), and no logic will ever be admitted to interact with a single item composing a set if the same logic will not be executed against all other items. Another principle about a set is that items do not have any order. Although, they do have an identifier; otherwise, duplication could occur.

Task parallelism with TPL

As mentioned earlier, task parallelism happens when dealing with parallel invocations of multiple methods/function. Within the .NET Framework, this can be obtained with the invocation of the `Parallel.Invoke` method, which needs to have as a parameter all parallelizable actions as a whole. Most techniques applicable here are also applicable in asynchronous programming with the `Task` or the `TaskFactory` class. So reading *Chapter 4, Asynchronous Programming* is mandatory to get the best of task parallelism.

The `Parallel.Invoke` method simply takes multiple remote methods to call procedures in a parallel way by accepting a `System.Action` array. Here is an example:

```
static void Main(string[] args)
{
    //short form with named methods
    Parallel.Invoke(Method1, Method2, Method3);

    //short form with anonymous methods
    Parallel.Invoke(
        () => { },
        () => { },
        () => { });
}

static void Method1() { }
static void Method2() { }
static void Method3() { }
```

In the following code example, we will process a picture resize in two different resolutions using task parallelism:

```
static void Main(string[] args)
{
    //add reference to System.Drawing assembly

    //an original image file
    byte[] originalImageData = File.ReadAllBytes("picture.jpg");
    byte[] thumb300x200 = null;
    byte[] thumb150x100 = null;

    //resize picture to 300x200px and 150x100px for thumbprint needs
    Parallel.Invoke(
        new Action(() =>
        {
            thumb300x200 = ResizeImage(originalImageData, 300,
200);
        }),
        new Action(() =>
        {
            thumb150x100 = ResizeImage(originalImageData, 150,
100);
        })
        );

    //save the resized images
    File.WriteAllBytes("pricture-300.jpg", thumb300x200);
    File.WriteAllBytes("pricture-150.jpg", thumb150x100);
}

static byte[] ResizeImage(byte[] original, int newWidth, int
newHeight)
{
    //creates a stream from a byte[]
    using (var sourceStream = new MemoryStream(original))
    //load a bitmap from source stream
    using (var originalBitmap = new Bitmap(sourceStream))
    //resize the original bitmap to a new size
    using (var resizedBitmap = new Bitmap(originalBitmap,
newWidth, newHeight))
    //creates a new in-memory stream from resized image
    using (var targetStream = new MemoryStream())
```

```
{
    //save resized image to the in-memory stream
    resizedBitmap.Save(targetStream, ImageFormat.Jpeg);
    //return a byte[] from the saved stream
    return targetStream.ToArray();
}
}
```

The `Parallel.Invoke` method will do the most work for us by actually creating a task for each action we need to process; thus obtaining the parallelization needed.

As with any task creation by the `TaskFactory` class, here we have the ability to configure some task creation options such as the maximum concurrent task number, giving a `CancellationToken`, and so on:

```
Parallel.Invoke(new ParallelOptions
{
    MaxDegreeOfParallelism = 2,
},
    () => Method1(),
    () => Method2(),
    () => Method3()
    );
```

An important fact that we always have to deal with when working with parallel programming is that this result has no order. Because of parallelization, we cannot predict task execution time. We must simply wait for completion.

A similar result is available through the `WaitAll` behaviour:

```
Task.WaitAll(
    Task.Run(
    () => Method1()),
    Task.Run(
    () => Method2()),
    Task.Run(
    () => Method3())
    );
```

Although this choice adds the ability to handle timeout as we wish, it provides a similar result because it lacks in task-group configuration, as what was offered by the `ParallelOptions` class. A solution is to use a custom class extending the `TaskFactory` class, but this choice will add nothing more than using the `Parallel.Invoke` method.

Please note that the focus when dealing with task parallelism is that the framework handles lot of things by itself; first of all, the task's creation and destruction. Because of this, the `WaitAll` method is a bit outside of the theory of task parallelism; it's only related to multiple asynchronous programming.

An interesting usage scenario for task parallelism is in **speculative execution**. This happens when we execute some task before it is actually needed, or in a more general way, when we do not need it. A canonical example is what happens when we execute multiple searches against our data source (or web) with different parameters. Here, only the fastest tasks win, so all other slower tasks are canceled. Here is an example:

```
static void Main(string[] args)
{
    //a cancellation token source for cancellation signalling
    using (var ts = new CancellationTokenSource())
    //tasks that returns a value
    using (var task1 = Task.Factory.StartNew<int>(TaskWorker,
ts.Token))
    using (var task2 = Task.Factory.StartNew<int>(TaskWorker,
ts.Token))
    using (var task3 = Task.Factory.StartNew<int>(TaskWorker,
ts.Token))
    {
        //a container for all tasks
        var tasks = new[] { task1, task2, task3 };
        //the index of the fastest task
        var i = Task.WaitAny(tasks);

        //lets cancel all remaining tasks
        ts.Cancel();

        Console.WriteLine("The fastest result is {0} from task
index {1}", tasks[i].Result, i);

        //bring back to the starting thread all task exceptions
        try
        {
            Task.WaitAll(tasks);
        }
        catch (AggregateException ax)
        {
            //let's handle all inner exceptions automatically
            //if any not OperationCanceledException exist
```

```
                //those will be raised again
                ax.Handle(ex => ex is OperationCanceledException);
            }
        }
    Console.ReadLine();
}

private static readonly Random random = new Random();
private static int TaskWorker(object token_as_object)
{
    //the token is available as object parameter
    var token = (CancellationToken)token_as_object;
    //do some long running logic
    var finish = DateTime.Now.AddSeconds(random.Next(1, 10));
    while (DateTime.Now < finish)
    {
        //if the cancellation has been requested
        //an exception will stop task execution
        token.ThrowIfCancellationRequested();
        Thread.Sleep(100);
    }
    return random.Next(1, 1000);
}
```

Please note that although we can obtain task parallelism with by simply using the `Parallel.For/ForEach/Invoke` methods, complex scenarios are available only by manually handling task creation, continuation, and waiting. Please remember that a task is simply a deferred job. Nothing more or less. It is how we use it that makes our design using parallelism or asynchronous programming.

Data parallelism with TPL

As already said, data parallelism with TPL happens only when we deal with a dataset (not the `DataSet` class). Within .NET, the easy way of doing this is with the `Parallel.For` and `Parallel.ForEach` methods from the `Parallel` module. The following example shows the basic usage of the `Parallel` module:

```
for (int i = 0; i < 10; i++)
{
    //do something
}

Parallel.For(0, 10, i =>
```

```
    {
        //do something
    });
```

The first thing that catches our eye is the singularity of logic. While in task parallelism we deal with multiple instances of logic; here, there is always only one type of logic. We simply execute it on multiple CPUs.

This example is obviously incompatible with the Set Theory previously exposed, because there is neither a simple collection of objects. In other words, the parallel For is an iterative structure as the normal For.

To parallelize some logic regarding just a simple collection, the Parallel class gives us the ForEach method:

```
var invoiceIdList = new[] { 1, 2, 3, 4, 5 };

Parallel.ForEach(invoiceIdList, InvoiceID =>
    {
        //do something
    });
```

This alternative made with the Parallel.ForEach method outclasses the very simple result achieved by the Parallel.For method implementation, giving us the chance to work against a collection that is a Set.

 Although a collection in .NET is not actually a Set, it is quite similar. The only missing requirement is that a collection does not guarantee the uniqueness of items.

Any collection of any size may be enumerated by the Parallel.ForEach method. Obviously, the best performance improvement is achieved by big collections because the more items there are, the more the TPL engine can split such items across multiple threads.

Parallelism in .NET executes on the TPL framework. This means that threads from ThreadPool are used to execute parallel jobs. Limitations and configurations of such behavior were exposed in the *Task-based Asynchronous Pattern* section in *Chapter 4, Asynchronous Programming*.

An added feature available in parallelism is the throttling configuration within the `ParallelOptions` class. `Parallel.Invoke/For/ForEach` methods accept an instance of this class, giving the ability to specify a maximum amount of parallel executions. Here's an example:

```
//our throttling configuration
var throttling = new ParallelOptions
{
    MaxDegreeOfParallelism = 2
};

//let's process the data in a parallel way
Parallel.ForEach(invoiceIdList, throttling, i =>
{
    //do something
});
```

ThreadPool tuning

Please bear in mind that TPL uses threads from `ThreadPool` to execute a task's code. This is why tuning `ThreadPool` is so important when using parallel programming extensively . In addition to what we saw in the *Task-based Asynchronous Pattern* section in *Chapter 4, Asynchronous Programming*, here we will try to show you what happens if we try to increase the thread pool size to an extreme, for example:

```
ThreadPool.SetMinThreads(256, 256);
ThreadPool.SetMaxThreads(4096, 4096);
```

The configuration shown asks the thread pool to increase its size from a minimum of 256 threads to a maximum size of 4096 (losing dynamic size management—the default value for the maximum size). Increasing the thread pool size at such high values will cost some CPU usage and memory because the operating system needs such resources in thread creation.

Obviously, such a high thread availability will give TPL the ability to parallelize hundreds of tasks (at least 256, as set earlier). Carefully increment so extremely global thread availability because of the increased possibility of cross-thread issues that we will need to handle with locks and signals, as seen in the *Multithreading Synchronization* section in *Chapter 3, CLR Internals*. In fact, with such an extreme concurrency level, when using locks to serialize specific code blocks, a huge overhead in terms of CPU time will occur because of the contest of the lock flag that all concurrent threads will try to obtain.

Parallel execution abortion

Within a parallel iteration, we cannot use the `break` keyword in any classic `for`/`foreach` statement. If we need a similar behavior, we can use an overload of the `foreach` method that will execute inner parallel code by using an `Action<T, ParallelLoopState>` class that in addition to the iterating item will also inject a `ParallelLoopState` object available to the inner code. This state object will provide information about the overall parallel state or let us request a premature stop of the full parallel execution. Here's a complete example:

```
static void Main(string[] args)
{
    //a big dataset
    var invoiceIdList = Enumerable.Range(1, 1000);

    int c = 0;

    Parallel.ForEach(invoiceIdList, (id, state) =>
        {
            //stop all ForEach execution if anything go wrong
            try
            {
                //execute some logic
                ExecuteSomeCode(id);

                //within the lambda/method we can know about stop
signalling
                if (state.IsStopped)
                    Console.WriteLine("Executed # {0} when
IsStopped was true", c++);
                else
                    Console.WriteLine("Executed # {0}", c++);
            }
            catch (Exception ex)
            {
                Console.WriteLine("Error: {0}", ex.Message);
                //stop al parallel process
                state.Stop();
                Console.WriteLine("Requested a parallel state
break!");
            }
        });

    Console.WriteLine("END");
```

```
        Console.ReadLine();
    }

    private static readonly Random random = new Random();
    private static void ExecuteSomeCode(int id)
    {
        //a random execution time
        Thread.Sleep(random.Next(1000, 2000));

        //an impredicted fail
        if (DateTime.Now.Millisecond >= 800)
            throw new Exception("Something gone wrong!");
    }
```

In this example, we used the `Stop` method that actually requests a stop to all subsequent parallel interactions and together will signal the running iterations that a stop has been requested by the `IsStopped` flag. This is the output of such an example (the results can vary a lot):

```
Executed # 0
Executed # 1
Executed # 2
Executed # 3
Executed # 5
Executed # 4
Executed # 6
Executed # 7
Executed # 8
Error: Something gone wrong!
Requested a parallel state break!
Executed # 9 when IsStopped was true
Executed # 10 when IsStopped was true
Error: Something gone wrong!
Requested a parallel state break!
Error: Something gone wrong!
Requested a parallel state break!
Error: Something gone wrong!
Requested a parallel state break!
Executed # 11 when IsStopped was true
Executed # 12 when IsStopped was true
Executed # 13 when IsStopped was true
Executed # 14 when IsStopped was true
END
```

As shown, after the initial normal execution of parallel statements (from #0 to #8), an error has occurred; this invoked the Stop method of the ParallelLoopState class, which is available in the state parameter within the lambda code. This prevented new interactions of the Parallel.ForEach method. Within the already executing interactions, the IsStopped flag is given a value of true, so (eventually) a proper logic may be applied.

Similar to the Stop method, the Break method can also stop the execution of a parallel statement but it will stop executing only the items that will follow the calling item in the underlying collection order.

If we have a collection of integers from 1 to 100, and when processing the 14th we called the Break method, only items from 15 to 100 will actually receive the IsStopped flag or will not run at all.

Partitions

Any time we deal with data parallelism, TPL will prepare data to flow in different tasks in small groups. Such groups are called **partitions**.

Two default partition logics are available within the .NET framework. **Range partitioning** happens against any finite collection. It divides the collection between all available threads, and any partition is then executed within its related thread. The following shows an example of the Parallel.For method that produces a finite indexer collection of values:

```
Parallel.For(1, 1000, item =>
    {
        Console.WriteLine("Item {0} Task {1} Thread {2}", item,
Task.CurrentId, Thread.CurrentThread.ManagedThreadId);
        Thread.Sleep(2000);
    });
```

This code produces the following output:

```
Item 1 Task 1 Thread 8
Item 125 Task 2 Thread 9
Item 249 Task 3 Thread 11
Item 373 Task 4 Thread 10
Item 497 Task 5 Thread 12
Item 621 Task 6 Thread 16
Item 745 Task 7 Thread 14
Item 869 Task 8 Thread 15
Item 993 Task 9 Thread 13
```

As visible, the index value collection has been divided by 9, as 8 is the number of the initial `ThreadPool` size, plus the one new thread created by `ThreadPool` is triggered by the huge pre-empted work. The same range partitioning logic is involved by using the `AsParallel()` method against any other finite collection such as an `Array`, `ArrayList`, `List<T>`, and so on.

Another built-in partition logic is the **chunk partitioning** logic, which takes place whenever we use the `Parallel.ForEach` method or the `AsParallel()` method against any enum without a finite length. This partitioning is based on an enumerator logic. It simply asks for some new item (usually the same amount as the number of CPU cores), creates a new task for this item group, and puts the execution on an available thread, and then waits for any new thread's availability to start its logic again. In chunk partitioning, the chunk size is known at start and totally handled by the TPL inner logic.

Chunk partitioning has a better balancing capability than the range partitioning because a chunk is often smaller than a partition.

If built-in partitioning logic is not enough for our needs, we can create a custom partitioner by inheriting from the `Partitioner<T>` class. A custom partition logic can avoid using locks, greatly improve overall resource usage, and lead to energetic efficiency within the whole solution. A complete guide is available on the MSDN website: `https://msdn.microsoft.com/en-us/library/dd997411(v=vs.110).aspx`.

Although chunk partitioning supports dynamic chunk sizes, this size is invariant during a single enumeration. If we need full dynamic partitioning, we need to create a partitioner. An example is shown on the MSDN website:

```
https://msdn.microsoft.com/en-us/library/dd997416%28v=vs.110%29.aspx
```

```
Further details about partitioning are explained in the Partitioning
optimization section later in this chapter.
```

Sliding parallel programming

An interesting behavior takes place when we combine sliding programming, just like when using a cursor from a stream or an enumerable with parallel programming. In this scenario, we add high computation speed together with a very low footprint in the memory because of the tiny memory usage made by the few pieces of data currently loaded in each thread. Here is an example:

```
static void Main(string[] args)
{
    var enumerable = GetEnumerableData();
```

```
        Parallel.ForEach(enumerable, new ParallelOptions
        {
            MaxDegreeOfParallelism = 2,
        }, i =>
            {
                //process the data
                Console.WriteLine("Processing {0}...", i);
                Thread.Sleep(2000);
            });

        Console.WriteLine("END");
        Console.ReadLine();
    }

    private static IEnumerable<int> GetEnumerableData()
    {
        //let's produce an enumerable data source
        //eventually use an underlying steam
        for (int i = 0; i < 10; i++)
        {
            Console.WriteLine("Yielding {0}...", i);
            yield return i;
        }
    }
```

This scenario gives tremendous computational power without having to keep in memory all data altogether, thus, only actually processing objects resides in memory.

The previous examples shows a single method using the `yield` keyword for manually enumerated values. The example may be improved by implementing multiple methods using the `yield` operator invoking each one to the other. The obtained architecture, will be able to handle extremely complex logic without never having to keep more than needed data in memory.

Integrated querying with LINQ

The **Language-Integrated Query (LINQ)** framework is what mostly changes the programming technique in the .NET world. LINQ is a framework that lives within the .NET language and helps us create complex queries against any data source, such as in-memory objects using the LINQ to object-provider or against an Entity Framework database using the LINQ to entities provider.

Almost anything that is enumerable in the world has its own provider within a simplified index, as shown at the following link:

http://blogs.msdn.com/b/charlie/archive/2008/02/28/link-to-everything-a-list-of-linq-providers.aspx

Any iteration for the `for` or `foreach` statements is now made with LINQ. The same is made against any relational database accessed by an O/RM or any non-relational database too. LINQ has its own pseudo SQL language that is accessible within any .NET language. Here is a LINQ statement example:

```
var query = from i in items
            where i >= 100
            orderby i descending
            select i;
```

By analyzing the preceding statement, you should understand that it represents a simple query that will make a filter for in-memory data, then will order the filtered data, and later will output the data. The key concept of LINQ is that LINQ creates queries. It does not executes such queries; it simply declares queries.

Any query has a proper type. The type of `query` mentioned earlier is `IOrderedEnumerable<int>`, which means that it is an ordered enumerable collection. Because of the verbosity of the query's result type, in conjunction with the frequent usage of anonymous types, the `var` keyword is widely used when typing a variable that will contain the query itself, as the previous example showed.

Please remember that anonymous types will be visible to **Intellisense** (Visual Studio's suggestion system of the text editor) only within the code block in which it was created. This means that outside the method where we created the anonymous type, we will lose the Intellisense support. The anonymous type will be visible only to the assembly where it was created.

This means that if we need to use an anonymous typed object outside our assembly, we should instead use a statically typed type (not anonymous), or we need to use the `Reflection` namespace to read the `internal` marked properties that compose our anonymous type.

Back to LINQ, the query itself will be executed in a lazy fashion only when iterated by any `foreach` statement or when using specific **Extension methods** that will materialize (produce results) the query in the `ToArray` or `ToList` methods:

```
var concreteValues = query.ToArray();
```

LINQ has a lot of extension methods to access its huge library. Actually, the preceding syntax is very limited compared to all the extension methods available from any enumerable collection. Here's an example:

```
var values = items
    .Where(i => i >= 100)
    .OrderByDescending(i => i)
    .ToArray();
```

All LINQ methods will work in a fluent way, appending any new altering method to the previous one. The Lambda expression is ubiquitous and is used to define new values, value mapping, filter predicates, and so on, so its syntactical deep knowledge is mandatory when using LINQ. The two examples provide identical results, although the second one will not store the query itself but only its concrete result.

The magic of LINQ is the ability to work in any application and query any kind of data, from variables to XMLs with a single syntax. Of course, some limitations are present when dealing with external resources such as databases, because some data providers cannot handle all LINQ methods. In such a case, an exception will be thrown by the provider itself. In modern .NET programming, any iterating logic is usually executed within a LINQ statement.

Another magic aspect of LINQ is the ability to return queries and not always data. This adds the ability to create new features without having to retrieve the same data more than once, or without having to write complex if/else statements with possible copy/paste programming. The following example shows how to split the query similar to what we have already seen in the previous example:

```
var query1= items as IEnumerable<int>;
var query2= query1.Where(i => i >= 100);
var query3 = query2.OrderByDescending(i => i);
var values = query3.ToArray();
```

The following example shows how to add new filters to the already filtered query. The two where statements will execute just like an and clause.

```
var query = items.Where(i => i >= 100);

if (SomeLogic())
    //another where is added to the LINQ
    query = query.Where(i => i <= 900);
```

Please note that using this query result can trigger an undesirably query materialization (execution) multiple times. If you want to work in values, it is always easier to materialize the LINQ with an ending that consists of the ToArray or ToList method.

LINQ offers, by default, any set operation such as Union, Distinct, Intersect, and Except; any aggregate operation such as Count, Sum, Max, Min, and Average; and any relational data operation such as Join, GroupJoin, and so on.

Transformation methods such as `Select` or `SelectMany` are also interesting because they give us the ability to change the object that flows from one LINQ step to the other letting us add/remove/change data. By the way, one of the greatest features of LINQ is the ability to append LINQ queries to another LINQ query, including when dealing with multiple LINQ data providers.

Here's an overview of LINQ's features:

```
//a dataset
var items = Enumerable.Range(1, 1000);

//a simple filter
var filter1 = items.Where(i => i <= 100);

//takes until matches a specific predicate
var filter2 = items.TakeWhile(i => i <= 100); //same as Where
above.

//shape the original data item in another one
var shape1 = items.Select(x => new { Value = items });

//shape multi-dimensional data in flattened data
//this will produce a simple array from 1 to 9
var shape2 = new[] { new[] { 1, 2, 3 }, new[] { 4, 5, 6 }, new[]
{7, 8, 9 } }.SelectMany(i => i);

//group data by divisible by 2
var group1 = items.GroupBy(i => i % 2 == 0);

//take only x values
var take1 = items.Take(10);

//take only after skipped x values
var skip1 = items.Skip(10);

//paginate values by using Take and Skip together
var page3 = items.Skip(2 * 10).Take(10);

//join values
var invoices = new[]
{
    new {InvoiceID=10, Total=44.50},
```

```
    new {InvoiceID=11, Total=34.50},
    new {InvoiceID=12, Total=74.50},
};
//join invoices with items array
//shape the result into a new object
var join1 = invoices.Join(items, i => i.InvoiceID, i => i, (a, b)
=> new { a.InvoiceID, a.Total, Index = b, });
```

All LINQ methods are combinable with any other data collection made by any other data provider. This means that we can actually make a join between two different database values, or between a database value and a file, or an XML, a Web Service, or a control on our UI, or anything else we could want. Obviously, things are not so easy when we want merge data from multiple LINQ data providers, especially because of the Entity Framework data provider that will try to translate anything written in LINQ into SQL. To help us avoid LINQ to SQL translation issues, there are techniques such as small materializations within the LINQ steps (like putting a `ToArray()` method before performing the join between different providers) or starting the query with an in-memory source instead of using an Entity Framework `DbQuery` class.

Entity Framework queries will be discussed later in *Chapter 7, Database Querying*. In the meantime, here is a simple example of a cross LINQ provider query:

```
var localDataset = new[]
{
    new { Latitude=41.88f, Longitude=12.50f, Location="Roma"},
    new { Latitude=45.46f, Longitude=9.18f, Location="Milano"},
    new { Latitude=59.32f, Longitude=18.08f,
Location="Stockholm"},
};

//within the TestDB there is a simple table as
//CREATE TABLE [dbo].[Position] (
//[Latitude] [real] NOT NULL,
//[Longitude] [real] NOT NULL)
using (var db = new TestDBEntities())
{
    //this query starts from the local dataset
    //and later creates a join with the table within the database
    var query = from p in localDataset
                join l in db.Position on new { p.Latitude,
p.Longitude } equals new { l.Latitude, l.Longitude }
                select new
                {
                    l.Latitude,
```

```
                    l.Longitude,
                    p.Location,
            };


    //materialize the query
    foreach (var position in query)
        Console.WriteLine("Lat {0:N2} Lon {1:N2}: {2}",
position.Latitude, position.Longitude, position.Location);
    }


    Console.ReadLine();
```

By executing the example given, you will know how to join two different data providers by specifying the only coordinate couple that we want see in the database table.

> Carefully use lambda expressions because any time we create an anonymous method with lambda, all variables available in the scope of the anonymous method are also available within the method itself. When we use some external variable within the anonymous method, those variables became *captured variables*, changing (extending) their lifecycle, and assuming the same lifecycle of the anonymous method that captures them.

Data parallelism with PLINQ

PLINQ is the framework required to use LINQ within the TPL parallel framework. In .NET, it is straightforward to use parallelism against any LINQ query because we simply need to add the `AsParallel` method at the root of the query to switch the execution from the simple LINQ engine to PLINQ with TPL support.

The following example will execute two different `where` conditions against an enumerable using PLINQ:

```
static void Main(string[] args)
{
    //a dataset
    var items = Enumerable.Range(1, 100);

    //multi-level in-memory where executed as data parallelism
    var processedInParallel = items.AsParallel()
        .Where(x => CheckIfAllowed1(x))
```

```
        .Where(x => CheckIfAllowed2(x))
        .ToArray();

    Console.ReadLine();
}

private static bool CheckIfAllowed2(int x)
{
    Console.WriteLine("Step 2 -> Checking {0}", x);
    //some running time
    Thread.Sleep(1000);
    return x % 3 == 0;
}

private static bool CheckIfAllowed1(int x)
{
    Console.WriteLine("Step 1 -> Checking {0}", x);
    //some running time
    Thread.Sleep(2000);
    return x % 2 == 0;
}
```

This is a partial result:

```
Step 1 -> Checking 1 //first chunk starts
Step 1 -> Checking 6
Step 1 -> Checking 3
Step 1 -> Checking 2
Step 1 -> Checking 4
Step 1 -> Checking 7
Step 1 -> Checking 8
Step 1 -> Checking 5
Step 1 -> Checking 9
Step 1 -> Checking 10
Step 2 -> Checking 4 //second chunk starts
Step 2 -> Checking 8
Step 2 -> Checking 2
Step 2 -> Checking 6
Step 1 -> Checking 12
Step 1 -> Checking 11
Step 1 -> Checking 13
```

The execution of the preceding example will easily show how PLINQ performed using the chunk partitioning logic. The first chunk of items (10 items) reached Step 1 in a simple way. Just later, the second chunk of items were executed all together. This second chunk contains items of the first chunk that succeeded in passing Step 1 and now are ready for Step 2, and new items for the Step 1.

There is the ability to use the AsParallel method without returning values with the ForAll method, as shown in the following code example:

```
items.AsParallel().ForAll(i =>
{
    //do something
});
```

After an AsParallel method invocation, the type of the enumerable changes in ParallelQuery<T>. This new type adds configurability for parallelism, such as forcing parallel-concurrency or forcing parallelism itself, although the heuristics of the TPL cannot be enabled if given an enumerable.

Forcing parallelism (with the WithExecutionMode method) is useful when the engine does not seem to understand that parallelism, it could add some execution time (latency time) reduction. This happens because anytime we use the AsParallel method, the engine makes a prediction of the reduced execution time, and if this is not positive, the engine can decide to not use parallelism at all. Here is an example:

```
//multi-level in-memory where executed as data parallelism
var processedInParallel = items.AsParallel()
    .WithExecutionMode(ParallelExecutionMode.ForceParallelism)
    .Where(x => CheckIfAllowed1(x))
    .Where(x => CheckIfAllowed2(x))
    .ToArray();
```

We can configure parallel concurrency by setting the maximum degree with the WithDegreeOfParallelism method. This method is useful for limiting (throttling) concurrency level, and for increasing it above the usual size as defined by the heuristic of the TPL. The maximum size is 64 for .NET 4 and 512 for .NET 4.5+, while the default value is the CPU core count. Here is an example:

```
var processedInParallel = items.AsParallel()
    .WithDegreeOfParallelism(100)
    .Where(x => CheckIfAllowed1(x))
    .Where(x => CheckIfAllowed2(x))
    .ToArray();
```

Another useful method of the `ParallelQuery<T>` class is `WithMergeOptions`, which gives us the ability to configure how the parallel engine will buffer (or not) data from the parallel partitions before collecting the result. The ability to disable buffering at all is interesting. This choice will give the parallel results to any enumerator consuming the parallel query as soon as possible, without having to wait for processing all parallel query items. The following shows an example that consists of parallel merge options:

```
items.AsParallel().WithMergeOptions(ParallelMergeOptions.NotBuffer
ed)
```

Partitioning optimization

The CLR gives us the ability to force a specific partitioning logic if the one exposed as the default is not optimal for our needs. The default partitioning logic is automatically chosen according to the data collection type given as an input through the `AsParallel` method. Here is an example:

```
//a dataset
var items = Enumerable.Range(1, 1000).ToArray();

//a customized partitioning logic
//range partitioning
var partitioner = Partitioner.Create<int>(items, false);

partitioner.AsParallel().ForAll(item =>
    {
        Console.WriteLine("Item {0} Task {1} Thread {2}", item,
Task.CurrentId, Thread.CurrentThread.ManagedThreadId);
        Thread.Sleep(2000);
    });
```

The preceding example shows a range partitioning logic within the `AsParallel` execution of PLINQ. Here, the result shows the partition size:

```
Item 1 Task 2 Thread 6
Item 751 Task 8 Thread 13
Item 501 Task 6 Thread 16
Item 251 Task 4 Thread 12
Item 376 Task 5 Thread 15
Item 626 Task 7 Thread 14
Item 876 Task 9 Thread 9
Item 126 Task 3 Thread 10
Item 377 Task 5 Thread 15
Item 877 Task 9 Thread 9
```

Instead, the following example shows a load-balancing logic that is obtainable by using the `Partitioner` class:

```
//a dataset
var items = Enumerable.Range(1, 1000).ToArray();

//a customized partitioning logic
//a load-balancing logic
var partitioner = Partitioner.Create<int>(items, true);

partitioner.AsParallel().ForAll(item =>
    {
        Console.WriteLine("Item {0} Task {1} Thread {2}", item,
Task.CurrentId, Thread.CurrentThread.ManagedThreadId);
        Thread.Sleep(2000);
    });
```

The following is the output:

```
Item 2 Task 2 Thread 10
Item 7 Task 6 Thread 11
Item 5 Task 5 Thread 15
Item 8 Task 8 Thread 16
Item 6 Task 7 Thread 13
Item 3 Task 4 Thread 12
Item 4 Task 3 Thread 17
Item 1 Task 9 Thread 9
Item 10 Task 7 Thread 13
Item 15 Task 5 Thread 15
```

When no partitioning logic fits your needs, the only choice available is writing your own partitioner by extending the `Partitioner<T>` or `OrderablePartitioner<T>` class:

```
class Program
{
    static void Main(string[] args)
    {
        //a dataset
        var items = Enumerable.Range(1, 1000).ToArray();

        //my partitioner
        var partitioner = new MyChunkPartitioner(items);

        partitioner.AsParallel().ForAll(item =>
```

```
                {
                    Console.WriteLine("Item {0} Task {1} Thread
    {2}", item, Task.CurrentId, Thread.CurrentThread.ManagedThreadId);
                    Thread.Sleep(2000);
                });

            Console.ReadLine();
        }
    }


    //only use for testing purposes
    public class MyChunkPartitioner : Partitioner<int>
    {
        //underlying data collection
        public IEnumerable<int> Items { get; private set; }
        public MyChunkPartitioner(IEnumerable<int> items)
        {
            Items = items;
        }


        //partition elaboration
        public override IList<IEnumerator<int>> GetPartitions(int
    partitionCount)
        {
            var result = new List<IEnumerator<int>>();

            //compute the page size in an easy way
            var pageSize = Items.Count() / partitionCount;

            for (int page = 0; page < partitionCount; page++)
                result.Add(Items.Skip(page * pageSize).Take(pageSize).
    GetEnumerator());

            return result;
        }
    }
```

Keep in mind that with custom partitioning logic, we have the opportunity to define partition size, and not partition count, because this count is passed as a parameter from outside.

Summary

In this chapter, you saw how to use task parallelism and data parallelism with the .NET framework's features and techniques. Asynchronous programming and parallelism together give any .NET programmer the ability to reach impressive performance goals with an easy-to use approach and reliable environment.

In next chapter, you will see how to implement everything that you learned in this chapter in the special case of mathematics or engineering elaboration.

6

Programming for Math and Engineering

This chapter will focus on computation that is mathematical and engineering oriented, such as digital signal filtering, or any other mathematical computation that may apply to any Big Data of (usually) simple items.

A lot of the examples within this chapter will use libraries such as `Math.NET Numerics` or `AForge.Math`. These libraries are available for free through **NuGet Package Manager**.

In this chapter, we will cover the following topics:

- Evaluating the performance of data types
- Real-time applications
- Case study: the Fourier transform
- Sliding processing

Introduction

Performance impact regarding complex computation is often a primary concern for mathematicians and engineers who deal with C# coding.

Throughput is usually the main performance goal when dealing with scientific data because the faster the application can do its job, the faster the result will be available to the user. This high computational speed improves updating a UI in a higher FPS or processing more asynchronous data for a non-UI application. This always affects the end user considerably.

As opposed to an enterprise world in which big datasets of complex data and logics with simple operations exist, in the mathematical or engineering world, these datasets are usually huge but always of primary types, such as floating-point numbers or sometimes timestamps.

Saving a single millisecond per item when processing 100,000 items per second means saving lot of time, so, fixing usually unintended mistakes or computations that are not optimized has become a main task of any programmer.

Evaluating the performance of data types

Years ago, when CPUs were very slow, the choice of the type of variable was actually an important choice. With modern managed programming languages, even the most primitive data types perform quite the same, but in some cases specific and different behaviors still exist regarding data type performance, in terms of throughput and resource usage.

The following is a sample application that is useful for checking data type speed in randomly generating and sum ten million data items of primitive values. Obviously, such sample code is not able to give any kind of absolute speed rating. It is a simple demonstration application that is useful for giving an idea of different data-type performance behavior:

```
//a random value generator
var r = new Random();

//repeat 10 times the test to have an averaged value
var stopwatchResults = new List<double>();

//a stopwatch for precision profiling
var w = new Stopwatch();

w.Start();
//change type here for testing another data type
var values = Enumerable.Range(0, 10000000).Select(i =>
(float)(r.NextDouble() * 10))
    .ToArray();

w.Stop();
Console.WriteLine("Value array generated in {0:N0}ms",
w.ElapsedMilliseconds);

for (int j = 0; j < 10; j++)
```

```
{
    w.Reset();
    w.Start();

    //change type here for testing another data type
    float result = 0;

    //sum all values
    foreach (var f in values)
        result += f;

    w.Stop();
    Console.WriteLine("Result generated in {0:N0}ms",
w.ElapsedMilliseconds);
        stopwatchResults.Add(w.ElapsedMilliseconds);
}

Console.WriteLine("\r\n-> Result generated in {0:N0}ms avg",
stopwatchResults.Average());
Console.ReadLine();
```

When executed, this application gives an average execution time. Here are some results per data type that were executed on my laptop, which has a quad-core Intel i7-4910MQ, running at 3.9Ghz in turbo mode.

 Please note that the following values are only useful in relation to each other and they are not valid speed benchmark results.

Type	Average result
Int32	37 ms
Int16	37 ms
Int64	37 ms
Double	37 ms
Single	37 ms
Decimal	328 ms

As expected, all data types with a footprint of 32 or 64 bits executed at the same on my 64-bit CPU within the CLR execution environment, but the Decimal data type, which is actually a 128 floating-point number, executed almost 10 times slower than all the other data types.

Although in most financial or mathematical computation the increased precision of a decimal is mandatory, this demonstrates how using a lower precision data type will really boost throughput and latency of any of our applications.

The `Decimal` datatype is able to drastically reduce rounding errors that often happen when using standard 64-bit or 32-bit (double or float) floating point data types, because most of the decimal memory footprint is used to increase precision instead of minimum/maximum numeric values. Visit the following link for more details: `https://msdn.microsoft.com/en-us/library/system.decimal.aspx`.

BigInteger

A special case is when dealing with arbitrary-sized data types, such as the `BigInteger` of the `System.Numerics` namespace (add reference to `System.Numerics` assembly in order to use the related namespace). This structure can handle virtually any numeric signed integer value. The size of the structure in memory will grow together with the internal value numeric size, bringing an always-increasing resource usage and bad throughput times.

Usually, performance is not impacted by the numeric values of two (or multiple) variables when involved in a mathematical computation. This means that computing `10*10` or `10*500` costs the same with regards to CPU usage. When dealing with arbitrary sized typed variables, this assertion becomes false, because of the increased internal size of the data being computed, which brings a higher CPU usage at each value increase.

Let us see how a `BigInteger` multiplication speed changes with the same multiplier:

Multiplier	Average result	Difference
10	332 ms	
100	348 ms	+ 5%
1000	441 ms	+ 26%
10000	640 ms	+ 45%
100000	658 ms	+ 3%

Things change a lot here. The `BigInteger` numeric structure performs in a similar way to the `Decimal` type, when the number is actually a small value. Compared with other data types, this type always performs worse as the value increases, although only by a small amount, because of the intrinsic implementation of the type that internally contains an arbitrary amount of small integer values that compose the full value. A `BigInteger` type has no bound limitations in the numeric value range.

Compared to a `Decimal` type that has very high precision with a good numeric value range, the `BigInteger` type has no precision (as an integer value) with no value range limitation. This differentiation simply states that we should only use the `BigInteger` type when we definitely need storing and computing calculations against a huge numeric value, possibly with no known upper/lower numeric range boundaries.

This behavior should discourage users from using such a data type, except when it is absolutely necessary. Consider that an arbitrary size numeric structure is hard to persist on any relational database without strong customizations or by using serialization features, with the high costs of lot of data extraction whenever we need to read/write such a value.

Half-precision data type

Although not available by default within the CLR, when dealing with unmanaged code, often referred to as unsafe code, this old data type becomes available.

A native implementation for .NET is made in this link: `http://csharp-half.sourceforge.net/`.

This implementation, as expected, uses native unsafe code from C++. To enable unsafe coding within C#, we need to select the `Allow unsafe code` flag within the **Build** pane of project property page.

Here, a 16-bit floating-point precision example is given with unsafe coding:

```
var doublePrecision = double.Parse("10.987654321");
Console.WriteLine("{0}", doublePrecision);

var singlePrecision = float.Parse("10.987654321");
Console.WriteLine("{0}", singlePrecision);

var halfPrecision = Half.Parse("10.987654321");
Console.WriteLine("{0}", halfPrecision);

//result:

10.987654321
10.98765
10.98438
```

When you lose precision by using a smaller data type, you reduce the characteristic digit count (the number of digits different from zero) of the contained value. As seen, the 64-bit example (the first row) clearly shows more digits than the other two types.

Another great disadvantage of using small precision datatypes is that because of the numeric characterization reduction, it may be possible that a specific value won't exist. In this case, the nearest value available is used in place of the original value. This issue also exists in 32-bit and 64-bit floating points. But when working with a very tiny 16-bit value, such as the half-precision data type, this issue becomes more evident.

All floating-point values have a characteristic number and a 10-based multiplier. This means that the more characteristic numbers we use upside the decimal separator, the fewer will remain available downside the decimal separator. And the opposite is also true.

Regarding performance, maybe because of this specific implementation, performances are actually poor with high computation times that become a visible issue on big datasets.

Using a 16-bit floating-point data type is discouraged because it is unable to give any performance improvement, but only in case if we definitely need such a 16-bit data type, that may be because of some legacy-application integration.

Real-time applications

Real-time computing happens when a system is able to guarantee its latency time, regardless of the system load. Obviously, low latency times are mandatory, but it is the ability to guarantee the same latency time as load increases that makes a fast system actually a real-time system. A more detailed definition is available here: http://en.wikipedia.org/wiki/Real-time_computing.

A canonical example is the ABS (anti-lock braking system) logic ubiquitously implemented in any automobile. Such logic must give results within a specific deadline (in a span of milliseconds), otherwise the system will go into a failed state.

Sometimes real-time systems may run at an acceptable service level, although with soft constraint specifications such as adding some tolerance to the deadline requirement. With such a near real-time requirement, we can code in .NET for Microsoft Windows as easily as we usually do for any other application type.

Bear in mind that within Microsoft Windows we cannot have full real-time computation, mainly because of the unavailability of any application to claim the 100 percent time of a CPU that is handled in time-share by the OS itself.

This does not mean that Windows or the CLR cannot run code fast enough for real-time, as real-time programming does not mean fast – it means with deterministic times. Windows cannot run real-time applications, simply because it cannot guarantee specific timing for (system – Win32) method invocations or thread start-up/stop times. The same happens regarding the CLR that cannot guarantee fixed timings about method execution and object destruction, for instance as has already been described in the *Garbage Collection* section in *Chapter 3, CLR Internals*.

When dealing with specific applications such as industrials systems for automations or robotics, it may be that we need near-real-time execution in C# to drive such automations. Although we cannot create a Computer Numerical Control (CNC) with C#, we can drive a CNC with remote invocations made in any .NET language. When driving a CNC, the best performing architecture in C# is made using task-parallelism or multi-thread based design.

If we have to create an application that reads a joystick position value, and then moves a robotic arm to a specific position, we should make at least a three-threaded application that can run at 60 FPS (Frame Per Second). This means that all C# code must execute in less than 16ms per cycle.

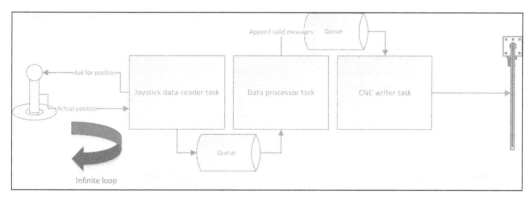

A real-time queued driver processor made with C#

The application consists of a task, or a thread in charge of asking the position of the joystick with an infinite-loop in a polling design. No logic can be placed here because if any kind of logic is placed here, it would reduce the read speed, which, in turn, would reduce the overall FPS rates of the application.

Successively, any value will be queued in a valid thread-safe in-memory queue that will propogate the value without having to couple the two tasks processing speeds.

The second task will eventually check for data integrity and avoid data duplication by knowing the actual CNC state and thus avoid sending the same position to the next step multiple times.

The last task will read messages from the previous step by reading another queue and will later send any queued message to the CNC in the right sequence, because the whole queued architecture guarantees the sequential transmission of all messages.

For instance, you can run the real time application and later run a telnet client by executing such command: [telnet localhost 8080]. When the telnet will enstabilish the connection to the real time application we can simply test it by writing some text in the telnet client one. All the text will be sent to the real time application and is later shown in the console..

```
static void Main(string[] args)
{
    //create all needed tasks and wait until any will exit
    //any task exit will be considered an error and will cause process
exit
    Task.WaitAny(
        Task.Factory.StartNew(OnDataReaderTask, TaskCreationOptions.
LongRunning),
        Task.Factory.StartNew(OnDataProcessorTask,
TaskCreationOptions.LongRunning),
        Task.Factory.StartNew(OnDataWriterTask, TaskCreationOptions.
LongRunning));

    Console.WriteLine("Abnormal exit!");
}

//a stopwatch for testing purposes
static readonly Stopwatch stopwatch = new Stopwatch();

//this task will read data from the reader source
//we will use a simple tcp listener for testing purposes
private static void OnDataReaderTask()
{
    //a listener for opening a server TCP port
    var listener = new TcpListener(IPAddress.Any, 8080);
    listener.Start();

    //the server client for communication with remote client
    using (var client = listener.AcceptTcpClient())
    using (var stream = client.GetStream())
        while (true)
        {
            //try reading next byte
```

```
            var nextByte = stream.ReadByte();

            //valid char
            if (nextByte >= 0)
            {
                AllMessagesQueue.Enqueue((char)nextByte);

                //start stopwatch
                stopwatch.Reset();
                stopwatch.Start();
            }

            Thread.Sleep(1);
        }
    }


//this queue will contains temporary messages going from reader
task to processor task
static readonly ConcurrentQueue<char> AllMessagesQueue = new
ConcurrentQueue<char>();

//this task will process data messages
//no data repetition will be admitted
private static void OnDataProcessorTask()
{
    char last = default(char);
    while (true)
    {
        char c;
        //if there is some data to read
        if (AllMessagesQueue.TryDequeue(out c))
            //only new values are admitted when sending
coordinates to a CNC
            if (c != last)
            {
                last = c;
                ValidMessagesQueue.Enqueue(c);
            }
            else
                //stop stopwatch
                stopwatch.Stop();

        Thread.Sleep(1);
    }
```

```
}

//this queue will contains temporary messages going from processor
task to writer task
static readonly ConcurrentQueue<char> ValidMessagesQueue = new
ConcurrentQueue<char>();

//this task will push data to the target system
//instead of a CNC we will use the Console for testing purposes
private static void OnDataWriterTask()
{
    while (true)
    {
        char c;
        //if there is some data to read
        if (ValidMessagesQueue.TryDequeue(out c))
        {
            //stop stopwatch
            stopwatch.Stop();
            Debug.WriteLine(string.Format("Message crossed tasks
in {0:N0}ms", stopwatch.ElapsedMilliseconds));

            //we will send such data to the CNC system
            //for testing purposes we will use a Console.Write
            Console.Write(c);
        }

        Thread.Sleep(1);
    }
}
```

The preceding example shows how to process data without ever making any tasks
wait for another. This solution will guarantee the message flow and executes in
not more than 10ms on my laptop, so its speed is actually higher than 60 FPS,
as required.

The usage of Thread.Sleep at 1ms will force CLR to pause the execution of the
thread. On Windows, this stop-and-resume time is variable.

Obviously, we cannot guarantee that under load, the system will process in the
same time, so this is definitely a near-real-time application with a soft constraint
on deadlines specification; although optimistically, for 99.99% of the time, it works
just fine.

Case study: Fourier transform

Fourier transform has several usages in engineering programming. The easiest usage is producing a rolling average value for a dataset by applying a digital filter on the given values as being frequency-domain values.

A low-pass filter is the one that stops high frequency values from passing. In audio engineering, it is used to drive a sub-woofer or any low-frequency speaker. When dealing with any other numerical value, such filters become useful to have an averaged value or to cut away any interference or parasite signal in our values.

Rolling average

The application of a `Fast Fourier Transform` (FFT) on any numerical value will produce a rolling average result like this:

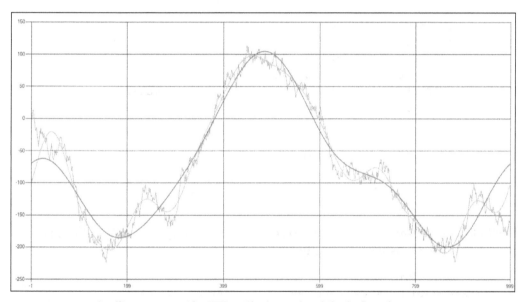

A rolling average with a FFT at 10hz (orange) and 4hz (red) cut frequency

A typical feature of a FFT filter is at the edges, where the filter follows the trend of the whole dataset instead of the local data. In the preceding picture, this error is visible on the right-hand side, where the FFT produces an increasing averaged value while the raw one is going down.

By using the `Math.NET Numerics` package from NuGet, the following is the code to make a low-pass with FFT:

```csharp
/// <summary>
/// Makes a low-pass digital filter against any floating point
data
/// </summary>
private static IEnumerable<float> LowPass(IEnumerable<float>
values, int cutHz)
{
    //convert raw data to Complex frequency domain-data
    var complex = values.Select(x => new Complex(x, 0)).ToArray();

    //start a fast Fourier transform (FFT)
    //this will change raw data in frequency data
    Fourier.Forward(complex);

    //low data is at edges so we clean-up
    //any data at the centre because we want
    //only low data (is a low-pass filter)
    for (int i = 0; i < complex.Count(); i++)
        if (i > cutHz && i < complex.Count() - cutHz)
            complex[i] = new Complex();

    //convert back data to raw floating-point values
    Fourier.Inverse(complex);

    return complex.Select(x => (float)x.Real);
}
```

The following example shows how to create the preceding chart in Windows Forms. The application starts with an empty `Form1` file.

```csharp
//for data initialization
private void Form1_Load(object sender, EventArgs e)
{
    var r = new Random();
    double d = 0;

    //randomly generated data
    var data = Enumerable.Range(1, 1000)
        .Select(i => (float)(r.Next() % 2 == 0 ? d += (r.NextDouble()
 * 10d) : d -= (r.NextDouble() * 10d)))
```

```
    .ToArray();

//namespace System.Windows.Forms.DataVisualization.Charting
var chart1 = new Chart();

//add the chart to the form
this.Controls.Add(chart1);
//shows chart in full screen
chart1.Dock = DockStyle.Fill;

//create a default area
chart1.ChartAreas.Add(new ChartArea());

//create series
chart1.Series.Add(new Series
    {
        XValueMember = "Index",
        XValueType = ChartValueType.Auto,
        YValueMembers = "RawValue",
        ChartType = SeriesChartType.Line,
    });
chart1.Series.Add(new Series
{
    XValueMember = "Index",
    XValueType = ChartValueType.Auto,
    YValueMembers = "AveragedValue10",
    ChartType = SeriesChartType.Line,
    BorderWidth = 2,
});
chart1.Series.Add(new Series
{
    XValueMember = "Index",
    XValueType = ChartValueType.Auto,
    YValueMembers = "AveragedValue4",
    ChartType = SeriesChartType.Line,
    BorderWidth = 2,
});

//apply a digital low-pass filter with different cut-off
frequencies
var lowPassData10hz = LowPass(data, 10).ToArray();
```

```
var lowPassData4hz = LowPass(data, 4).ToArray();

//do databinding
chart1.DataSource = Enumerable.Range(0, data.Length).Select(i
=> new
    {
        Index = i,
        RawValue = data[i],
        AveragedValue10 = lowPassData10hz[i],
        AveragedValue4 = lowPassData4hz[i],
    }).ToArray();
chart1.DataBind();

//window in full screen
WindowState = FormWindowState.Maximized;
}
```

Low-pass filtering for Audio

Low-pass filtering has been available since 2008 in the native .NET code. **NAudio** is a powerful library helping any CLR programmer to create, manipulate, or analyze audio data in any format.

Available through NuGet Package Manager, NAudio offers a simple and .NET-like programming framework, with specific classes and stream-reader for audio data files.

Let's see how to apply the low-pass digital filter in a real audio uncompressed file in WAVE format. For this test, we will use the Windows start-up default sound file. The chart is still made in a legacy Windows Forms application with an empty `Form1` file, as shown in the previous example.

```
private async void Form1_Load(object sender, EventArgs e)
{
    //stereo wave file channels
    var channels = await Task.Factory.StartNew(() =>
        {
            //the wave stream-like reader
            using (var reader = new WaveFileReader("startup.wav"))
            {
                var leftChannel = new List<float>();
                var rightChannel = new List<float>();

                //let's read all frames as normalized floats
```

```
            while (reader.Position < reader.Length)
            {
                var frame = reader.ReadNextSampleFrame();
                leftChannel.Add(frame[0]);
                rightChannel.Add(frame[1]);
            }

            return new
            {
                Left = leftChannel.ToArray(),
                Right = rightChannel.ToArray(),
            };
        }
    });

    //make a low-pass digital filter on floating point data
    //at 200hz
    var leftLowpassTask = Task.Factory.StartNew(() =>
LowPass(channels.Left, 200).ToArray());
    var rightLowpassTask = Task.Factory.StartNew(() =>
LowPass(channels.Right, 200).ToArray());

    //this let the two tasks work together in task-parallelism
    var leftChannelLP = await leftLowpassTask;
    var rightChannelLP = await rightLowpassTask;

    //create and databind a chart
    var chart1 = CreateChart();

    chart1.DataSource = Enumerable.Range(0, channels.Left.Length).
Select(i => new
        {
            Index = i,
            Left = channels.Left[i],
            Right = channels.Right[i],
            LeftLP = leftChannelLP[i],
            RightLP = rightChannelLP[i],
        }).ToArray();

    chart1.DataBind();

    //add the chart to the form
```

```
        this.Controls.Add(chart1);
    }

    private static Chart CreateChart()
    {
        //creates a chart
        //namespace System.Windows.Forms.DataVisualization.Charting

        var chart1 = new Chart();

        //shows chart in fullscreen
        chart1.Dock = DockStyle.Fill;

        //create a default area
        chart1.ChartAreas.Add(new ChartArea());

        //left and right channel series
        chart1.Series.Add(new Series
        {
            XValueMember = "Index",
            XValueType = ChartValueType.Auto,
            YValueMembers = "Left",
            ChartType = SeriesChartType.Line,
        });
        chart1.Series.Add(new Series
        {
            XValueMember = "Index",
            XValueType = ChartValueType.Auto,
            YValueMembers = "Right",
            ChartType = SeriesChartType.Line,
        });

        //left and right channel low-pass (bass) series
        chart1.Series.Add(new Series
        {
            XValueMember = "Index",
            XValueType = ChartValueType.Auto,
            YValueMembers = "LeftLP",
            ChartType = SeriesChartType.Line,
            BorderWidth = 2,
        });
        chart1.Series.Add(new Series
```

```
    {
        XValueMember = "Index",
        XValueType = ChartValueType.Auto,
        YValueMembers = "RightLP",
        ChartType = SeriesChartType.Line,
        BorderWidth = 2,
    });

    return chart1;
}
```

Let's see the graphical result:

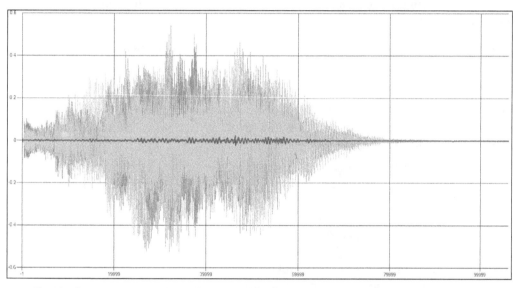

The Windows start-up sound waveform. In bolt, the bass waveform with a low-pass filter at 200hz.

The usage of parallelism in elaborations such as this is mandatory. Audio elaboration is a canonical example of engineering data computation because it works on a huge dataset of floating points values. A simple file, such as the preceding one that contains less than 2 seconds of audio sampled at (only) 22,050 Hz, produces an array greater than 40,000 floating points per channel (stereo = 2 channels).

Just to have an idea of how hard processing audio files is, note that an uncompressed CD quality song of 4 minutes sampled at 44,100 samples per second * 60 (seconds) * 4 (minutes) will create an array greater than 10 million floating-point items per channel.

Because of the FFT intrinsic logic, any low-pass filtering run must run in a single thread. This means that the only optimization we can apply when running FFT based low-pass filtering is parallelizing in a per channel basis. For most cases, this choice can only bring a 2X throughput improvement, regardless of the processor count of the underlying system.

Sliding processing

As already seen in *Chapter 3*, *CLR Internals*, CLR has some limitations in memory management.

Working with engineering data means having to deal with a huge dataset of more than a million records.

Although we can load a simple integer array with millions of items in memory, the same thing will be impossible when the number rises by a lot, or the data type becomes heavier than a simple integer value.

The .NET has a complete enumerator-like execution model that can help us handle a billion items without ever having to deal with all such items in memory, all together. Here is an example on sliding processing:

```
static void Main(string[] args)
{
    //dataset
    //this dataset will not be streamed until needed
    var enumerableDataset = RetrieveHugeDataset();

    //start using the enumerable
    //this will actually start executing code within
RetrieveHugeDataset method
    foreach (var item in enumerableDataset)
        if (item % 12 == 0)
            Console.WriteLine("-> {0}", item);

    //parallel elaboration is also available
    enumerableDataset
        .AsParallel()
        .Where(x => x % 12 == 0)
        .ForAll(item => Console.WriteLine("-> {0}", item));

    Console.ReadLine();
```

```
    }

    static readonly Random random = new Random();

    //return an enumerable cursor to read data in a sliding way
    static IEnumerable<int> RetrieveHugeDataset()
    {
        //easy implementation for testing purpose
        for (int i = 0; i < 10000; i++)
        {
            //emulate some resource usage
            Thread.Sleep(random.Next(50, 200));

            //signal an item available to the enumerator
            yield return random.Next(10, 100000);
        }
    }
}
```

Although this is a simple example, the ability to process a huge dataset with data-parallelism, without storing the whole dataset in memory, is often mandatory when dealing with special data elaboration such as what is produced by CNC systems or audio ADCs. When dealing with a high frequency sampler dataset, it is easy to store more than a billion of items. Because dealing with such a huge dataset in memory may easily cause an OutOfMemoryException issue, it is easy to see that sliding elaboration is the only design that can avoid memory issues altogether, with the ability to process in a parallel manner.

Keep in mind that LINQ queries against in-memory objects work with exactly the same implementation as the preceding code. Most LINQ methods, such as an altering method, or a filtering method, will internally execute in a sliding way. By executing a LINQ expression against another enumerator, such as our RetrieveHugeDataset method, we start a completely new world of programming in which the data flows between enumerator steps without having to being stored somewhere in memory in a fixed-length container.

A canonical example of such sliding elaboration also uses a source or target (or together) a stream-based class, as a FileStream or NetworkStream. The combination of all such sliding processor classes is infinite and greatly powerful.

Summary

In this chapter, we discussed classical mathematic and engineering concerns about data processing using practical examples and real-world solutions, such as the Fast Fourier Transform and near-real-time elaboration.

In the next chapter, we will see how to persist/de-persist data at high speed with modern ADO.NET techniques such as Entity Framework O/RM.

7
Database Querying

Accessing a database for persisted data retrieval is usually a time-consuming operation. Within the .NET framework, **ADO.NET** is the sub-framework responsible for database access. In 2008, Microsoft introduced **Entity Framework (EF)** as a multiplatform object relational-mapping (O/RM) database access subsystem within ADO.NET itself.

Although classical ADO.NET (low level) database access techniques have been superseded by EF's features, some specific usage is still a prerogative of such legacy programming classes.

In this chapter, we will take a tour of EF's querying capabilities, trying all available techniques to emphasize the performance results of each one. We will cover the following topics in this chapter:

- Overview of ADO.NET
- Overview of Entity Framework
- Entity Framework querying optimization
- Entity Framework persistence optimization
- Performance comparison
- ADO.NET specific features

Introduction

The **ActiveX Data Objects (ADO)** .NET is the main data provider for database access for any CLR-based application. ADO.NET was designed to supercede the old ADO. ADO used to be another framework for database access and manipulation. It works as a middleware, similar to a control or component, able to make available underlying database features as simplified features. It uses ActiveX technology (which is the heir to COM and OLE) to encapsulate its features as reusable cross-language features. This is why ADO was able to work in applications made with Visual Basic 6 or C++. ADO.NET, instead, is available only to CLR-based applications. As the ADO could, ADO.NET can also interact with any database using a specific data provider or cross provider, such as OLEDB or ODBC.

ADO.NET is completely extensible with a full interface-based architecture, relying on the abstract factory pattern. This makes the framework usable in situations other than in a classical tightly-coupled scenario with path to the specific database, as well as in an agnostic way without having to know exactly which data provider is actually running.

Made for ADO.NET, Entity Framework is the main O/RM created by Microsoft to interact with any database in an object-oriented way. The usage of EF relies on the data provider's ability to translate C# queries in specific SQL-dialect, such as TSQL or others. Thus, the underlying ADO.NET data provider must be compliant with EF. At this time, almost all database engines have a specific EF-compliant data provider, each one optimized for its database language.

Within ADO.NET, we have the ability to use all specific database features, even if they are not standardized across all database producers. On the contrary, Entity Framework uses only standardized features to give you the ability to change the data provider at any time.

Overview of ADO.NET

ADO.NET components access the database in two ways: in a *connected* way and in a *disconnected* way. In the connected access method, we deal with synchronous communication with a database instance, sending any instances of **data definition language (DDL)** or **data manipulation language (DML)**. In the disconnected access method, we store a pseudo-copy of data and schema of any table locally, with the ability to save changes (if any) asynchronously.

In the end, any time we deal with ADO.NET, as with low level classes, or with high level OR/M classes, we always produce some SQL statement. This statement may be the result of an OR/M data provider that translate object-oriented code in SQL code or may be the result of our direct text entry like when we write the SQL by ourselves or like when we simply invoke a stored procedure (an SQL statement stored on the database itself). Eventual parameters may be used to parameterize the SQL execution. Never concatenate strings to produce an SQL statement because of poor performance execution of the string-format-like value formatting, heavily increased attack surface for SQL-injection exploits, and bad testability.

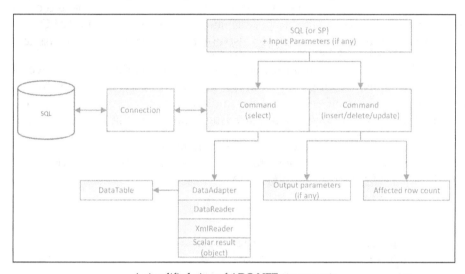

A simplified view of ADO.NET components

The simplest database access is when we make a simple SELECT statement against our persistence storage and try to read its result, later. If the result is in a tabular form, we must use a DataReader object, which is an enumerator-like class that uses a client-side cursor to stream data rows, giving us the ability to read columns data as we wish, by column index or name. As a simplified option, we can read the first row's first column data of any SELECT with a direct request, without having to stream the result-set with a cursor. Here is an example:

```
//a connection with specific connection-string
using (var cn = new SqlConnection("data source=(local);initial
catalog=TestDB;integrated security=true;"))
//a command with custom SQL statement
using (var cm = new SqlCommand("SELECT [Number],[Date] from
[Invoice]", cn))
{
    //open the connection
    cn.Open();
```

```
    //execute the command statement and catch the result-set into
a data reader
    using (var dr = cm.ExecuteReader())
        //read until cursor signal new rows availability
        while (dr.Read())
            //reads columns data
            Console.WriteLine("Number:{0}\tDate:{1:d}", dr[0],
dr["Date"]);
    }
```

Because of the extremely high customizability of the ADO.NET connected classes architecture, it could easily run into performance issues. A poor-quality SQL statement made by the developer could also create another performance issue.

If the using keyword is not used properly, the preceding code can open several database connections, wasting client and server resources and limiting future usage of the database server itself because of the limited number of connections available. This is another example showing a scalar request made against the database:

```
//a connection with specific connection-string
using (var cn = new SqlConnection("data source=(local);initial
catalog=TestDB;integrated security=true;"))
//a command with custom SQL statement
using (var cm = new SqlCommand("SELECT @a+@b+@c", cn))
{
    //add parameters value to the command
    //the usage of the "@" is not mandatory
    cm.Parameters.AddWithValue("a", 10);
    cm.Parameters.AddWithValue("b", 10);
    cm.Parameters.AddWithValue("@c", 10);

    //open the connection always at the last time
    cn.Open();
    var result = (int)cm.ExecuteScalar();
}
```

In this case, a direct binary value flows to the client from the database. The usage of an input parameter is actually straightforward.

Another specific feature of the Command class is the ability to return an XML value made in the database. Even if such a feature has bad performance for both XML encoding and decoding, sometimes it is useful. Moreover, if applied together with XML serialization from .NET, this could make a (very) basic O/RM tool. Here is an example:

```csharp
//an XML serializer/deserializer for Invoice class
var serializer = new XmlSerializer(typeof(Invoice));

using (var cn = new SqlConnection("data source=(local);initial
catalog=TestDB;integrated security=true;"))
//a command with XML result
using (var cm = new SqlCommand("SELECT [Number], [Date] from [Invoice]
FOR XML AUTO", cn))
{
    cn.Open();

    //instead of returning a binary result-set this returns an
XmlReader
    using (var reader = cm.ExecuteXmlReader())
        //read until an Invoice is available
        while (!reader.EOF && reader.ReadToFollowing("Invoice"))
        {
            //the single row as xml string
            string xml = reader.ReadOuterXml();
            //another reader to read the single row
            using (var subReader = reader.ReadSubtree())
            {
                //the deserializer can parse the xml row and retrieve
needed values as defined by the decorator pattern (attributes) against
the Invoice class
                var invoice = serializer.Deserialize(subReader);
            }
        }
}
```

The following example shows the Invoice class decorated to supply XmlSerializer
needs:

```csharp
[XmlRoot("Invoice")]
public class Invoice
{
    [XmlAttribute]
    public string Number { get; set; }

    [XmlAttribute]
    public DateTime Date { get; set; }
}
```

When executing such an example in **SQL Management Studio**, the rows are
returned as an XML instance, shown as follows:

```
<Invoice Number="001/2015/GR" Date="2015-01-01T00:00:00" />
```

Any other operation that does not need data retrieval will return the affected row
count, as shown in the following example:

```
using (var cn = new SqlConnection("data source=(local);initial
catalog=TestDB;integrated security=true;"))
//a command with a insert-select using parameters
using (var cm = new SqlCommand("INSERT INTO [Invoice](CustomerCustomer
ID,Number,Date) SELECT @customerid,
@number, @date", cn))
{
    //parameter definition and population
    cm.Parameters.AddWithValue("customerid", 1);
    cm.Parameters.AddWithValue("number", "2015/test/test");
    cm.Parameters.AddWithValue("date", DateTime.Now.Date);

    //open the connection
    cn.Open();

    //checks for the right insert result
    if (cm.ExecuteNonQuery() != 1)
        throw new ArgumentException("No insert made within
database server. Check values");
}
```

The other way of dealing with ADO.NET classes is by accessing the database
in disconnected mode, in which we bring the data and schema locally in our
application state, without having to maintain a connection open to the database
server. The following code shows an example:

```
//a temporary datatable to contains
//read data and schema
using (var dt = new DataTable())
{
    //a connection with specific connection-string
    using (var cn = new SqlConnection("data source=(local);initial
catalog=TestDB;integrated security=true;"))
    //a command with custom SQL statement
    using (var cm = new SqlCommand("SELECT [Number], [Date] from
[Invoice]", cn))
    //a data adapter to fill a datatable and
    //handle eventual change tracking
```

```
using (var da = new SqlDataAdapter(cm))
    //the connection this time is handled by the adapter
    da.Fill(dt);

//thanks to the using keyword
//at this row anything related
//to the database connection and
//command execution is being
//disposed

//do some work on disconnected data
//the DataRow usage is similar to a DataReader
foreach (DataRow dr in dt.Rows)
    Console.WriteLine("Number:{0}\tDate:{1:d}", dr[0],
dr["Date"]);
}
```

Although such usage is actually substituted by O/RM data access techniques, the ability to execute SQL code without the need to know the shape of returned data during design is still a killer feature of such legacy (2001) data-access framework. An example is reading a pivot table from a database *view* or a *stored procedure*.

An overview of Entity Framework

First released in 2008, EF has improved heavily during the four major releases deployed over the last 5 years. At the time of writing, the stable release is the Version 6.x and has the ability to connect to any relational database with three main connection architectures: **database-first**, **model-first**, and **code-first**. The first two are similar, except for the need to connect to an already-existing database or creating one with EF itself. Code-first, instead, is a completely new approach to access and maintain a database structure during application's lifetime. This relies on classes and a lot of **decorator pattern** (attributes) to specify physical names, constraints, and types. This design, together with the classical validation and UI-formatting oriented decorations from the **DataAnnotation** namespace, definitely makes it an easy-to-write persistence layer class that can flow up to the UI (MVC has great advantages due to approach) to create simple data-driven applications.

Oddly, when using super decoupled architectures such as **domain-driven design (DDD)**, it offers great advantages when all application layers (database itself) are developed in the same way and coded in the same language (without any SQL).

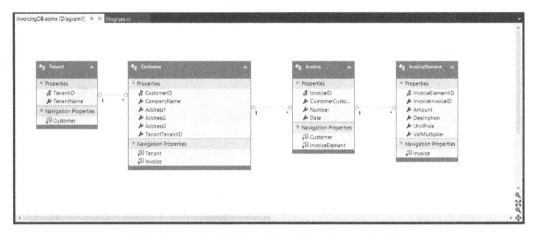

EF in diagram view of a (very) simple invoicing application

When using an O/RM, making a SELECT query in a database means using items from the collection that represent the table. It is quite impossible to make a one-to-one comparative between classical ADO.NET and EF because of the completely different approach in database iteration. What definitely is important to understand is that until materialized, anything is still a query when dealing with an O/RM; otherwise, a large number of performance issues may arise.

The materialization happens when we actually iterate with an enumerator by using the for-each statement, or when we flow the result in a finite collection, such as an Array or List<T> by using the LINQ extensions methods such as ToArray, ToList, ToDictionary, or anything similar. Here's an example:

```
using (var context = new InvoicingDBContainer())
{
    var query = context.Invoice;
    Console.WriteLine("query: {0}", query.ToString());

    var data = context.Invoice.ToArray();
    Console.WriteLine("data: {0}", data.ToString());
}
```

Luckily and easily, if we invoke the .ToString() method on a query, we would have the real SQL output as proof of being a simple query (similar to a command in classical ADO.NET object hierarchy). On the other hand, if we invoke the same method on the materialized data stored in an array, we obviously take the class name of the array itself. Here is an example:

```
query: SELECT
    [Extent1].[InvoiceID] AS [InvoiceID],
    [Extent1].[CustomerCustomerID] AS [CustomerCustomerID],
    [Extent1].[Number] AS [Number],
    [Extent1].[Date] AS [Date]
    FROM [dbo].[Invoice] AS [Extent1]
data: EntityFrameworkWorkbanch.Data.Invoice[]
```

In Entity Framework, the context is definitely not a simple data proxy or container. It never caches data or contains data. Its main job is to implement the **Unit of Work** pattern. The goal of this pattern is tracking changes to any entity (data item) within the context so that it is capable of persisting changes that have occurred in entities autonomously. The following is an example of a Unit of Work pattern:

```
//the unit of work context
using (var context = new InvoicingDBContainer())
{
    //an invoice
    var invoice = context.Invoice.FirstOrDefault();
    //editing the Date property
    invoice.Date = invoice.Date.AddDays(-1);
    //ask the context for persist detected changes
    context.SaveChanges();
}

//the unit of work context
using (var context = new InvoicingDBContainer())
{
    //add a new invoice
    context.Invoice.Add(new Data.Invoice
        {
            Date = DateTime.Now.Date,
            Number = "NUMBER",
            CustomerCustomerID = 1,
        });
    //ask the context for persist detected changes
    context.SaveChanges();
}

//the unit of work context
using (var context = new InvoicingDBContainer())
{
    //an invoice
    var invoice = context.Invoice.FirstOrDefault();
```

```
    //register for removal
    context.Invoice.Remove(invoice);
    //ask the context for persist detected changes
    context.SaveChanges();
}
```

The bigger difference when using those two frameworks is that when we use connected ADO.NET, we deal with a remote server speaking SQL language, while when we use EF, we work on objects that map data. This means that if we need to edit any data, we have to deal with the local object states, not with the remote server itself.

Advanced querying

The best of EF is seen when querying data. Although the comfort of editing data with objects definitely offers some great advantages in terms of data quality and issue prevention, data querying with EF and LINQ raises the level of quality and the maximum level of complexity of such queries, without actually increasing the complexity in code. This is because of the great power of querying with LINQ.

A big advantage when working with objects is the ability to produce a dynamic object-oriented query with all related benefits, such as type safe values, constraint validation, and so on.

```
using (var context = new InvoicingDBContainer())
{
    //a simple user filter
    string filter = null;

    //base query
    var query = context.Invoice
        .Where(x => x.Date >= new DateTime(2015, 1, 1))
        .Where(x => string.IsNullOrEmpty(filter) || x.Number.
Contains(filter));

    if (true)//some dynamic logic
        query = query.OrderBy(x => x.Date);
    else
        query = query.OrderByDescending(x => x.Date);

    //query materialization
    var data = query.ToArray();
}
```

The same example executed in connected ADO.NET would need concatenated SQL strings with obvious increased attack surface for SQL injection and a general reduction in design quality of the whole code.

Another great advantage when using **LINQ to Entities** (LINQ when applied to an EF data provider) as a querying language is the ability to easily make a nested query with full support from IntelliSense, and the auto-completion of Visual Studio with the full list of querying features of LINQ, such as aggregations, computations, interactions, filters, and so on. Here's an example on advanced querying:

```
using (var context = new InvoicingDBContainer())
{
    string filter = null;

    var query = context.Invoice
        //an hard-coded filter
        .Where(x => x.Date >= new DateTime(2015, 1, 1))
        //a dynamic filter from user
        .Where(x => string.IsNullOrEmpty(filter) || x.Number.
Contains(filter))
        //it is time to shape data with needed aggregations
        .Select(x => new //new anonymous type
        {
            CustomerID = x.CustomerCustomerID,
            x.Number,
            x.Date,
            //InvoiceElement is the navigation property to
            //the InvoiceElement table containing invoice elements
            //the navigation makes associated table data available
like if we had done a JOIN on the child table
            ElementCount = x.InvoiceElement.Count(),
            BaseAmount = x.InvoiceElement.Sum(e => e.Amount *
e.UnitPrice),
            VATAmount = x.InvoiceElement.Sum(e => e.Amount *
e.UnitPrice * (e.VatMultiplier - 1d)),
            //instead of writing here the TotalAmount duplicating
calculations we will write it in next step
        })
        .Select(x => new
        {
            x.CustomerID,
            x.Number,
            x.Date,
            x.ElementCount,
            x.BaseAmount,
```

```
            x.VATAmount,
            TotalAmount = x.BaseAmount + x.VATAmount,
        })
        .OrderBy(x => x.Date)
        .ThenBy(x => x.Number);

    var data = query.ToArray();
}
```

This ability to create new objects within any query is called query shaping. By using anonymous types, we can create as many query levels as we need to achieve our result with object querying. Never use old interaction logic (`for`/`for-each` on locally materialized objects) with EF because it has no pros; it only seems too familiar to someone who is used to LINQ to entities queries.

Entity Framework querying optimization

First, when trying to understand EF performance, we need to know what stages EF operates on in order to actually query the database server with our object query. We always must keep in mind that EF is an object model mapped to a physical model that is produced from database's metadata. When we make a query, it is made across the entity objects that are mapped to the known physical layer within the EF itself. This mapping later produces the right SQL, which is sent to the database server. This means that if a change is made against the database metadata, the known metadata in EF may become invalid and produce runtime errors.

Talking about performance, we must dive deep into SQL materialization. This knowledge of the stage list made by EF becomes critical.

Querying execution lifecycle

The first step when we make a query from scratch with EF involves *metadata loading*. This step reflects all entity class metadata and related mapping to the physical layer. When made, the result is cached in all application domains. This step definitely incurs high cost. Luckily, it takes place only once in an application's lifetime, but only in the case when we deal with multiple application domains.

The second step that occurs any time we perform any kind of database access (query or edit) is the connection opening (later closed immediately when the result is materialized). Although this does not cost so much because of CLR connection pooling, it adds some minor latency times to the first database connection, when the first connection is added to the pool.

Once the connection is available, Entity Framework needs compiling an in-memory query, representing the SQL query in object-oriented way. This in-memory query, called **query view**. For performance purposes, this query view is cached by Entity Framework itself per each AppDomain. This means that subsequent executions of the same query, will not produce a new query view, simply the previous query view is used and the related SQL statement is sent to the database server.

Now it is time for EF to create the proper SQL statements (related to the specific database dialect) by analyzing the expression tree of all LINQ expressions used for the object query. This adds some execution time, and is still cached for a single query.

The following steps are less incisive in terms of performance. These are SQL execution on database (out of our performance concern scope) entity type load by reading the metadata from step one, metadata validation, change-tracking activation (it's possible to disable this step if not needed), and finally, object materialization. The last step may increase execution time if multiple objects are materialized together.

Without any caching, EF would definitely perform 10 times worse or more than connected ADO.NET would in the data retrieval scenario, in which the query view compilation would always take quite some more time than the database SELECT execution itself.

Although the connection pooling reduce connection open/close times by caching such connections, any time we reuse a connection from the pool, some handshake happens (at least the authentication). When we deal with Internet accessed SQL Servers, like SQL Azure, a frequent connection pooling can produce a significant delay if we insert (for instance) hundreds of items with a new connection opening handshake per item. In this case, a connection retention like storing a single connection in a static variable, will avoid pooling overhead.

> More detail on ER performance consideration can be found at https://msdn.microsoft.com/en-us/library/cc853327.aspx.

Querying approaches

Entity Framework gives us the ability to query with different designs. By default, the approach of EF is to execute in the main query what we actually write in the query. Because of the object-oriented approach of EF entities, later, we can later access its properties, such as the navigation properties, to associate entities without having to put such navigation imperatively in the main query. The execution is available until the context is available. This also means that another statement is sent to the database server and another connection open/close happens per main item iterated, producing many database round trips. This default approach, named **lazy loading**, can also be disabled in the design view of EF itself. In such a case, if we want to access a navigation property with disabled lazy loading, we will need to manually load it or else we will simply get a null value.

Another querying approach is by preloading all the required navigation properties using an approach called **eager loading**. By executing an EF query in eager loading against a master-detail relationship, the result in terms of database querying is a SELECT statement producing a Cartesian product of all tables involved in the executed queries. This may produce a huge result set within the database server. Once such a set comes to EF, it creates a sort of in-memory data grouping to give objects the right hierarchical shape. With eager loading, no multiple round trips happen, but the big dataset may easily result in great network usage and client (EF side) materialization costs.

The eager and the lazy loading approach gives us the ability to use interesting OOP designs. For example, we could add computational properties or methods to any entity centralizing such logic. This becomes very useful for data-driven applications. Here's an example:

```
partial class InvoiceElement
{
    public double BaseAmount { get { return Amount * UnitPrice; }
}
    public double TotalAmount { get { return Amount * UnitPrice *
VatMultiplier; } }
}

partial class Invoice
{
    public double BaseAmount { get { return InvoiceElement.Sum(x
=> x.BaseAmount); } }
    public double TotalAmount { get { return InvoiceElement.Sum(x
=> x.TotalAmount); } }
}
```

This means that anytime we will need to know the total invoice amount, it will simply be available as a computed property. However, this also means that we always have to take in memory all invoice elements, even if we simply need a total amount.

The last available approach uses query shaping. Instead of executing a query on standard inferred entities from a physical database, we use EF to materialize only the required data, as happens when dealing with a View on a database server. Here is an example:

```
//the AsNoTracking disable change tracking
//this avoid wasting some time and resources
using (var db = new Data.InvoicingDBContainer())
{

    //the lazy execution - the default one
    var lazy_query = db.Invoice.AsNoTracking();

    //the eager execution
    //this will pre-execute in a super-join all requested
navigation properties
    var eager_query = db.Invoice.AsNoTracking()
        .Include("Customer")
        .Include("InvoiceElement");

    //a new query with a new shape
    //this give us the ability to get
    //from the database server only what we need
    //without wasting network resources and
    //moving computation across the remote server
    var shaped_query = from i in db.Invoice.AsNoTracking()
                       select new
                       {
                           i.Number,
                           i.Date,
                           CustomerName = i.Customer.CompanyName,
                           BaseAmount = i.InvoiceElement.Sum(x =>
x.Amount * x.UnitPrice),
                           TotalAmount = i.InvoiceElement.Sum(x
=> x.Amount * x.UnitPrice * x.VatMultiplier),
                       };

    Console.WriteLine("Simple (lazy) query");
    TraceTime(() =>
    {
        //enumerate the result to execute the query
```

```
        foreach (var item in lazy_query)
        {
            var date = item.Date;
            var total = item.TotalAmount;

            //accessing navigation property in lazy way
            //will trigger context to load the related
            //navigation property for each entity in resultset
            var companyname = item.Customer.CompanyName;
        }
    });

    Console.WriteLine("Simple (eager) query");
    TraceTime(() =>
    {
        //enumerate the result to execute the query
        foreach (var item in eager_query)
        {
            var date = item.Date;
            var total = item.TotalAmount;

            //with eager loading no multiple round-trips are made
            //but at beginning a bigger result-set is loaded
            var companyname = item.Customer.CompanyName;
        }
    });

    Console.WriteLine("Shaped query");
    TraceTime(() =>
    {
        //enumerate the result to execute the query
        foreach (var item in shaped_query)
        {
            //all needed data is already within
            //query materialization
        }
    });
}
```

Performance thoughts

Analyzing performance concerns of the three approaches is not so easy. The first thing to learn is that each approach may perform well in different scenarios.

The following table shows the pros and cons of lazy loading, eager loading, and shaped query:

Approach	Pros	Cons
Lazy loading	• All local properties always available and ready to be edited • Full OOP programming against navigation and local properties • Local-side execution of logic once data is materialized	• Navigation available only until the context is available • Wastes many resources when a property is not needed, as lazy loading always makes a sort using `SELECT *` on the base entity • Lots of round trips to the DB for each entity navigation property during first usage
Eager loading	• All local properties always available and ready to be edited • Full OOP programming against navigations and local properties • Local-side execution of logic once data is materialized • No round trips to DB	• Lot of resources are wasted anytime a property is not needed because makes always a sort of `SELECT *` on base entity • High execution cost for network and object materialization
Shaped query	• Server-side execution of logics within the query • No round trips to DB • Minimal resource usage on network and EF side • Only needed data is materialized	• Unable to centralize logics within objects because of the data-driven approach • Read-only objects

Oddly, lazy loading always loads all entity data to reduce eventual round trips to the database by applying a **Data Transfer Object (DTO)** pattern with the database server, while navigation properties use the **Lazy Load** pattern, which is exactly the opposite of DTO.

The execution of the following example will give us interesting evidence of how EF performs different query approaches:

```
First execution
Simple (lazy) query
-> in 1,717 ms
Simple (eager) query
-> in 189 ms
Shaped query
-> in 181 ms

Second execution
Simple (lazy) query
-> in 1,153 ms
Simple (eager) query
-> in 97 ms
Shaped query
-> in 10 ms
```

The example executed on my laptop includes fake data of 100 invoices, each with 84 elements. Absolute values are definitely useless, while relative data analysis gives us several interesting features. First, we need to observe how EF metadata and query view generation add sensible time cost to each querying approach.

In terms of real execution time — visible from the second execution and later — by using lazy loading, the request of all invoice elements per invoice adds huge round-trip times to the whole querying mechanism. This elaboration time is more than 10 times than that of eager loading and more than 20 times that of shaped loading.

Compared to lazy loading, the eager loading approach performs better when considering latency time of a single round trip. However, upon analyzing the produced database query in SQL Server Profiler, we can see the concrete SQL statement produced. A huge and resource-wasting statement! Here is an example:

```
SELECT
    [Project1].[InvoiceID] AS [InvoiceID],
    [Project1].[CustomerCustomerID] AS [CustomerCustomerID],
    [Project1].[Number] AS [Number],
    [Project1].[Date] AS [Date],
    [Project1].[CustomerID] AS [CustomerID],
```

```
    [Project1].[CompanyName] AS [CompanyName],
    [Project1].[Address1] AS [Address1],
    [Project1].[Address2] AS [Address2],
    [Project1].[Address3] AS [Address3],
    [Project1].[TenantTenantID] AS [TenantTenantID],
    [Project1].[C1] AS [C1],
    [Project1].[InvoiceElementID] AS [InvoiceElementID],
    [Project1].[InvoiceInvoiceID] AS [InvoiceInvoiceID],
    [Project1].[Amount] AS [Amount],
    [Project1].[Description] AS [Description],
    [Project1].[UnitPrice] AS [UnitPrice],
    [Project1].[VatMultiplier] AS [VatMultiplier]
    FROM ( SELECT
        [Extent1].[InvoiceID] AS [InvoiceID],
        [Extent1].[CustomerCustomerID] AS [CustomerCustomerID],
        [Extent1].[Number] AS [Number],
        [Extent1].[Date] AS [Date],
        [Extent2].[CustomerID] AS [CustomerID],
        [Extent2].[CompanyName] AS [CompanyName],
        [Extent2].[Address1] AS [Address1],
        [Extent2].[Address2] AS [Address2],
        [Extent2].[Address3] AS [Address3],
        [Extent2].[TenantTenantID] AS [TenantTenantID],
        [Extent3].[InvoiceElementID] AS [InvoiceElementID],
        [Extent3].[InvoiceInvoiceID] AS [InvoiceInvoiceID],
        [Extent3].[Amount] AS [Amount],
        [Extent3].[Description] AS [Description],
        [Extent3].[UnitPrice] AS [UnitPrice],
        [Extent3].[VatMultiplier] AS [VatMultiplier],
        CASE WHEN ([Extent3].[InvoiceElementID] IS NULL) THEN
CAST(NULL AS int) ELSE 1 END AS [C1]
        FROM    [dbo].[Invoice] AS [Extent1]
        INNER JOIN [dbo].[Customer] AS [Extent2] ON
[Extent1].[CustomerCustomerID] = [Extent2].[CustomerID]
        LEFT OUTER JOIN [dbo].[InvoiceElement] AS [Extent3] ON
[Extent1].[InvoiceID] = [Extent3].[InvoiceInvoiceID]
    )  AS [Project1]
    ORDER BY [Project1].[InvoiceID] ASC, [Project1].[CustomerID] ASC,
[Project1].[C1] ASC
```

This statement produces a result-set of 8,400 rows. However, an execution time of 97 milliseconds is good for a set this size. Let's consider that the query is executed on a local database. If the same query were executed across a network, it would lead to a lot of wastage of network resources, as well as a higher execution time. Hence, it is important to use eager loading carefully.

Obviously, the shaped query performed the best with respect to latency times and overall resource usage. Take into consideration that although there are advantages, it is lacking in terms of scalability. In a system design where we have a single database system and multiple application servers—because of the database-side execution of computations—once the relational database ends its computational resources, it will be impossible to have better performance. It will be impossible improving performances although adding hundreds of application servers running our .NET application.

Regarding the quality of the SQL statement, a shaped query produce the most beautiful code. Here's an example:

```
SELECT
    [Project1].[InvoiceID] AS [InvoiceID],
    [Project1].[Number] AS [Number],
    [Project1].[Date] AS [Date],
    [Project1].[CompanyName] AS [CompanyName],
    [Project1].[C1] AS [C1],
    (SELECT
        SUM([Filter2].[A1]) AS [A1]
        FROM ( SELECT
            [Extent4].[Amount] * [Extent4].[UnitPrice] *
[Extent4].[VatMultiplier] AS [A1]
            FROM [dbo].[InvoiceElement] AS [Extent4]
            WHERE [Project1].[InvoiceID] =
[Extent4].[InvoiceInvoiceID]
        ) AS [Filter2]) AS [C2]
    FROM ( SELECT
        [Extent1].[InvoiceID] AS [InvoiceID],
        [Extent1].[Number] AS [Number],
        [Extent1].[Date] AS [Date],
        [Extent2].[CompanyName] AS [CompanyName],
        (SELECT
            SUM([Filter1].[A1]) AS [A1]
            FROM ( SELECT
                [Extent3].[Amount] * [Extent3].[UnitPrice] AS [A1]
                FROM [dbo].[InvoiceElement] AS [Extent3]
                WHERE [Extent1].[InvoiceID] =
[Extent3].[InvoiceInvoiceID]
            ) AS [Filter1]) AS [C1]
        FROM [dbo].[Invoice] AS [Extent1]
        INNER JOIN [dbo].[Customer] AS [Extent2] ON
[Extent1].[CustomerCustomerID] = [Extent2].[CustomerID]
    ) AS [Project1]
```

Entity Framework persistence optimization

When dealing with DML statements, EF shows some limitations due to its object orientation. An example on all comes with a DELETE statement made in EF. This example shows how to make a master-detail delete operation:

```
int InvoiceID = 11;

using (var db = new InvoicingDBContainer())
{
    //materialize an invoice
    //this will produce a SELECT statement
    var invoice = db.Invoice
        .Include("InvoiceElement") //eager-load elements for
deletion
        .FirstOrDefault(x => x.InvoiceID == InvoiceID);

    //manually load elements for deletion
    //no lazy-load works for cascade delete objects
    //db.Entry(invoice).Collection("InvoiceElement").Load();

    //informs EF context to remove invoice from database
    db.Invoice.Remove(invoice);

    //asks EF context to persist changed entities
    //this will produce the DELETE statement
    db.SaveChanges();
}
```

Obviously, the whole selection of the Invoice and of all InvoiceElement instances (both for eager or lazy loading approaches is the same) is mandatory before asking the context to delete them, marking them as removed. This leads to a big resource wastage and heavily increases the execution time of any DELETE statement.

Please note that without specifying the cascade-delete operation on the Invoice and the InvoiceElement relation in EF designer, we will have to iterate all invoice elements of the correct navigation property from the invoice variable.

 Notice that lazy loading in cascade-delete does not work at all.

Do not think that EF has poor `DELETE` operation performances. Also, note that for the case of manipulating data by hand, any application will need data retrieval before knowing what item to delete. So, the entity instances required to be deleted are, for the most times, already available to your application.

Specifically for data deletion, a simple workaround comes to the rescue:

```
var ElementID = 9;

using (var db = new InvoicingDBContainer())
{
    //create a disconnected instance with needed key
    var element = new InvoiceElement
        {
            //manually set the primary-key value
            InvoiceElementID = ElementID,
        };

    //asks the context for attaching the disconnected instance
    db.InvoiceElement.Attach(element);

    //mark element with removed status within context change tracker
    db.InvoiceElement.Remove(element);

    //asks EF context to persist changed entities
    //this will produce the DELETE statement
    db.SaveChanges();
}
```

It is also possible to make deletions in master-detail scenarios, but the reduced strength of the whole design should convince you to avoid this choice. The same behavior occurs when dealing with the `UPDATE` statement:

```
var InvoiceID = 15;

using (var db = new InvoicingDBContainer())
{
    //materialize an invoice
    //this will produce a SELECT statement
    var invoice = db.Invoice
        .FirstOrDefault(x => x.InvoiceID == InvoiceID);

    //a simple edit
    invoice.Number = "updated nr";
```

```
        //asks EF context to persiste changed entities
        //this will produce the UPDATE statement
        db.SaveChanges();
    }

    using (var db = new InvoicingDBContainer())
    {
        //a fake invoice for updating data
        var invoice = new Invoice
        {
            InvoiceID = InvoiceID,
        };

        //attach the fake invoice to the context
        //this will start the change tracking of  such entity
        db.Invoice.Attach(invoice);

        //a simple edit
        invoice.Number = "updated again";

        //asks EF context to persiste changed entities
        //this will produce the UPDATE statement
        db.SaveChanges();
    }
```

In the first example, EF will make a SELECT operation and later an UPDATE operation, setting the only edited column to the new value. In the second example, the workaround shows how to have the same result without having to make a SELECT operation. Obviously, as was said before, sometimes such SELECT operations will always be required because we need a valid ID.

This workaround works fine because the change tracker can produce the SQL statement of only the changed properties, leaving all the others intact on the database server.

About the INSERT operation: when dealing with EF, this adds no cost overhead, so no performance concerns exist more than with a legacy SQL statement that is manually written.

Performance comparison

Comparing two different frameworks for database interaction is actually difficult. An O/RM that provides increased simplicity in database querying/persisting and extreme team working improvements from the intrinsic object-oriented programming makes EF the best choice in several scenarios. This, along with the knowledge of performance bottlenecks that occurs in such a framework, will help in avoiding dangerous issues when in the production stage, when the application load increases more than expected.

The following is a comparison of all performance results of connected ADO.NET with SQLClient data provider and EF using the same data provider. Absolute values are always useless, while relative ones give us significant information about the performance results:

	SqlClient	EF	EF + Workaround
INSERT (1000 items)	215ms	1716ms (+ 698 %)	none
UPDATE (1000 items)	268ms	1672ms (+ 524 %)	914ms (+ 241 %)
DELETE	1ms	7ms (+ 600 %)	40ms (+ 3900 %)
SELECT	1ms	1ms	

- The INSERT test is executed by adding to an Entity Framework entity Set all items with a single SaveChanges invocation at the operation ending, by using a single always-opened SQL Connection.

- The UPDATE test is executed with a different connection or context for ADO or EF per item to update.

- The DELETE test executed against a single row deletion. Although EF made a SELECT query before a DELETE operation, the workaround with the disconnected item attachment adds significant execution time, making its usage valid only to avoid item materialization for complex (or big) entities.

- The SELECT test is executed with a top 1000 against the only invoice table.

As evident in the preceding table, EF actually performs fast in data reading along with the ability to produce complex queries with multiple execution scenarios. In contrast, when dealing with data manipulation, connected ADO.NET classes perform much better.

Stream-like querying

It is not about how much memory we have, it is about conserving it. If we have to execute a custom **ETL** (**Extract, Transform, Load**) workflow application or any other application that needs accessing, and usually persists the data, it doesn't mean that we have to keep all the data in the application state. A sliding approach becomes mandatory anytime we deal with huge datasets. However, when the dataset is not so huge, reducing resource usage without sacrificing any other performance aspect is important.

This design is available as with Entity Framework classes as with connected ADO. NET classes. By using EF we have the ability to manipulate data items in object-oriented way, and while using connected ADO.NET classes we don't. Here is an example of the stream-like data manipulation using the two frameworks (EF and ADO.NET):

```
//a source and target context
using (var sourceContext = new InvoicingDBContainer())
using (var targetContext = new InvoicingDBContainer())
    //iterate a query without a collection materialization
    foreach (var invoice in sourceContext.Invoice.Take(100000).
AsNoTracking())
        //a simple client-side logic
        if (invoice.Number.EndsWith("0"))
        {
            targetContext.Invoice.Add(new Invoice
                {
                    Date = invoice.Date.AddDays(4),
                    Number = string.Format("{0}/BIS",
invoice.Number),
                    CustomerCustomerID =
invoice.CustomerCustomerID,
                });
            targetContext.SaveChanges();
        }
```

The following is the same example with connected ADO.NET:

```
//a couple of connections for data copying
using (var sourceConnection = new SqlConnection("data
source=(local);initial catalog=TestDB;integrated security=true;"))
using (var targetConnection = new SqlConnection("data
source=(local);initial catalog=TestDB;integrated security=true;"))
{
    sourceConnection.Open();
```

```
        targetConnection.Open();

    //a source command and result-set
    using (var sourceCommand = new SqlCommand("SELECT TOP 100000 *
FROM Invoice", sourceConnection))
    using (var sourceReader = sourceCommand.ExecuteReader())
        while (sourceReader.Read())
        {
            //by scrolling a data reader we scroll a client cursor
            //this cursor works on a light row batch produced
            //by the data provider itself
            //we don't have all data materialized here

            var InvoiceID = (int)sourceReader["InvoiceID"];
            var CustomerCustomerID = (int)sourceReader["CustomerCusto
merID"];
            var Number = (string)sourceReader["Number"];
            var Date = (DateTime)sourceReader["Date"];

            //some sliding client-side logic
            if (Number.EndsWith("0"))
                //the target insert
                using (var targetCommand = new SqlCommand("INSERT
INTO [Invoice](CustomerCustomerID,Number,Date) SELECT @customerid,
@number, @date", targetConnection))
                {
                    targetCommand.Parameters.
AddWithValue("customerid", CustomerCustomerID);
                    targetCommand.Parameters.AddWithValue("number",
string.Format("{0}/BIS", Number));
                    targetCommand.Parameters.AddWithValue("date",
Date.AddDays(4));
                    targetCommand.ExecuteNonQuery();
                }
        }
}
```

ADO.NET bulk copy

In modern database access programming, the use of an object-oriented approach similar to the one available throughout EF is obvious. Although in most scenarios EF performs very well, there are specific cases when we want to use ADO.NET, for instance, when we want use some specific feature of the data provider or the database itself. Obviously, this choice is available at the cost of sacrificing the simplicity and reliability of dealing with an object-oriented data access layer. Although for custom database features we have to deal with the SQL language, often such features are available as data provider-specific features within ADO.NET classes.

Bulk copy is a great feature offered by the `System.Data.SqlClient` data provider. It allows the insertion of a lot of data within a database table without having to fulfill all `INSERT` validations or execution times. This boosts the throughput of the whole operation heavily. Here's an example of bulk copying:

```
//create a temporary data-table for new data
using (var dt = new DataTable())
{
    //the name of columns is not important
    //the type is useful
    //the right order is mandatory
    dt.Columns.Add("", typeof(int));
    dt.Columns.Add("", typeof(int));
    dt.Columns.Add("", typeof(string));
    dt.Columns.Add("", typeof(DateTime));

    for (int i = 0; i < 1000000; i++)
        dt.Rows.Add(new object[]
            {
                null, //primary key is identity on DB
                1, //the customer id
                string.Format("2015/001/{0}",i), //the number
                new DateTime(2015,1,1).AddDays(i), //the date
            });

    //the target connection
    using (var cn = new SqlConnection("data source=(local);initial
catalog=TestDB;integrated security=true;"))
    {
        //open the connection
        cn.Open();
```

```
        //the bulk copy engine
        var machine = new SqlBulkCopy(cn);
        //the batch size - if desired
        machine.BatchSize = 1000;
        //the destination table name
        machine.DestinationTableName = "Invoice";
        //start the bulk copy
        machine.WriteToServer(dt);
    }
}
```

Using the `Bulk Insert` feature is the best choice when we need to add a lot of data. This feature is often used in data import/export even by the database. For instance, SQL Server Integration Services makes extensive use of the Bulk Insert feature for its ETL workflows.

 More information about Bulk Insert can be found at `https://msdn.microsoft.com/en-us/library/ms188365.aspx`.

Summary

In this chapter, we saw how to deal with ADO.NET features for data access and manipulation. Within ADO.NET, Entity Framework adds some extremely useful features in a purely object-oriented approach, giving us the ability to write complex and dynamic queries with the reliability and ease of object-oriented programming.

In the next chapter, we will see how to handle Big Data specific data items and performance concerns with core .NET classes.

8
Programming for Big Data

In the previous chapter, we covered database access programming with Entity Framework and ADO.NET. In this chapter, we will cover solutions for small **big data** applications, based on core .NET framework and Entity Framework.

Although big data applications can fulfill government and/or scientific needs, those solutions will need customization at every level; this is beyond the scope of this book. This chapter will focus on small big data application scenarios, such as **IoT** (**Internet of Things**) or long-ranged enterprise applications that have been collecting data for decades.

This chapter will cover the following topics:

- What is big data
- Architecting big data solutions
- Microsoft Azure for big data
- Simplified grid-computing
- Lookup programming

What is big data?

A big data application deals with large volumes of fast-growing data. This is the most widely accepted definition and the most basic one too. Although a unique academic definition for big data does not exist, a more detailed definition of a big data application states is inclusive of the following criteria:

- It handles huge *volumes* of data, to take care of its size on every usage such SQL SELECT queries or similar. As the word *Big* suggests, to deal with big data, the total data size must be huge. These days, any database that is less than 100 GB in size cannot be considered as a valid big data storage.

- It handles fast-growing data in the meaning of *velocity* of growth. Real big data architecture and solutions are applicable only to fast-growing data; otherwise, we are simply dealing with a huge dataset. Any ever-growing large data store can be handled easily by any application in a few hours or days, depending on the scale of the data. The important thing to note here is that eventually, we will always be able to finish the computation. It is the rapidly increasing data that forces developers to come up with and use specific techniques and technologies to handle such data properly. This is different from the methods used to process standard data because these techniques are unable to deal with data that is both large and rapidly growing.

- It handles a great variety of non-homogeneous data types. Because of the intrinsic data handled by any big data application, a data item can be of many different types. It frequently happens that same data types exist in multiple versions, incrementing the overall data type number.

Although more complex or specific definitions of big data actually exist, we will stick to the more canonical one. This choice is necessary because of the poor uniformity of the definition among scientists and IT organizations that deal with big data.

Now that we have an idea of what big data is, it's time to take a look at related technologies and techniques. In terms of data storage, a huge big data solution will rely on NoSQL databases because of their intrinsic high speed data read/write capability. This does not mean that relational databases are not fast enough for big data because often, they are also used in similar designs. However, when dealing with very large applications, any small improvement in speed can result in crucial improvements in the overall application performance.

In big data applications, most of the development effort focuses on data analysis. In terms of analysis computation, extreme parallelism is the key to success when dealing with big data applications. As seen in *Chapter 2, Architecting High-performance .NET Code*, the most parallelizable design is based on grid-computing techniques that are made across heavy distributed programming technologies. Ideally, the most powerful big data design in terms of throughput heavily uses grid and parallel programming, together with an asynchronous design regarding data analysis and persistence.

Because this book is not addressed to scientists from NASA or NSA, we will still use a relational RDBMS with examples showing you how to handle a table with a billion rows with SQL-based data sources.

For more information on big data and its definitions, please visit:

- `https://en.wikipedia.org/wiki/Big_data`
- `http://timoelliott.com/blog/2013/07/7-definitions-of-big-data-you-should-know-about.html`

Architecting big data solutions

When dealing with a huge dataset, non-functional requirements definitely become a primary concern. We cannot place our primary focus on a domain, leaving non-functional requirements as a secondary concern, because a single system that can fulfill a big data application's needs by itself simply does not exist.

When dealing with big data solutions, a lot of the work of a developer is predicting usage patterns and sizing the whole environment for correct short-term and long-term future usage. Never think of how to design and maintain the initial system size; always think of how to design and maintain it after a year or more of data throughput. The whole system must be able to grow not only in size but also in complexity; otherwise, the system will never fit the future needs of business and will soon become obsolete (because of the need for data type variety of previously seen tenets).

Let's make some usage predictions. For instance, let's consider a satellite antitheft-system that is always probing your position in the world. Such systems usually send data to the central data center from one to five times per hour, with a dataset of hundreds or more positions per instance.

A binary position packet is made up of a device ID, a UTC GPS fix, latitude, and longitude. This means 4 x 32-bit data fields for a sum of 16 bytes per position packet multiplied 120 times (2 positions per minute), which results in 1920 bytes per hour. Now, think of it as a car that runs for an average of 5 hours per day plus a lot of parking time, with obvious data-sending optimizations. This produces a size of 600 *in-moving* packets per day with a size of 9600 bytes per day in the network. Anyone could think it is easy to manage such network usage for any kind of Internet bandwidth. Of course, if you multiply such usage for 1000 cars (or more in the real world), this becomes 600,000 new packets per day in our database, with a constant network usage in the *in-moving* time of 9.15 MB/s.

Continuing our usage prevision, things start becoming a little harder to manage with a database of 219 million rows (600k x 365 days) per year, which means 3.26 GB (219 m x 16 bytes) of increased size per year (plus indexes). Keep in mind that that this preview is related to a small client market share of only 1000 cars, while in the real world, any car rental company that has thousands of cars must manage a database greater than the one that we have just predicted.

The first thing to keep in mind when designing fast-growing solutions is that the datatype choice is crucial for the life of the whole system. Using 32 bits instead of 16 bits in a single data-packet field means increasing the network usage for nothing. The same thing happens if we increase the database column size. Another drawback of the database design is the increased size of all indexes or keys using the wrong-sized column, with obvious increase in the index seek/scan time. Also, keep in mind that in such large databases, altering the column size later (by years in a production environment) means hours or days of system downtime for maintenance.

Another critical aspect is breaking dependencies from different system modules and tiers. Never directly make a synchronous database `INSERT` from a Web Service operation. Always decouple by using a persisted queue, such as the one used in **Azure Service Bus**. This makes it easier to design the whole system and adds the benefit of increasing the system's reliability and scalability.

When trying to use a relational database, the key to success for big data systems is planning multiple instances of splitting data of different functional types, or (if possible) balancing content across multiple available tables of the same logical database across multiple physical servers.

Another important design to implement often in big data solutions is the **Reporting Database** pattern, as described by Martin Fowler, a british software engineer. Within such suggested designs, there are database instances for data-insert and others, which are asynchronously filled, for data querying. The added feature here is the ability to denormalize or reshape data specifically for querying in the ETL workflow used to move asynchronous data to the query databases. Obviously, the usage of read-only databases also adds the great advantage of easily balancing database usage on multiple servers.

 To learn more about the Reporting Database pattern, visit `http://martinfowler.com/bliki/ReportingDatabase.html`.

Case study – automotive big data system

It is easy to infer that cloud computing is the easiest way to handle big data solutions. Here, you have space to deploy all the different tiers of your application, persisted-queues to let tiers communicate with each other, huge space for databases, and easy access to the right number of virtual machines to be used in grid computing, if applicable to your needs.

Let's evaluate a practical satellite-based anti-theft system that is always connected, with advanced logistic management sized for 10,000 devices, and that can produce 6 million packets per day or more. We choose to release the solutions across the Microsoft Azure cloud provider. In the overall architecture design, we will consider using idioms and specific technology provider (Azure) oriented features to optimize all the performance aspects we can. Instead, exploiting maximum provider-specific solutions and technology is a primary requirement. Here, the main functional and non-functional requirements are as follows:

- Store a device packet positioned in a history table for three years:
  - Develop a low-level binary server to read device packets
  - Develop a data delete engine to purge data that is older than 3 years

- Asynchronously analyze and store device routes

- Always be aware of the last position of each device:
  - ○ Decouple last-position item storage from history to another table in order to avoid frequent SELECT operations on a huge table
  - ○ Notify system managers when a device goes out of the scope for more than 30 minutes on usual routes and more than 15 minutes on new routes
- Always be aware of device entering/exiting from any point of interest (POI)
- Show simplified device data for end users
- Show detailed device data for system managers

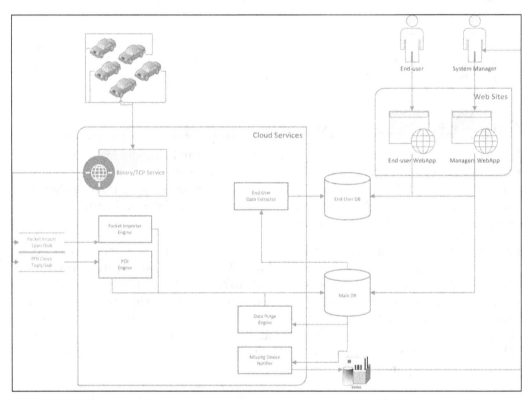

A decoupled big data solution, suited for Windows Azure

The preceding system architecture can handle thousands of incoming messages per second, flowing through the binary service released as **Worker Role** within the Microsoft Azure Cloud Services. The usage of the **Service Bus Topic** with two different subscriptions — one for the packet importer engine and one for POI engine — decouple the two different logic that handles different execution times. With this choice, the data-packet will flow into the history database as soon as possible, while the POI logic execution could even be executed a bit later. The primary concern for design here is to catch all messages. Instead, the primary concern regarding performance is the high scalability provided by the eventual scale-out of the VM count of the two engines, and obviously a high overall throughput in receiving device packets.

> An Azure Service Bus Topic is a special FIFO queue with a single entrance and multiple exits. Those exits are called subscriptions because their usage is the same as publish/subscribe scenarios, where multiple receivers expect the same message from a single message queue. The usage is exactly the same as having multiple FIFO message queues with the commodity of sharing some configuration, plus the obvious (and important) benefit of not having to deal with multiple messages sent to the sender side, as a single copy of the message flows into the Topic. It will multiply the message across all subscribers by itself.

Later, the data packet will flow within the business logic lying in the Packet Importer and POI engines. Those will then create proper persistence objects, which will then flow within the main database (or multiple physical ones). This ends the overall workflow of the packet input.

Asynchronously, the **Data Purge Engine** will evaluate and, if needed, will clean up old data from the main database. Still asynchronously, the **Missing Device Notifier** will evaluate its logic against the persisted data, and if needed, it will notify system managers if something interesting or wrong is happening. Because this logic may became heavy to compute against a huge dataset, multiple VM instances will eventually be required here.

The **End-User Data Extractor** will execute the reporting database logic to produce simplified data for the end user by simplifying data structure and reducing data size. This is because the end-user database must contain three years of data by requirement; instead, the main database (or multiple physical instances) could even contain more data. This is our choice according to local laws. This logic may also become CPU-intensive, so here, multiple VM instances could be required.

At the end of the system, two web applications exist for the two main types of users. We could even create a single web application with multiple authorization roles, but this choice would produce trickier business logic with less ability to optimize the two different business and data access logic. Remember that in big data, this optimization is a primary concern. The logic centralization, instead, becomes a secondary concern. By the way, also remember that a lot of logic and modules are still shareable between those two web applications and packaged in libraries with our preferred granularity.

Although web applications will not require high computational power, they will access lot of data frequently, so a well-designed cache strategy is mandatory.

Microsoft Azure offers different cache providers and solutions. We can use **AppFabric** cache within our cloud services in specific VMs, or together with Worker/Web Roles VMs to save some money (and performance). The same cache is available in a managed multitenant offer by Azure itself with preconfigured size slots. The same offering is also available with the **Redis** cache engine. My personal tests showed that the two caches are similar in all primitive-data-based scenarios. Redis became better when using its special features, such as caching data lists or flags; AppFabric, instead, became better while handling huge datasets because of the higher memory size limit due to its balanced design (Redis has only an active/passive failover).

Microsoft Azure for big data

Cloud computing is the principal technology provider for any big data solution from small to mid-sized applications, although it is also available for huge big data needs with different cloud features.

In the previous chapter, we saw some usage of Microsoft Azure. Let's see how to develop solutions using such technologies.

Within the Microsoft Azure offering, we will focus on the Service Bus sub-offering. Within this category, we can find technologies such as the **Relay** (a WCF router service for cross-premise communication), **Queue** and Topics (one-to-one or one-to-many messaging queues), ACS (a federated security service), Event Hub (a multistream-like event router similar to a queue), and a centralized and customizable Push Notification service.

Service Bus Topic

To use a Topic within Microsoft Azure, we must create a Service Bus and get an access key for the specific Topic. To create a Service Bus item within Microsoft Azure, following the wizard on the website will suffice. Once created, the connection information can be found through the button on the lower part of the page with the name **Connection Information**.

The Service Bus page of the Microsoft Azure web portal

In the information popup, we will find the full connection string:

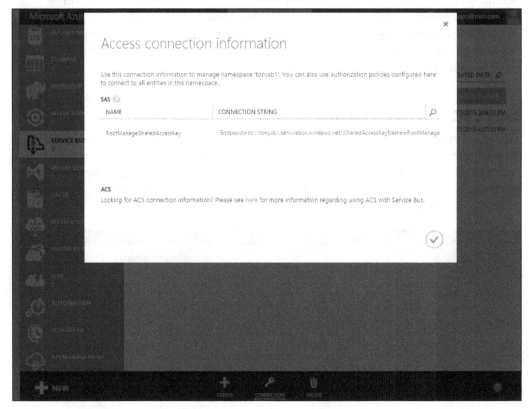

Connection information popup of a Service Bus account

Once we have the Service Bus name and the full connection string, we simply need to add a name to a Topic (always following the wizard). Here's an example of how to do this:

```
//topic connection string
static string connectionString = "[CONNECTIONSTRING]";

//the topic name
static string topicName = "[TOPICNAME]";

static void Main(string[] args)
{
    //a topic client
```

```
        var client = TopicClient.CreateFromConnectionString(connectionStri
ng, topicName);

        StartSubscription1Async();
        StartSubscription2Async();

        while (true)
        {
            Console.Clear();
            Console.WriteLine("Write a message");
            var message = Console.ReadLine();

            //send the message to the topic
            client.Send(new BrokeredMessage(message));

            Console.WriteLine("RETURN TO CONTINUE");
            Console.ReadLine();
        }
    }


    //a helper for handling all subscribers
    private static Task SubcribeToTopicAsync(string subscriptionName,
    Action<BrokeredMessage> messageHandler)
    {
        return Task.Factory.StartNew(() =>
        {
            //the subscription client
            var client = SubscriptionClient.CreateFromConnectionString(con
    nectionString, topicName, subscriptionName);

            //always dequeue messages...
            while (true)
            {
                //try dequeue message from subscription's inner queue
                var msg = client.Receive(TimeSpan.FromSeconds(3));
                if (msg != null)
                    //handle message with subscription specific logic
                    messageHandler(msg);

            }
        }, TaskCreationOptions.LongRunning);
    }


    private static void StartSubscription2Async()
```

```
{
    var subscription = "sub1";
    SubcribeToTopicAsync(subscription, msg =>
        {
            //read message body containing user message
            var body = msg.GetBody<string>();

            //some subscriber specific logic
            Thread.SpinWait(1000000);

            Console.WriteLine("{0} -> {1}",
SubscriptionClient.FormatSubscriptionPath(topicName,
subscription), body);

            //once completed, the message is flagged as completed
            //otherwise the message will flow again in the next
            //message subscriber available
            msg.Complete();
        });
}

private static void StartSubscription1Async()
{
    var subscription = "sub2";
    SubcribeToTopicAsync(subscription, msg =>
    {
        //read message body containing user message
        var body = msg.GetBody<string>();

        //some subscriber specific logic
        Thread.SpinWait(2000000);

        Console.WriteLine("{0} -> {1}", SubscriptionClient.FormatSubsc
riptionPath(topicName,
subscription), body);

        //once completed, the message is flagged as completed
        //otherwise the message will flow again in the next
        //message subscriber available
        msg.Complete();
    });
}
```

For more information on Bus Topic, please visit `http://azure.`
`microsoft.com/it-it/documentation/articles/service-`
`bus-dotnet-how-to-use-topics-subscriptions/`.

AppFabric Cache

The AppFabric cache is available for the Windows Server operating system. In Azure, the same caching engine is available within the cloud services offering or as a **Managed Cache Service**, where we can buy a portion of a cache in a pay-per-use way. The API is always the same.

```
//cache provider

    //will use the "default" configured cache
    //within the .config file
    var cache = new DataCache();

    var key = "time";

    while (true)
    {
        //retrieve cached value
        var value = (DateTime?)cache[key];

        //if not available, drill the cache with a new value
        if (value == null)
        {
            value = DateTime.Now;

            //adds the value to the cache with a TTL of 5 seconds
            cache.Add(key, value, TimeSpan.FromSeconds(5));
        }

        Console.WriteLine(" {0}", value);

        //slow down
        Thread.Sleep(1000);
    }
```

Using the AppFabric API is easy. A lot of configuration is available, but is not mandatory.

A great benefit in using such an API is the ability to put anything that is serializable within the cache. Another great benefit is the local cache feature that adds an in-memory cache within the running executable memory, for example, as the *MemoryCache* class does from the System.Runtime.Caching namespace.

When enabled, this local cache becomes a primary-level cache that reduces the usage of the cloud cache, which acts as a second-level cache. This dual caching reduces the network usage of the remote cache service, also reducing the latency considerably.

 To know more about creating cache for Azure Managed Cache Service, refer to https://msdn.microsoft.com/en-us/library/dn448831.aspx.

Redis Cache

Redis was born as an object-oriented NoSQL database. Later, because of the high throughput and reduced latency offered by the Redis database — because of its intrinsic architecture of being an in-memory database — Redis became a cache provider that is widely used across multiple programming languages and platforms.

Unlike the easiness of the AppFabric cache, Redis has a verbose API with the ability to do several things that are unavailable within the AppFabric SDK, such as locking an item or using a cache item, such as the Interlocked class. By default, the Redis API for .NET serializes only strings and primitive numbers or binary data. Date and time is not supported. Here is an example:

```
//redis connection string
var cs = "[URL],ssl=true,password=[PWD]";

//cache connector
var client = ConnectionMultiplexer.Connect(cs);

//cache proxy
var cache = client.GetDatabase();

var key = "time";

while (true)
{
    //retrieve cached value
    var value = (string)cache.StringGet(key);

    //if not available, drill the cache with a new value
```

```
    if (value == null)
    {
        value = DateTime.Now.ToString();

        //adds the value to the cache with a TTL of 5 seconds
        cache.StringSet(key, value, TimeSpan.FromSeconds(5));
    }

    Console.WriteLine(" {0}", value);

    //slow down
    Thread.Sleep(1000);
}
```

The two biggest drawbacks of the Redis cache are the missing support for built-in serialization of custom types and the unavailability of a built-in local cache.

Caching must happen at the layer/tier boundary. Sharing cache data is important; this is why distributed cache systems exist. However, avoiding wastage of network usage is important. A second-level cache is mandatory when dealing with highly accessed data. Within .NET, the help to create such a local cache comes with the MemoryCache class, the following is an example:

```
//local cache
var local = new MemoryCache("local");

//redis connection string
var cs = "[URL],ssl=true,password=[PWD]";

//cache connector
var client = ConnectionMultiplexer.Connect(cs);

//cache proxy
var cache = client.GetDatabase();

var key = "time";

while (true)
{
    //retrieve value from local cache
    string value = (string)local[key];

    if (value != null)
        Console.WriteLine("local -> {0}", value);
```

```
        //if unavailable retrieve if from
        //second level cache from cloud
        else if (value == null)
        {
            value = (string)cache.StringGet(key);

            if (value != null)
                Console.WriteLine("redis -> {0}", value);
        }

        //if not available, drill both caches with a new value
        if (value == null)
        {
            value = DateTime.Now.ToString();

            Console.WriteLine("new -> {0}", value);

            //as an example we will use different TTLs
            cache.StringSet(key, value, TimeSpan.FromSeconds(8));

            local.Add(key, value, new CacheItemPolicy {
    AbsoluteExpiration = DateTime.Now.AddSeconds(5) });
        }

        //slow down
        Thread.Sleep(1000);
    }
```

This example produces the following result:

```
new -> 22/03/2015 17:50:18
local -> 22/03/2015 17:50:18
local -> 22/03/2015 17:50:18
local -> 22/03/2015 17:50:18
local -> 22/03/2015 17:50:18
redis -> 22/03/2015 17:50:18
redis -> 22/03/2015 17:50:18
new -> 22/03/2015 17:50:26
local -> 22/03/2015 17:50:26
local -> 22/03/2015 17:50:26
```

Carefully use multilevel cache because of the increased difficulty in synchronizing cache items' expiration.

A complete guide on using the Azure Redis cache is available at `http://azure.microsoft.com/en-us/documentation/` `articles/cache-dotnet-how-to-use-azure-redis-cache/`.

Simplified grid computing

Cloud computing gives us enough power and technologies to do almost anything. Such a statement is true until we do not deal with real-world limits. As discussed in the *Parallel programming* section in *Chapter 1, Performance Thoughts* in, some overhead that limits the system's scalability always exists. This is **Amdahl's law**. Although this sentence is definitely true, we can avoid many such limitations. Grid computing is the art of parallelizing computation with a large number of systems.

Although specific frameworks or languages do exist, we will see how to create a small grid computing system from scratch in C#.

The first thing to do is have a huge dataset divided into smaller datasets. This improves scalability at the highest level. Once we have the data, we also have to bind each data portion with the related execution logic. By creating multiple messages, we can handle any business logic step. This fine granularity helps to achieve the highest scalability and adds great reliability because anything could eventually go wrong at any time. Such a message architecture will let the forgotten message flow to another available engine, which can resume from the last failed point. Indeed, designs that frequently save partial states refer to those messages as **persistence points**.

Let's imagine that we have to work for an automotive solution. Now, we need to handle millions of position packets per day, and for each packet, calculate the full street address if it is not already available in our system.

Different designs are available with increasing difficulty and eventually impacts performance results. Usually, the more scalable a design is, the more overload it could bring if executed in a small system. However, such overall overload is a necessary cost if we want to scale to hundreds of systems or more.

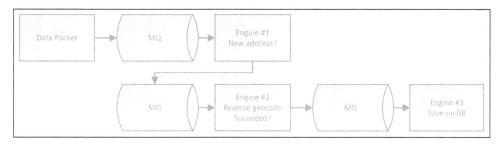

A queue-based automotive solution for grid computing

The message structure is the main creation. Although the structure itself is quite the same, using different message names helps in making the business needs very clear. Otherwise, a single message name is also possible with the addition of a message status. The tree messages represent the tree computational stages: data input, reverse geocode, and data saving. Here is an example:

```
/// <summary>
/// stage 1
/// a position is found in history db
/// a street address search starts across streets database
/// </summary>
public class SearchForAddressMessage
{
    public SearchForAddressMessage()
    {
    }

    public SearchForAddressMessage(float latitude, float
longitude)
    {
        Latitude = (float)Math.Round(latitute, 4);
        Longitude = (float)Math.Round(longitude, 4);
    }

    public float Latitude { get; set; }
    public float Longitude { get; set; }

    public override int GetHashCode()
    {
        return new { Latitude, Longitude }.GetHashCode();
    }
}

/// <summary>
/// stage 2
/// a new address need to be parsed from
/// found coordinates against a reverse-geocode service
/// </summary>
public class GeocodeNewAddressMessage : SearchForAddressMessage
{
}

/// <summary>
/// stage 3
```

```
/// a street address has been found and must
/// flow to the street database
/// </summary>
public class SaveNewAddressMessage : SearchForAddressMessage
{
    public string StreetAddress { get; set; }
}
```

Some helper methods increment productivity and make it easier to understand the code:

```
public static class QueueClientExtensions
{
    /// <summary>
    /// Helper method for sending any message
    /// to the queue with type name as ContentType
    /// </summary>
    public static void SendBody<T>(this QueueClient client, T arg)
    {
        client.Send(new BrokeredMessage(arg)
        {
            //by specifying the message type
            //the receiver will know what logic to execute
            //and how to deserialize the message body
            ContentType = arg.GetType().Name
        });
    }

    /// <summary>
    /// Helper method for sending any message
    /// to the queue with type name as ContentType
    /// </summary>
    public static void SendBody<T>(this QueueClient client,
IEnumerable<T> args)
    {
        client.SendBatch(args.Select(arg => new BrokeredMessage(arg)
        {
            //by specifying the message type
            //the receiver will knows what logic to execute
            //and how to deserialize the message body
            ContentType = arg.GetType().Name
        }));
    }
}
```

To improve the realism of demonstration, I read thousands of positions from a CSV file I created with pseudo-random values. The CSV file only contains two columns: latitude and longitude. Here's an example of how to read it:

```
//the queue client needs connection string and queue name
var queue = QueueClient.CreateFromConnectionString(
SERVICEBUS_CONNECTIONSTRING, QUEUE_NAME);

//emulate data packet input
Task.Factory.StartNew(() =>
    {
        //a csv file with positions
        var fname = @"C:\Temp\positions_export.csv";

        //skip line nr 1 containing column names
        //take only 100 items for testing purpose
        //split string for semicolon char
        var positions = File.ReadAllLines(fname).Skip(1).Take(100)
            .Select(row => row.Split(';'))
            //parse csv data as "latitude;longitude"
            .Select(x => new { Latitude = float.Parse(x[0]),
Longitude = float.Parse(x[1]) })
            //avoid unnecessary duplications
            .Distinct()
            //create stage 1 messages
            .Select(x => new SearchForAddressMessage(x.Latitude,
x.Longitude));

        //upload all messages to the queue
        queue.SendBody(positions);
    });
```

Each process step will send a message to the following one throughout a queued message. Based on those steps, engines will execute their internal logic without interfering with other engines, because each one will handle only a single message per instance.

Now, start the sequence of sending messages to the queue and retrieving them from the queue that acts as a persistence system for temporary data, adding failover logic and the asynchronous distributed programming feature. The queue will automatically send a message to another engine if one will not confirm that it has been successfully handled. Such logic execution is a type of *milestone-based programming*.

Those small persistence messages are often referred to as persistence points when used in other technologies, the Microsoft Biz Talk Server has a similar design. For this example, a simple database with the following table structure has been created:

```
CREATE TABLE [dbo].[StreetAddress](
  [Latitude] [real] NOT NULL,
  [Longitude] [real] NOT NULL,
  [Position] [geography] NOT NULL,
  [FullAddress] [varchar](250) NOT NULL,
 CONSTRAINT [PK_StreetAddress] PRIMARY KEY CLUSTERED
(
  [Latitude] ASC,
  [Longitude] ASC
)WITH (PAD_INDEX = OFF, STATISTICS_NORECOMPUTE = OFF,
IGNORE_DUP_KEY = OFF, ALLOW_ROW_LOCKS = ON, ALLOW_PAGE_LOCKS = ON)
ON [PRIMARY]
) ON [PRIMARY] TEXTIMAGE_ON [PRIMARY]
```

All grid engines will execute an *always-running* logic that reads messages from the queue, and then checks the message content type name to route the message to the right stage logic.

```
while (true)
{
    //try dequeue some message

    var msg = queue.Receive(TimeSpan.FromSeconds(1));
    if (msg == null)
        break;

//continue…
```

In the following example, the Stage 1 takes the message from the queue and checks if the address is present in our database. If not, a new message of Stage 2 is produced and sent to the queue:

```
if (msg.ContentType == "SearchForAddressMessage")
{
    //stage 1
    var body = msg.GetBody<SearchForAddressMessage>();

    // existence check for address
    using (var db = new StreetAddressDBEntities())
        if (!db.StreetAddress.Any(a => a.Latitude == body.Latitude
&& a.Longitude == body.Longitude))
            //if the address is unavailable in our database
```

```
                //a stage 2 message is sent to the queue
                //to trigger the reverse geocode logic
                queue.SendBody(new GeodoceNewAddressMessage
                {
                    Latitude = body.Latitude,
                    Longitude = body.Longitude
                });

        //signal the message as completed
        //so it will be deleted by the queue
        msg.Complete();
}
```

Once a message arrives at Stage 2, a reverse geocode request is sent to a **Geographic Information System (GIS)**, such as Bing Maps. Once the street address is found, we will enqueue (add to the queue) a new message for Stage 3:

```
else if (msg.ContentType == "GeodoceNewAddressMessage")
{
    Console.WriteLine("# {0} -> Found GeodoceNewAddressMessage",
i);

    //stage 2
    var body = msg.GetBody<GeodoceNewAddressMessage>();

    //a request for reverse-geocode is available
    //a WS is available for Bing Maps here
    //http://dev.virtualearth.net/webservices/v1/geocodeservice/
geocodeservice.svc

    //the found street
    string street = null;

    using (var client = new GeocodeServiceClient("BasicHttpBinding_
IGeocodeService"))
        try
        {
            //ask bing for the street address
            var response = client.ReverseGeocode(new
ReverseGeocodeRequest
            {
                //bing credential key
                Credentials = new Credentials { ApplicationId =
BING_KEY },
```

```
                //given position
                Location = new Location { Latitude =
        body.Latitude, Longitude = body.Longitude }
            }).Results.FirstOrDefault();

            if (response != null)
                street = response.Address.FormattedAddress;
        }
        catch (Exception ex)
        {
        }

    //if reverse geocode succeded
    if (street != null)
        //send a message for saving position to the street db
        queue.SendBody(new SaveNewAddressMessage
            {
                Latitude = body.Latitude,
                Longitude = body.Longitude,
                StreetAddress = street,
            });
    else
        Debug.WriteLine(string.Format("No street found for {0}
    {1}", body.Latitude, body.Longitude));

    //signal the message as completed
    //so it will be deleted by the queue
    msg.Complete();
}
```

Once a message reaches Stage 3, we will save the newly found street address to our database for future data caching and any other need:

```
else if (msg.ContentType == "SaveNewAddressMessage")
{
    Console.WriteLine("# {0} -> Found SaveNewAddressMessage", i);

    //stage 3
    var body = msg.GetBody<SaveNewAddressMessage>();

    using (var db = new StreetAddressDBEntities())
    using (var tr = db.Database.BeginTransaction())
    {
        //always make a double check
```

```
        if (!db.StreetAddress.Any(a => a.Latitude == body.Latitude
    && a.Longitude == body.Longitude))
            db.StreetAddress.Add(new StreetAddress
            {
                Latitude = body.Latitude,
                Longitude = body.Longitude,
                FullAddress = body.StreetAddress,
            });

        db.SaveChanges();
        tr.Commit();
    }


    //signal the message as completed
    //so it will be deleted by the queue
    msg.Complete();
}
```

This solution, although a simple prototype, could even handle millions of messages.

Further optimizations could split the single queue into multiple queues, one per stage or business logic. Often, a grid system executes different logic altogether or the same logic with different versions.

Lookup programming

As mentioned earlier, complete dataset retrieval is something that is poorly optimized in any application scenario. When dealing with a huge dataset, trying to load more than a million rows together in the same materialized Entity Framework query or something similar will surely result in an OutOfMemoryException output.

As seen in the *Stream-like querying* section in *Chapter 7, Database Querying*, ADO.NET gives us the ability to execute queries without having to put all the data together in our memory, as we would have to with the old DbCommand class or new Entity Framework ones. Sometimes, we are in the need of executing a lot of logic that needs frequent lookups at a data source. Let's talk about the previous example again.

What if a GPS device always sends the same position? In our system, we will take this position, produce a Stage 1 message, send it to the Stage 1 queue, and then down to our grid engine, which will make a request to our database to check whether such a position is already known to us or not, and eventually skip it.

The best solution to avoid such round trips is to know that in the first stage, the GPS position is already present in our system, thus being able to skip duplicated items as quickly as possible. Obviously, a second check at a lower level is mandatory, but this pre-check stage will easily boost latency of the whole application.

Instead of directly checking data duplication at the first stage with a direct database query, we can use a cache or a huge collection. In our solution, storing all coordinates could soon break any system. This is not a practical method, but we can use the opportunity to evaluate how different local data-storing classes behave.

Again, we will read a simple CSV file for testing purposes — this time without any CSV extraction limitation with the `Take` method:

```
var fname = @"C:\Temp\positions_export.csv";

//skip line 1 containing column names
//take only 100 items for testing purpose
//split string for semicolon char
var positions = File.ReadAllLines(fname).Skip(1)
    .Select(row => row.Split(';'))
    //parse csv data as "latitude;longitude"
    .Select(x => new { Latitude = float.Parse(x[0]), Longitude =
float.Parse(x[1]) })
    //avoid unnecessary duplications
    .Distinct()
    //produce a temporary key as a unique string taken from
    //the hash code of the anonymous instance (although
GetHashCode does not guarantee a complete uniqueness like any
hashing, we will use it for testing purposes)
    .Select(x => new { x.Latitude, x.Longitude, TempID =
x.GetHashCode().ToString() })
    .ToArray();
```

With the help of a `Stopwatch` class, let us evaluate how much it costs LINQ to have objects in our memory find each item by themselves, by value and not by reference:

```
s.Start();
foreach (var p in positions)
{
    var found = positions.FirstOrDefault(x => x.Latitude ==
p.Latitude && x.Longitude == p.Longitude);
}
s.Stop();

Console.WriteLine("By lat/lon {0:N0}ms", s.ElapsedMilliseconds);

s.Reset();
```

```
s.Start();
foreach (var p in positions)
{
    var found = positions.FirstOrDefault(x => x.TempID ==
p.TempID);
}
s.Stop();

Console.WriteLine("By string equals {0:N0}ms",
s.ElapsedMilliseconds);
```

Do consider that the cost is directly proportional to the number of rows. The following is the time each item takes to find itself by evaluating a by-value equality, with less than 6,000 rows in our CSV:

```
By evaluating lat/lon: 662ms
By evaluating the string key: 757ms
```

Are you wondering that the cost is because of the double integer key (lat/lon)? No! A single string costs more than a couple of integers. Remember that LINQ simply parses all objects in memory. It is not a database index seek.

So, how can we reproduce the logic of a database index seek in our .NET code? Simple! With the old Hashtable class, or the newly created dictionary or the HashSet classes (HashSet is the most recent).

Here, we give the dictionary a key by writing an anonymous Func<Myparam, object>:

```
var dictionary = positions.ToDictionary(x => x.TempID, x => new {
x.Latitude, x.Longitude });

s.Reset();
s.Start();
foreach (var p in positions)
{
    var found = dictionary[p.TempID];
}
s.Stop();

Console.WriteLine("By string dictionary {0:N0}ms",
s.ElapsedMilliseconds);
```

The result? The time taken to find each item again on its own, by asking the dictionary, seeking by the string key for the same number of items in memory, is 0ms! The drawback is still that we cannot put a whole table within a dictionary instance. The other option is to use a local cache object to contain the lookup data. Such a cache instance will contain as many items as possible without ever breaking an application's stability. Obviously, this does not contain the whole table in memory (which is a bad idea), but this choice will boost the latency time of your engines substantially by bringing the whole system to a higher throughput speed.

The following example shows how to preload an in-memory cache and check for missing cache items by verifying that all items are definitely within the cache. Bear in mind that a cache has its own memory management that tries to optimize storing, most used entries (items within the cache) or newly added items. Here's an example:

```
//try putting all items within the cache

foreach (var p in positions)
    cache.Add(p.TempID, p, DateTimeOffset.Now.AddMinutes(30));

//cache miss counter
int miss = 0;

s.Reset();
s.Start();
foreach (var p in positions)
{
    var found = cache[p.TempID];
    if (found == null)
        miss++;
}
s.Stop();

Console.WriteLine("By MemoryCache {0:N0}ms with {1:N0} misses",
s.ElapsedMilliseconds, miss);
```

The result comes to a latency of 3ms, with zero misses. This proves that although dictionary always remains the fastest class in item retrieval, a MemoryCache is not so bad.

In this example, the cache has been drilled together at the start. In the real world, this is a good practice, and although it creates some initial latency time, this initial time cost will later boost the cache checks. However, if such a design does not fit your needs, the lazy approach is available. It does not drill the cache at the beginning, but at any cache check.

Summary

In this chapter, we dived into the big data world. When dealing with billions of records increasing at a fast rate, usual techniques and technologies are useless. We had the opportunity to lay our hands on the basic grid computing techniques and designs that will guide us to the right path anytime we need to handle huge datasets.

In the next chapter, we will take a tour around the profiling and performance analysis tools available within Microsoft Visual Studio. We have already seen all kinds of architectures, strategies, and technologies in all eight chapters, including this one; although important, we need analysis tools to thoroughly understand how they behave in terms of various performance aspects.

Analyzing Code Performance

9

In this chapter, we will have an overview of performance analysis and software testing techniques. When trying to get the best out of our code, nothing is more useful than profiling our work. Profiling means analyzing code performance results, routine by routine, trying to find bottlenecks, which gives us the ability to identify performance consumption patterns.

Another important aspect of the software development lifecycle is testing our application. In this chapter we will see various kinds of tests and features, as offered by the Visual Studio test engine (**MsTest**). Tests are useful to analyze how our application behaves regarding performance, may help with trying to simulate the end-user feeling, or may help with analyzing the reliability of our application, or its ability to scale out.

We will cover the following pointers in this chapter:

- Software profiling
- Profiling with Visual Studio 2013
- Testing with Visual Studio 2013
- Static program analysis

Software profiling

Testing application results against the main performance aspects such as resource usage, latency, throughput, availability, scalability and efficiency is definitely the way any performance engineering fulfills its goals by comparing such results to the desired performance levels.

As developers, we need a numerical expression of all performance aspects to infer if something is working incorrectly, or simply if some optimization may improve a performance aspect. Never consider simply aggregated values. Always go deep in the performance analysis of any software. This is the key to success to developing a performing application.

Profiling is the technique used to analyze at runtime how our software behaves regarding resource usage (CPU or memory consumption), with details aggregated per routine/function. This means that a profiling engine will explicitly inform you which routine is consuming the most CPU time in our application, which is a huge help in bottleneck identification.

Obviously, a profiling tool is not mandatory. For instance, we could use our instincts to deduce that if a web application is taking lot of time to respond, maybe the database behind is slow to respond, or is receiving bad performing queries, or the web application is wasting time in doing its job. Although using a profiling tool is not mandatory, often we will need to find where a bottleneck is happening. By using a profiling tool, we can find the bottleneck quickly.

Today, any performance analysis tool should give us a detailed report of how our application executes. By using good profiling technology, we should never ask ourselves what the cause of bad performance is because we should already know it. If we have a slow responding web application, by profiling its execution in Visual Studio, we will know exactly which method(s) needs optimization.

Profiling supports different techniques. For instance, an instrumentation profiling injects special instructions in our method body (usually at the beginning and the end). This behavior happens when CLR executes its JIT compiler, so we cannot see such code in our Visual Studio text editor.

Profiling with Visual Studio

Visual Studio has a great profiling tool integrated within its usual IDE.

The main menu root is **ANALYZE**. Here, we find all we need to understand an application's performance details, together with interesting static analysis tools to verify a programmer's skill.

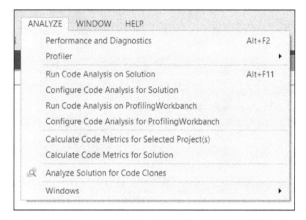

The ANALYZE menu as visible within Visual Studio 2013 update 4

Here's a brief guide to how to start profiling our application:

1. Within the menu, click on the **Performance and Diagnostics** menu item. This link opens the main window to start profiling our applications. Using the performance wizard helps us in selecting the best profiling technique and configuration for our needs. Specific profilers also exist for specific application kinds, such as JavaScript memory usage or GPU power usage.

Analysis Target

Startup Project

ProfilingWorkbanch

Change
Target ▾

Available Tools   Show target specific tools

☐ CPU Usage   ☐ Memory Usage
See where the CPU is spending time executing your code.   Investigate application memory to find issues such as memory
Useful when the CPU is the performance bottleneck.   leaks

☑ Performance Wizard
CPU Sampling, Instrumentation, .NET Memory allocation, and
Resource Contention

Not Applicable Tools ⌃

☐ Energy Consumption   ☐ GPU Usage
Examine where energy is consumed in your application   Examine GPU usage in your application. Useful to determine
                                                               whether CPU or GPU is the performance bottleneck. Only
                                                               available on supported graphics cards.

☐ HTML UI Responsiveness   ☐ JavaScript Function Timing
Examine where time is spent in your website or application   See the elapsed time and call counts of your JavaScript
                                                               functions. Useful when your code is waiting on I/O or other
                                                               non-CPU intensive operations

☐ JavaScript Memory   ☐ XAML UI Responsiveness
Investigate the JavaScript heap to help find issues such as   Examine where time is spent in your application
memory leaks

The performance and diagnostics window, ready to start profiling a WPF application

2. By pressing the start button at the bottom of the window, we will see the **Performance Wizard** asking us which profiling technology we want to use. We will leave the default selection that will **start CPU sampling**. This profiling technique will try to predict the CPU usage or our software, with good results.

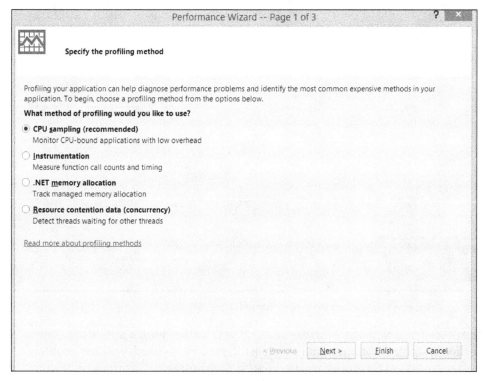

The performance wizard

3. Select the profiling method, the executable project to analyze, and if needed, start immediately, or simply save this configuration.

At this point, our application starts, along with the profiling process. We can now do anything in our software, such as the usual operations that give the profiling engine a way to understand our application usage. Obviously, right now the profiling engine is simply recording our steps and application feedback. When we exit our application, the profiling engine will then analyze the recorded data and produce a navigable detailed report.

The result is immediately shown to the developer in a simplified graphical way containing a CPU usage chart, a summary of hot paths, and the most CPU-consuming methods within our application, as shown in the following screenshot:

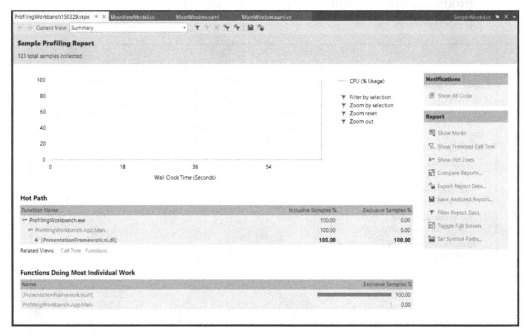

A profiling report for CPU sampling

In the preceding example, I profiled a WPF application with a single data-bindable collection, populated in memory. As a result, no CPU is used, and the profiler correctly shows that the only method that is consuming CPU time is within PresentationFramework.dll. This is because the WPF engine is outside of our code; in fact, at the place of the method name, there is the assembly name between the square brackets.

We could say that this is the ideal profiling result.

The same result could be visible by profiling an application by trying to load thousands of items in a single WPF control. Although a profiler will surely show that our code is expending zero percent of the total, because the 100 percent of CPU time cost is within the WPF library, this does not mean we cannot optimize anything else. Instead, this means that we have to change presentation architecture, maybe trying to load fewer items per time, or changing the control setup, or not changing the control at all. Although profiling does not care about such performance issues, they eventually can be analyzed within other tools like the WPF Performance Suite. Some details can be found at the following URI:

https://msdn.microsoft.com/en-us/library/
aa969767%28v=vs.110%29.aspx

The profiling result is available for future analysis within the **Performance Explorer** window usually docked to the left of the IDE. If we do not find it, it is simply available within the **ANALYZE** menu under the Windows item. The window lets us see all profiling configurations used for our application and historic reports. By clicking on the profiling method, we can start another recording session.

Back to the performance report, in the **Hot Path** box, we will find methods that consumed the most CPU time. A high CPU consuming example is available with the invocation of the Thread.SpindleWait method, which will waste CPU cycles.

```
public static IEnumerable<SimpleModel> GenerateMocks()
{
    var r = new Random(DateTime.Now.GetHashCode());
    return Enumerable.Range(1, 1000).Select(i =>
        {
            Thread.SpinWait(r.Next(100000, 1000000));
            return new SimpleModel
            {
                Name = string.Format("ITEM #{0}", i),
                Value = r.NextDouble() * (double)i,
            };
        })
        .ToArray();
}
```

As visible in the following screenshot, the CPU usage increases by up to 15 percent of the overall system. Analyzing the **Hot Path** box, we will see that our `GenerateMocks` method is responsible for the most CPU usage of the whole application (85 percent). Actually, as visible, the CPU usage happens in the `System.Core` external assembly, the one containing the `Thread` class of the core framework. The remaining 15 percent of the application's CPU time usage is because of WPF rendering:

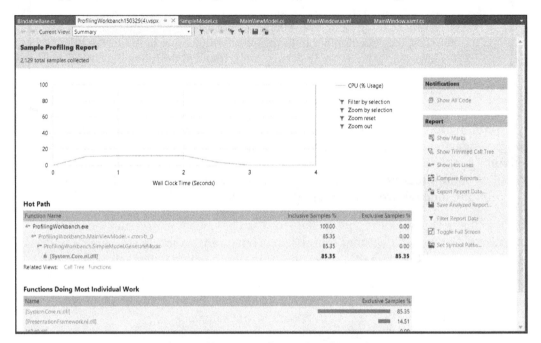

A sampling profiling report of some Thread.SpinWait usage

When reading at the **Hot Path** box (and other similar boxes), we have the ability to click on a single function that is CPU consuming. The click will bring us to the referred code block, if we have such a code file, otherwise (as happens when we click a core framework assembly name) if the consumption is for an external assembly, although by just clicking on its name we will be unable to read external code. In the preceding example, we can click the **GenerateMocks** item. This will bring us to a new view with a lot of interesting information, as can be seen in the following figure:

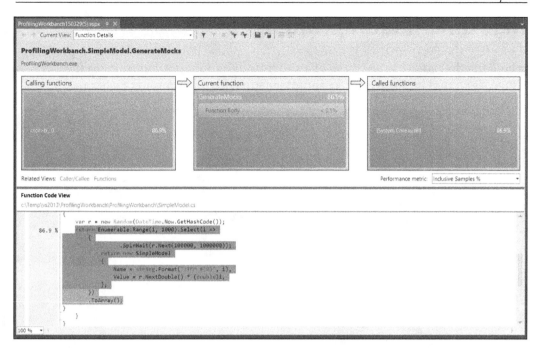

CPU sampling profiling results across code editor

By analyzing the profiling result offered by this window, we can immediately see which code row will have higher CPU usage. We can also see that our code block actually uses 0.1 percent of the CPU, maybe because of the Random.Next invocation, while the real CPU consumption comes from the method of the Core.dll.

This ability to dive into hierarchical invocation details and back to the root is the key feature of profiling our code.

Within the profiling report window, in the toolbox we have a drop-down list that names the **Current View** that gives us the ability to select different analysis results, all based on the recorded data from the profile. We will always see the same data, but with the ability to group it in different ways, be it in a per-function basis, or hierarchical basis, or by another way.

Instrumentation profiling

Executing the **Performance Wizard** again, we can use the **instrumentation profiling** technique that adds the ability to analyze the method invocation count to the CPU usage, as shown in the previous example made with the sampling technique.

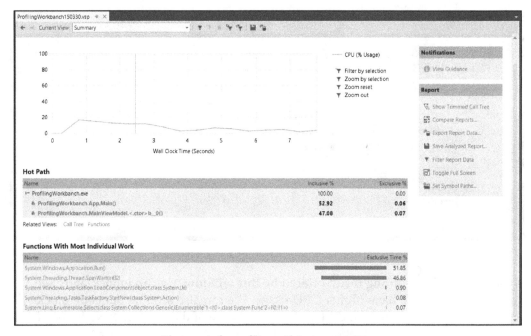

The report of a profiling with instrumentation

With instrumentation, the report summary is quite similar to the sampling one, while the detailed data available by selecting the proper view in the **Current View** is completely different. We still have the ability to find the most CPU consuming methods, but we also have the ability to see the invocation count. This information is priceless because it helps with finding development mistakes, other than the obvious CPU consummation.

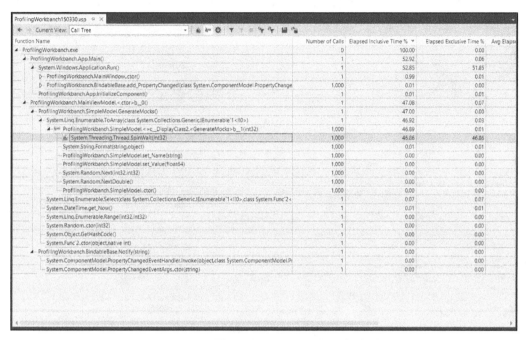

An instrumentation profiling call tree view with method call counters

Executing the Performance Wizard again, we have the ability to try the **Memory Usage** profiler. This profile records real-time memory usage during runtime. This gives us the ability to understand if there are critical patterns in resource usage, such as a memory leak (infinite memory usage increment), or if there are issues regarding garbage-collection timings.

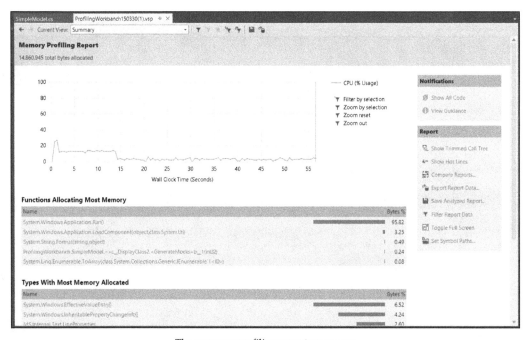

The memory profiling report summary

Within the Call Tree view, we can see memory usage in bytes and in a relative percentage. In the previous instance, the highest consuming method is the `Application.Run` method, executed by the WPF engine that iterates 1000 items collection and instantiates a template generation 1000 times. This results in 14MB memory consumption.

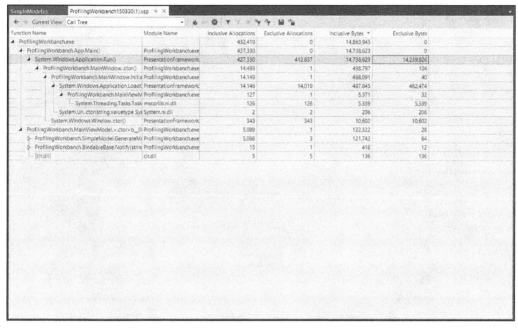

The call tree detailed view of a memory profiling report

Another great help comes with **Concurrency Profiler**, which is always available by executing the Performance Wizard. Such a profiler shows exactly how many race conditions happen in our code when multiple threads fight to get access to the same resource.

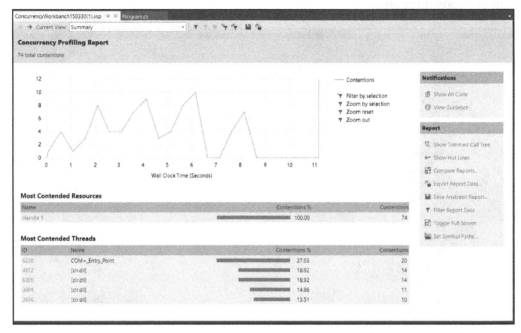

Concurrency profiling report showing race condition count

The same information is available throughout the **Resource Details** chart, which is shown in the following chart. On the Y side of the chart, we have thread IDs, while on the X side, we have the time. This chart is actually a Gantt chart of race condition that is happening within threads during time.

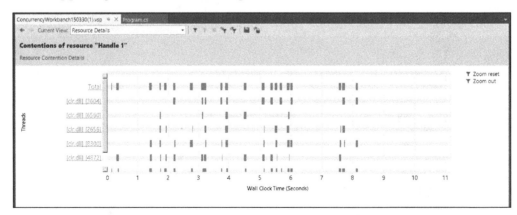

Concurrency profiling resource detail showing resource contention per thread

In the figure below, there is the **Call Tree** view that shows exactly how many times a race content occurred per method.

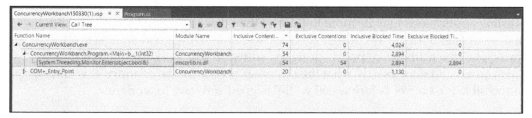

Concurrency profiling call tree showing that the most racing method is the Monitor.Enter method that is the underlying executing method for the lock C# keyword

The analysis report comparison

Another great feature of Visual Studio is the report comparison. This feature gives us a clear view of how our application performance results change over time.

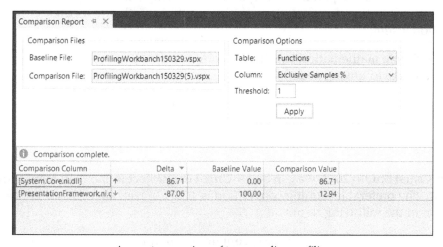

A report comparison of two sampling profiling

In the preceding example, the first report is about the demo code without any CPU wastage, while in the second report, the `Thread.SpinWait` method has been added. The result shows that the `System.Core.ni.dll` in the second report consumes more than 86 percent of the relative CPU, while the WPF rendering engine consumes a lot less, in comparison.

Testing with Visual Studio 2013

Software testing is what saves the life of any software development project.

Testing applications may be more important than designing good software. Although a developer should always design good software following good architectural principles, the truth is that poorly designed software will work fine if it has hardly been tested and does exactly what the customer needs. On the contrary, it is almost impossible for a never before tested well-designed software to work fine.

Software testing is available at multiple levels. The lower level of testing, the most tightly coupled with our code, is the **unit test**. Such kinds of tests have the goal of testing a single functional (or sometimes technical) method. If we need to test our Fourier transform method, a unit test is the starting point. When unit testing, it is good practice to give such method data for testing purposes. Such dummy data, called a **mockup**, is actually useful to point out our code (the subject of the test), isolating its execution from any external inference that real data could bring. In other words, a mockup parameter helps by testing only a method per time, indeed, this is real unit testing. In contrast, by testing multiple methods, we are doing integration testing.

Here is a simple mathematical function to compute the Pow of any Single number, as shown in the following code:

```
public static float Pow(float a, float b)
{
    return (float)Math.Pow(a, b);
}
```

Within Visual Studio 2013, we can add a **Unit Test Project** in the **Add New Project** window. The preferable naming convention is [TO_BE_TESTED_ASSEMBLY].Test, as shown in the following figure

Once created, we will find a test class, containing all unit tests coupled to a business class or by functional needs. Within such classes, all our unit tests will be available as simple methods, each agnostic against the other, as if each is a simple console application.

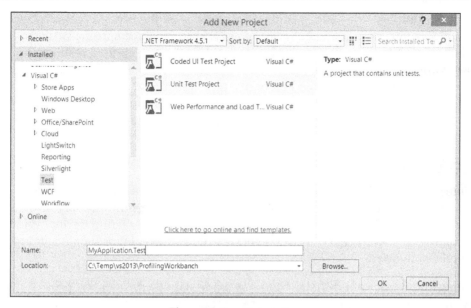

The unit test project creation

The unit test itself is actually easy, but we should always try to write tests with some ideal case and some real (not ideal) case. When writing a unit test, we should try to break the target method with any unusual parameter, trying to expose our methods to difficulties. For instance, when testing a Pow(a,b) function, we could test its usage by trying to use huge numbers, or negative numbers, or any other number that could bring an exception. Otherwise, a test that's too easy will definitely be useless. Here is an example:

```
[TestClass]
public class HelperTests
{
    [TestMethod]
    public void PowTest1()
    {
        var a = 10;
        var b = 10;
        var pow = Helpers.Pow(a, b);
        Assert.AreEqual<float>(pow, (float)Math.Pow(a, b));
    }
}
```

Within our unit test, the `Assert` static class gives us all the needed prebuilt helpers to signal `MsTest` (the test engine) that we are asking for some specific verification (or deny it). In the preceding example, we checked the `Pow` method result against a known value. The input parameters (a and b) are mock values. When dealing with complex input parameters, such as any real business object, a mock framework helps a lot to create dummy objects along with an Inversion of Control container to create mock data or real data, depending on the executing behavior.

The Integration test

An integration test helps to test how different software modules behave when working altogether. Any time we test multiple methods or multiple software modules (with a lot of methods), we are actually doing integration testing. With such testing, mock-up data may also leave space for the real world data coming from other modules.

Creating a unit test within Visual Studio is made with the proper test project. In contrast, there is no wizard or project template regarding integration testing. Such kinds of tests are totally related to the developer's work.

We have the choice of testing different modules by following the use cases step lists precisely, or we can use the software modules in a creative way, trying to find a condition when software hangs.

When dealing with software module integration testing, if we use real world data, an integration test may become a user-acceptance test, with the goal of trying to get the user approval of our development work.

Performance-related tests

Regarding performance, different kinds of tests exist.

We start a **performance test** if we try to analyze how the system responds regarding different performance aspects, such as scalability, latency, throughput, and so on.

Alternatively, we start a **load test** if we try to analyze how the application behaves regarding a huge user load, or if we try to identify the higher user load allowed with a static system setup.

Stress testing, although similar to a load test, instead this is more related to understanding how the system recovers from a system fault, or from a huge user load that will create some form of application fault.

All such tests, such as the integration test, are available to the developer as free developing tests. Those kinds of tests, although available within Visual Studio for some application types, are not universally available. For instance, in Visual Studio we have the Web Test (a test of website navigation) and the ability to create a Load Test by executing multiple Web Tests. The same tests are not available for other application types.

TDD

Test-driven development (TDD) is how the sword was centuries ago for fighters. It is not technical knowledge. It gives us the methodology to test in advance, during, and after we develop an application. In other words, it is like developing with the test in mind. The choice of using or not such methodology in your own development project, is related to team needs and wishes. Using TDD increases software quality, but following the TDD way is not the only way to create good tests.

Test and Continuous Integration

When working with complex projects or big teams, implementing the Continuous Integration within our **Application Lifecycle Management (ALM)** system, such as **Team Foundation Server (TFS)**, will be invaluable.

Continuous integration is the ability to verify that committed changes against our source control compiles without any error. The goal of such features is to verify code quality of the overall team, trying to avoid mistakes in which a developer somehow interfere with the work of another developer.

Within Visual Studio, great integration is available with TFS. This makes setting up Continuous Integration easy. An added feature of TFS is the ability to avoid the committed changes that are definitely committed against the overall source control. Usual Continuous Integration simply tries building our application projects at each check-in to verify code compilation. Within Visual Studio, a more restrictive version exists that is named as **Gated Check-in**. With this feature, a code that does not build is simply rejected to the developer. This totally avoids bad coding being stored within TFS.

Another great feature available within TFS is the ability to automatically execute all our tests together with the compilation of the Continuous Integration. We then have the ability to notify someone of test results, or prevent the developer committing changes from being saved in the main code, similar to what happens when using the gated check in feature.

This great feature helps increase the software quality a lot because of the automation of the whole testing job. In addition, we will have historical information about testing success/fail count. This can be a testing report itself, or give the development team a practical regression test result in time.

Static program analysis

Contrary to all tests or analysis against a running application, that names **dynamic analysis**, the static analysis focuses on our code when it is still at the design stage (when we develop within Visual Studio). In other words, it is the analysis of our code design (of the code, not of the application).

Static analysis helps to understand worst practices, such as an incorrect implementation of an event handler or the incorrect extension of the `IDisposable` interface within our class.

Static program analysis also helps with finding common mistakes and basic forgetfulness.

A lot of frameworks and methodologies actually exist when doing static program analysis. In this chapter, we will focus on the implementation available within Visual Studio itself.

Although static analysis is something that does not boost any performance of our applications by itself, it is obvious that an automated code analyzer makes writing good code easier. Good code always reduces bottlenecks, so we can definitely say that static analysis reduces common mistakes and helps in writing better-performing code.

You can also refer to the following link:
`http://en.wikipedia.org/wiki/Static_program_analysis`

Code analysis

Within Visual Studio's **ANALYZE** menu, we can execute the **Run Code Analysis on Solution** menu item. The analysis starts immediately for the entire solution currently opened. If anything is perfect, we will see within the **Code Analysis** window, the statement **No Code Analysis issues were detected**, otherwise a lot of warning messages will explain what we did wrong in our coding, as shown in the following screenshot.

Please note that static analysis is not an absolute truth. We can choose which kind of analysis checks to do on a project basis. Indeed, when choosing which analysis to activate or not, we could activate checks that for other software architects are irrelevant or the opposite, or we can enable a more or less verbose analysis checklist, depending on the project being analyzed:

The Code Analysis window, showing a possible issue with related description

The code analysis configuration is available in the last tab of the project properties window.

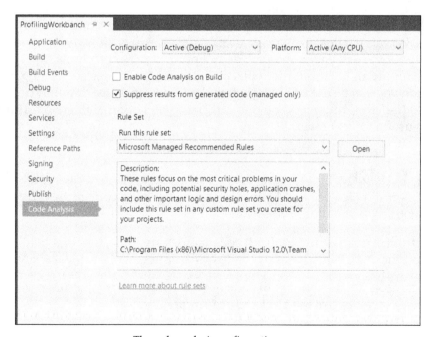

The code analysis configuration pane

Here, we have the ability to trigger a code analysis on the project build, otherwise (by default) we can start the code analysis execution when we need it.

More importantly, here we can configure which Rule Set (list of code analysis rules) to use to produce analysis issues, with the ability to open such sets for inspection or editing.

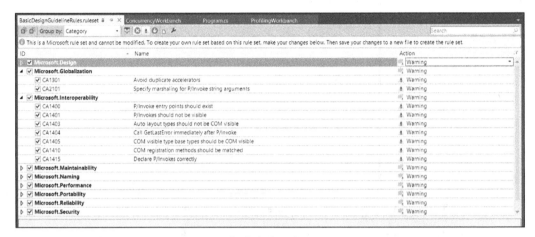

The Rule Set editor

When opening a Rule Set for editing, we have the ability to enable or disable the rule execution and change rule behavior. Although the default configuration lets us produce a **Warning** when an analysis check fail happens, such warnings usually do not pop up for the developer and they do not prevent project compilation. Instead, we can configure an **Error** output in place of the warning. These errors stop project compilation and can be used to link (together with the analysis on build) code analysis to the TFS Continuous Integration. The combination of the two features is definitely useful for team membership.

Code metrics

Another interesting feature that helps you to develop good code is the code metric analysis against our solution/projects.

Different from classical static analysis, code metrics are indicators that help us to understand the overall quality of our code by executing mathematical analyses.

Typical examples are the number of code lines, the number of inheritance levels, and other statistical values like the **Cyclomatic Complexity**.

Within Visual Studio 2013, we have the ability to execute a Code Metric analysis, accessed by the usual menu root **ANALYZE**. Here, we find the **Calculate Code Metrics** for solution menu item that will start the analysis immediately without any wizard or confirmation:

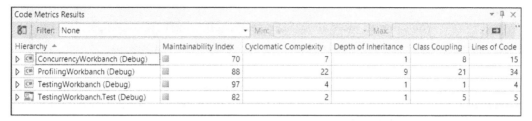

The Code Metrics Results window showing metric results

Within the **Code Metrics Results** window, we will see the results on a per project basis.

The complete explanation of the metrics analyzed, as shown in the preceding screenshot, is available through the MSDN website:

`https://msdn.microsoft.com/en-us/library/bb385914.aspx`

Although such indicators are useful to give numeric details on our software, never try to keep such indicators to their best value, because such a practice is something that can bring a lot of trouble. Indeed, well reviewed software regarding metrics could bring you a poorly designed and poorly performing application. Take such indicators as they actually are. They are useful indicators that can give a potential representation of our job, and give developers like us the time to rethink our application's behavior. The time to rethink, could bring about better software and not by trying to reach 100 in the **Maintainability Index**.

Another useful tip is regarding the `Lines of Code` indicator. Thirty years ago, the number of lines of code was a measure of working effort (such analysis is called SLOC). Today, writing so many lines of code means creating something difficult to maintain and often means we have simply wasted time in developing useless things.

Please note that when we extremely decouple our code with a C# interface per class, if such decoupling does not bring *real* benefits in future maintenance, this will actually only bring more overall work, in the present and in the future. The key to success is writing the right number of source lines without creating useless components, supporting future needs without predisposing features that we already know we don't need. Always compare your software module results regarding code metrics in order to keep a matrix index history.

For instance, if we develop a business library of thousands of lines of code, that is fine, while if we find that a simple assembly responsible for a few functional tasks has a thousand lines of code, there is something wrong. The question we should ask ourselves is *how can my logging library be so verbose, compared to my business one?*

You can read more about SLOC at the following link:
`http://en.wikipedia.org/wiki/Source_lines_of_code`

An interesting metric is the **Depth of Inheritance**, also visible in the preceding screenshot. When using polymorphic behavior, a high level of inheritance could cause difficulty in maintaining and using code.

For further reading refer to:
`http://en.wikipedia.org/wiki/Software_metric`

Summary

In this chapter, you received priceless information about good team working practices, along with advanced performance testing skills. Abilities such as profiling code and setting up a unit test project give tremendous advantages in software performance results and the overall perceived quality.

I hope you have learned useful skills and methodologies by reading this book. I thank you and hope you will deepen your knowledge of everything that you learned with the help of this book.

Index

Symbols

3-tier architecture
about 19, 45, 46
performance concerns 48, 49
.NET Remoting API 56

A

ActiveX Data Objects.NET (ADO.NET)
about 195, 196
bulk copy 221, 222
overview 196-201
Amdahl's law 239
APM
about 114-118
Delegate 114
AppDomains
IDisposable interface 91
working with 86-90
AppFabric Cache
about 37, 65, 235
URL 236
**Application Lifecycle Management
(ALM) 269**
AsParallel() method 161
ASP.NET MVC
about 33
performance concerns 35-40
async/await pattern
about 143, 144
URL 144
asynchronous programming
about 111
theory 112, 113

Asynchronous Programming Model. *See*
APM
async method 143

B

background thread 92
batch mode 84
big data
about 224
AppFabric cache 230
Automotive Big Data system 227-230
Data Purge Engine 229
End-User Data Extractor 230
lookup programming 246-249
Missing Device Notifier 229
Redis cache engine 230
solutions, architecting 225-227
URL 225
Worker Role 229
BigInteger data type
about 178
performance, evaluating 178, 179
BizTalk ESB Toolkit 55
BizTalk Server 55
BLOB storage 64
business-to-business (B2B) 32
business-to-consumer (B2C) 32

C

chunk partitioning 161
class of applications
about 9
performance aspects, of desktop
application 10

profiling
  about 252
  instrumentation profiling 260-264
  report comparison 265
  software profiling 252
  with Visual Studio 253-259

Q

querying approaches
  about 208
  eager loading 208
  lazy loading 208
  performance analysis 211-213
**querying optimization, Entity
    Framework (EF)**
  about 206
  approaches 208
  execution lifecycle, querying 206, 207

R

race condition 105
range partitioning 160
Rapid Application Development (RAD) 34
real-time applications
  about 180, 181
  testing 184
real-time computing
  about 180
  reference 180
Redis Cache
  about 236-238
  URL 239
Reporting Database pattern
  about 227
  URL 227
request-reply pattern 30

S

Service Bus Topic
  about 231, 232
  URL 235
Service-Oriented Architecture (SOA)
  about 50, 51
  service abstraction 53
  service autonomy 54

service composability 55
  service discoverability 55
  service loose coupling 52
  service reusability 53
  service statelessness 54
  standardized service contract 52
set 151
shaped query
  cons 211
  pros 211
short coding
  about 70
  URL 71
Simple Object Access Protocol (SOAP) 55
single responsibility principle 26
Single Thread Apartment (STA) 138
sliding processing
  about 192
  example 192, 193
Small office Home office (SoHo) 33
software architecture
  about 22, 23
  comparing 57
  performance concerns 24, 25
software design 3
software profiling 252
software testing, with Visual Studio 2013
  about 266, 267
  integration test 268
  load test 268
  performance related tests 268, 269
  report comparison 265
  stress test 268
  Test and Continuous Integration 269, 270
  test-driven development (TDD) 269
speculative execution 154
SQL Management Studio 200
starvation 105
static program analysis
  about 270
  code analysis 270, 272
  code metrics 272-274
  URL 270
system architecture 3, 28

Thank you for buying
Learning .NET High-performance Programming

About Packt Publishing

Packt, pronounced 'packed', published its first book, *Mastering phpMyAdmin for Effective MySQL Management*, in April 2004, and subsequently continued to specialize in publishing highly focused books on specific technologies and solutions.

Our books and publications share the experiences of your fellow IT professionals in adapting and customizing today's systems, applications, and frameworks. Our solution-based books give you the knowledge and power to customize the software and technologies you're using to get the job done. Packt books are more specific and less general than the IT books you have seen in the past. Our unique business model allows us to bring you more focused information, giving you more of what you need to know, and less of what you don't.

Packt is a modern yet unique publishing company that focuses on producing quality, cutting-edge books for communities of developers, administrators, and newbies alike. For more information, please visit our website at www.packtpub.com.

About Packt Enterprise

In 2010, Packt launched two new brands, Packt Enterprise and Packt Open Source, in order to continue its focus on specialization. This book is part of the Packt Enterprise brand, home to books published on enterprise software – software created by major vendors, including (but not limited to) IBM, Microsoft, and Oracle, often for use in other corporations. Its titles will offer information relevant to a range of users of this software, including administrators, developers, architects, and end users.

Writing for Packt

We welcome all inquiries from people who are interested in authoring. Book proposals should be sent to author@packtpub.com. If your book idea is still at an early stage and you would like to discuss it first before writing a formal book proposal, then please contact us; one of our commissioning editors will get in touch with you.

We're not just looking for published authors; if you have strong technical skills but no writing experience, our experienced editors can help you develop a writing career, or simply get some additional reward for your expertise.

C# Multithreaded and Parallel Programming

C# Multithreaded and Parallel
Programming

Develop powerful C# applications to take advantage of today's
multi-core hardware

Rodney Ringler

C# Multithreaded and Parallel Programming

ISBN: 978-1-84968-832-1   Paperback: 344 pages

Develop powerful C# applications to take advantage
of today's multicore hardware

1. Make use of the latest Visual Studio debugging
    tools, to manage and debug multiple threads
    running simultaneously.

2. Learn how to use the Thread, Task, and Parallel
    libraries in your C# applications.

3. Explore the evolution of multithreaded
    development in C#, starting with
    BackgroundWorker classes and moving on to
    threads and tasks and finally covering Async.

Visual Studio 2013 and
.NET 4.5 Expert Cookbook

Over 30 recipes to successfully mix the powerful capabilities of
Visual Studio 2013 with .NET 4.5

Abhishek Sur

Visual Studio 2013 and .NET 4.5 Expert Cookbook

ISBN: 978-1-84968-972-4   Paperback: 308 pages

Over 30 recipes to successfully mix the powerful
capabilities of Visual Studio 2013 with .NET 4.5

1. Provides step-by-step instructions, helping
    you to learn the various components and
    technologies of .NET development with
    Visual Studio 2013.

2. Filled with examples that clearly illustrate
    how to integrate with the technologies and
    frameworks of your choice.

3. Helps you keep pace with the fast growing
    IT industry and gain expertise on upcoming
    technologies, common forms of debugging
    and software testing.

Please check **www.PacktPub.com** for information on our titles

.Net Framework 4.5 Expert Programming Cookbook

ISBN: 978-1-84968-742-3   Paperback: 276 pages

Over 50 engaging recipes for learning advanced concepts of .NET Framework 4.5

1. Explores the advanced features of core .Net concepts in step-by-step detail.

2. Understand great ways to enhance your website by securing against cross-site scripting attacks, enabling third party authentications, and embedding maps.

Multithreading in C# 5.0 Cookbook

ISBN: 978-1-84969-764-4   Paperback: 268 pages

Over 70 recipes to help you learn asynchronous and parallel programming with C# 5.0 quickly and efficiently

1. Delve deep into the .NET threading infrastructure and use Task Parallel Library for asynchronous programming.

2. Scale out your server applications effectively.

3. Master C# 5.0 asynchronous operations language support.

Please check **www.PacktPub.com** for information on our titles